Studia Fennica
Ethnologica 16

The Finnish Literature Society (SKS) was founded in 1831 and has, from the very beginning, engaged in publishing operations. It nowadays publishes literature in the fields of ethnology and folkloristics, linguistics, literary research and cultural history.

The first volume of the Studia Fennica series appeared in 1933. Since 1992, the series has been divided into three thematic subseries: Ethnologica, Folkloristica and Linguistica. Two additional subseries were formed in 2002, Historica and Litteraria. The subseries Anthropologica was formed in 2007.

In addition to its publishing activities, the Finnish Literature Society maintains research activities and infrastructures, an archive containing folklore and literary collections, a research library and promotes Finnish literature abroad.

Studia fennica editorial board
Pasi Ihalainen, Professor, University of Jyväskylä, Finland
Timo Kaartinen, Title of Docent, Lecturer, University of Helsinki, Finland
Taru Nordlund, Title of Docent, Lecturer, University of Helsinki, Finland
Riikka Rossi, Title of Docent, Researcher, University of Helsinki, Finland
Katriina Siivonen, Substitute Professor, University of Helsinki, Finland
Lotte Tarkka, Professor, University of Helsinki, Finland
Tuomas M. S. Lehtonen, Secretary General, Dr. Phil., Finnish Literature Society, Finland
Tero Norkola, Publishing Director, Finnish Literature Society
Maija Hakala, Secretary of the Board, Finnish Literature Society, Finland

Editorial Office
SKS
P.O. Box 259
FI-00171 Helsinki
www.finlit.fi

Eerika Koskinen-Koivisto

Her Own Worth

Negotiations of Subjectivity in
the Life Narrative of a Female Labourer

Finnish Literature Society · SKS · Helsinki

Studia Fennica Ethnologica 16

The publication has undergone a peer review.

The open access publication of this volume has received part funding via a Jane and Aatos Erkko Foundation grant.

© 2016 Eerika Koskinen-Koivisto and SKS
License CC-BY-NC-ND

A digital edition of a printed book first published in 2014 by the Finnish Literature Society.
Cover Design: Timo Numminen
EPUB Conversion: Tero Salmén

ISBN 978-952-222-609-9 (Print)
ISBN 978-952-222-753-9 (PDF)
ISBN 978-952-222-618-1 (EPUB)

ISSN 0085-6835 (Studia Fennica)
ISSN 1235-1954 (Studia Fennica Ethnologica)

DOI: http://dx.doi.org/10.21435/sfe.16

This work is licensed under a Creative Commons CC-BY-NC-ND license.
To view a copy of the license, please visit http://creativecommons.org/licenses/by-nc-nd/4.0/

A free open access version of the book is available at http://dx.doi.org/10.21435/sfe.16 or by scanning this QR code with your mobile device.

Contents

Preface 9

1. Introduction: Understanding Her Life 12

Research Aims and Questions 12
Studying the Life of an "Ordinary" Individual 15
Elsa's Life Context 16
    The Life of Elsa Koskinen 16
    Inha Ironworks – The Factory Village 18
    Factory Workers' Families 22
Concepts and Theoretical Framework 24
    Narrated Life and Personal Experiences 24
    The Life Narrative as a Negotiation of Subjectivity 25
    Intersections of Gender, Class and Work 27
Outline of this Book 29

2. The Dialogic Research Process and Analysis 31

The Interviews and Intimacy 32
    Interviews with Elsa 32
    Studying a Relative – Subjective Knowledge and Validity 36
    Blind Spots and Reflexivity 38
    The Challenges of Intergenerational Dialogue 41
Research Ethics 44
Tools of Analysis 48
    Micro-narratives and Key Dialogues 48
    Narrative Positioning 49
    Cultural Ideals 51

3. A Working Woman: The Negotiation of Gendered Ideals 53

Family Dynamics, Generations and Gendered Ideals 54
 The Model of the Heroic Mother 54
 The Working Mother as Homemaker 59
 The Woman I Want (You) to Be 63

Gender and Humour in the Factory Environment 66
 Dirty Work, Dirty Talk 66
 Absurd Ideals: Working, Resting and Taking Care of the Home 71
 A Female-Rebel or Young People Having Fun? 73

Women in Manual Labour 78
 Strength and Self-control 79
 Embodied Femininity: Pretty Girls in Dirty Overalls 80

4. Social Class: Identification and Distinction 83

Narrated Worlds: Social Dynamics in the Factory Community 84
 The Days of the Paternalistic Factory Owner 84
 The Stereotype of the Rough and Drunken but Genuine Worker 90
 Youth, Solidarity and Sense of Community 92
 Social Mobility: Making and Breaking Boundaries 95

The Self Defined by Class 98
 Material Scarcity and Social Ranking 98
 Relegated to a Lower Class: Dominance and Humiliation 104
 Skills and Dignity: "I knew the job" 108
 Worker Identity and "a greasy skin" 112

5. Change and Continuity in a Life Narrative 117

Embodied Change: Experiences of Advance and Loss 117
 Modernizing Factory Work: Embodied Experience and the Worker Identity 118
 An Easier Life Equals a Better Life? 121
 Sites (Dis)Connecting People 125
 Disappearing Landscapes – The Amputated Sites of the Factory Community 129

Travelling Selves – Narrative Strategies and Biographical Time 133
 Beginnings: The Solidarity of the Family and the Community 133
 The Young and Wild Elsa 135
 The Shy and Worrying Elsa 142
 The Funny Elsa 144
 Completion: the Humorous Storyteller 147

6. Conclusions 149

Narrating Subjectivity: Continuity and Renegotiation 150
Reflections on Narrative Means, Strategies and Agency 153
The Potential of Micro-level Analysis and a Dialogic Approach in Life Narrative Research 155

Notes 158

References 175

Appendixes 196

Abstract 210

Index 212

Preface

This book is based on my PhD research. During the research process I learned a lot from the experienced masters craftsmen of different "factories and units" and received help from many fellow workers.

From our first meeting, I have admired the energy and enthusiasm for conducting research of my supervisor Laura Stark. She has worked tremendously to support her students in finding research funding and always has had time to discuss and advise us on the path to becoming researchers. In the context of mentoring, she has involved me in her research projects and has urged me to go abroad. I have learned a lot from her, and want to thank her for her help and support. I would also like to thank my other supervisor, PhD Saara Tuomaala-Sarpong, for her encouraging and constructive comments concerning my texts through the entire process. When we first met, she and I were strangers, but she took her role seriously and remained a constant help despite everything that life brought along. Your support and trust were of crucial importance to me. Thank you.

I wish to particularly thank the reviewers Professor Ulf Palmenfelt and Docent Teemu Taira for their thorough and constructive evaluations. I met Ulf in 2007 at the first international conference I ever attended. Prof. Palmenfelt's work on narrators and narration has inspired me a great deal. I was honored to be able to end this process with his evaluation. While writing my Master's thesis, I heard a lecture by Teemu Taira on autobiographies and was impressed. I am honored that he agreed to act as my opponent at the defense and thank him for his remarks and for the challenging and enlightening discussion.

Docent and lecturer Pertti Anttonen helped me especially at the beginning of my research process. He encouraged critical thinking and took seriously the attempts of a young doctoral student to discuss theoretical issues. Pertti also gave me comments which helped me rework the manuscript after the defense. I take this opportunity to express my thanks to him.

During my PhD studies, I was a member of the research project *Strategic Practices: Hidden Histories of Gender in Finland 1880–2005*. In addition to my supervisor Laura Stark, the leader of the project, and my other supervisor Saara Tuomaala-Sarpong, I wish to thank Docent Marja Kokko, PhD Pasi Saarimäki, PhD Arja Turunen and Phil.Lic. Heli Niskanen for their inspiring thoughts and collegial support. I would also like to thank Professor

Hanna Snellman, the director of the project *Happy Days? – Everyday Life and Nostalgia in the Extended 1950s* (SA 137923) in the context of which I began my postdoctoral research, and which made it possible to revise this manuscript. The co-operation with all of the members of the Happy Days network has been a pleasure. Thanks go to Lena Marander-Eklund, Simo Laakkonen, Leena Paaskoski, Arja Turunen, Laura Hirvi, Kirsi-Maria Hytönen, Keijo Rantanen, Tytti Steel and Antti Wallius as well as Kalle Kallio and Teemu Ahola from Werstas and Iina Wahlström from Sarka.

In addition to project groups, I had the privilege of being a member of the Graduate School of Cultural Interpretations, a joint graduate school of folklore and religious studies. I am grateful to the directors and coordinators of the graduate school for the well-organized program, and to all the friends and fellow graduate students who gave critical comments, pushed my work ahead, and provided joyful evening gatherings.

Further, I want to express warm thanks to my own working community, the Department of History and Ethnology at the University of Jyväskylä, whose staff and students have been an inspiring group to work with. Special thanks to the director, Professor Jari Ojala, for creating an excellent working environment. I also want to thank Professor Pirjo Korkiakangas for leading the doctoral seminar of ethnology, and all the participants of the doctoral seminars as well as those of the annual seminar of the department for their comments that helped me to improve my work. In addition, I greatly benefitted from the meetings and discussions of our gender studies research cluster led by Professors Pirjo Markkola and Tiina Kinnunen. And I wish to thank my closest colleagues who have also become dear friends in sharing with me both the joys and worries of life. Thank you Kirsi-Maria Hytönen, Laura Hirvi, Pilvi Hämeenaho and Arja Turunen.

I also need to send thanks to the other side of the Atlantic. In 2009–2010 I spent a year as a Fulbright grantee in the Center for Folklore Studies at Ohio State University in Columbus, Ohio. That year was significant in many ways. I am grateful to Professor Dorothy Noyes for her invitation to visit the Center and to Professors Amy Shuman, Katherine Borland, Sabra Webber, Ray Cashman and Patrick B. Mullen for their time and insightful comments to my texts. I also wish to thank Barbara and Timothy Lloyd for introducing me to the American folklore community and for offering me their friendship and support. During my stay in Columbus, I also enjoyed the wonderful company of many fellow graduate students.

Research also requires financial support. I wish to thank all the institutions who have funded my research: the Ellen and Artturi Nyyssönen Fund, the Graduate School of Cultural Interpretations, the Finnish Academy, the Fulbright Center, the Eino Jutikkala Fund, Palkansaajasäätiö, the Finnish Cultural Foundation, the Emil ja Lempi Hietanen Fund, and the Faculty of Humanities as well as the Department of History and Ethnology at the University of Jyväskylä. I would also like to thank Gerard McAlester and Joan Nordlund for proofreading the parts of this manuscript. I would like to thank Ethnologia Scandinavica for the permission to use parts of my article "Disappearing Landscapes. Embodied Experience and Metaphoric

Space in the Life Story of a Female Factory Worker" published in volume 41 in Chapter 5 of this book. I also want to thank the anonymous reviewers for their comments.

This text took its final form thanks to the insightful comments of two anonymous reviewers. I am also grateful to the editor of this series, Professor Katriina Siivonen, for her help and to Maija Hakala and Eija Hukka from the Finnish Literature Society's publishing department for all the instructions and co-ordination. Thank you for your collaboration.

At this point, I would also like to thank friends who helped me while I commuted back and forth between Riihimäki and Jyväskylä: Riikka Aro, Kirsi-Maria Hytönen, Arja and Olli Turunen. I am very grateful also to those who have supported me sharing happy and dark moments of life. Thank you Essi and Tamás Gruborovics, Essi Ikonen, Sini-Mari and Antti Lepistö, Tiina and Timo Piispanen and Pauliina Tujula. My family, on their part, has offered me moments during which I could forget my research work. A special thanks is owed to my father Asko for helping me to gather information on the Inha Ironworks and on Elsa's life. And last but not least, there are no words that could express my gratitude towards my husband Ilja who has followed me to other side of the world because of this work, has read numerous versions of my text, listened to my worries and ideas, and stayed by my side during the difficult times. Thank you for believing in me!

And finally, this research would not have been possible without my grandmother Elsa Koskinen, who shared with me her life narrative. Not everyone has the privilege to know a grandparent so well as a human being. I wish to dedicate this work to her.

Madison October 30th, 2014

Eerika Koskinen-Koivisto

1. Introduction

Understanding Her Life

> I worked. I said I have greasy skin. I am a greasy-skinned worker. Let others study. But I have done OK. (Interview 10, 9, p.8)

Research Aims and Questions

The world has changed tremendously over the past century. Science and technology have taken huge steps, human mobility has increased in scale and speed, and market economics has taken over most of the globe. Finnish society is totally different from what it was a hundred years ago: the everyday life of regular Finns is rather secure and financially comfortable; most citizens live in urban areas and have access to high education. It is even said that Finns form one big middle class. This is, of course, a generalization like any shared narrative of social change. It excludes controversies, struggle, and tragedies that narratives of personal experiences could reveal. What would individual people have to say about life in the 20th century? What kind of story would you tell about your life to a representative of the younger generation? What aspects of life would you emphasize and what accounts would you narrate?

In this study, I examine the life narrative of a female worker who also happens to be my grandmother, Elsa Sanelma Koskinen (née Kiikkala). I analyze her account of her experiences related to work, class and gender because I seek to gain a better understanding of how changes in these aspects of life influenced the ways in which she saw her own worth at the time of the interviews, and constructed her subjectivity. I am also interested in the power dynamics in modernizing Finland: social norms and values, intersecting identities and varying social positions that limit individual choices but at the same time are constantly renegotiated in shifting social situations. A life narrative, which consists of several smaller narratives, offers views on both of these dimensions: the process of individual meaning making and the power of social norms and ideals.

I chose to study Elsa[1] for a number of reasons. First, early on she expressed a willingness to share her experiences with me. Trust, mutual understanding and the depth of our many years of interaction allowed her to open up to me, the interviewer, on sensitive topics such as social hierarchy, her family life and her sense of shame and dignity.[2] In addition, Elsa's life touches upon many of the core aspects of 20th-century social change: changes in women's roles, the entrance of middle-class women into working life, women's increasing participation in the public sphere, feminist movements, upward social mobility, the expansion of the middle class, the growth of welfare and the appearance of new technologies not only in industrial working life but also in daily life: the kitchen, the laundry room and the hospital. These complex constellations of socio-economic transformation have been designated "the process of modernization" (Felski 1995, 12–13). During the course of modernization in Finland, the number of narratives entering people's lives expanded via newspapers, literature, schoolbooks, popular culture, and plays performed by civic groups and in school galas (Stark 2006a, 11–14, 17). Reading, writing, social movements and education encouraged modern citizens to reflect upon their own encounters with material novelties, new technologies, novel ideologies, developments and social changes. Many interesting experiences of encounters with these innovations are recounted in life stories of 20th-century Europeans. Individual life stories such as Elsa Koskinen's offer hundreds of smaller narratives for analysis.

This study takes an ethnographic approach to life narrative and applies dialogic methodology both in the interview method and in the analysis of the interview material. The folklorist Patricia Sawin (2004), who has examined the songs and life of female Appalachian singer and storyteller Bessie Eldreth (born in the 1910s), provides us with a brilliant example of this kind of ethnographic analysis. Eldreth had been interviewed and taped several times before Sawin started to collect oral traditions from her. At first, Sawin did not expect to find herself engaged in the project of studying Eldreth and her self-representation. Sawin's aim was simply to study Eldreth's songs and singing practice. During the research process, Sawin ended up using dialogic methodology. Hearing more and more about Eldreth's life and listening to her multi-vocal stories, Sawin became interested in Eldreth's creation of a gender- and class-determined sense of self. Eldreth, who grew up in rural Appalachia, supported her family (a husband and eleven children) by doing various, often physical, jobs such as farm work, cutting timber, cleaning and cooking. Eldreth constructs her subjectivity mostly around labour and gender. In her study, Sawin considers how Bessie Eldreth positions herself in relation to internalized societal discourses. Describing her research process and methodology, she uses the term *the ethnography of subjectivity* and explains:

> "My approach thus challenges the assumptions that underpin biography or life history, in that biography treats the subject as self-evidently significant, life history presents the subjective as representative of a group and both not only accept the subject as performed and self-consistent but also obscure the process whereby various bits of information drawn from multiple sources and originally inflected by multiple voices are melded into 'the story' of a person's life. *The ethnography of subjectivity*, in contrast, locates significance in exposing the process through which the subject creates herself through interaction and in interrogating the traces from which we can track that process." (Sawin 2004, 2; Emphasis E.K-K.)

The subject and aim of this study are parallel to Sawin's: to study the life story of one woman who is a skilled narrator, who has performed hard physical labour and who had situated herself as belonging to a lower rank in her social hierarchy. Sawin's intention to respect the informant and their relationship and her desire to seek a profound understanding of the other person are similar to my own, and called for a dialogic approach[3].

My interest in life narratives and the folklore of worker communities began at an early stage of my academic studies, when I started writing my Master's thesis. My focus in this thesis (2005) was on Elsa's life-story narration, her repertoire of narratives and her world view. In order to collect material for the thesis I interviewed Elsa repeatedly during the years 2001–2004. In all, I conducted 12 interviews with her, although in my Master's thesis I analyzed only nine of these interviews. This study includes all 12 interviews (about 12 hours of audiotape). The issues I analyze here – gender, class and work – were prominent in the interviews, which together form Elsa's life story as she chose to tell it to me. During the interview process, Elsa told me about her life at the Inha Ironworks (*Ruukki*, as she still calls it).[4] In the course of her life and working career, Elsa witnessed the heyday of the ironworks, when a traditional patriarchal style of management predominated in the metal industry. She lived through the transformation undergone by the factory community and its production due to the emergence of new technologies and modern practices of automation, increased supervision and the ever-spreading power of the market economy.[5] Elsa also experienced changes in women's role in society, and enjoyed a degree of social mobility and a dramatic improvement in her standard of living after the Second World War. It is important to note that these changes were neither unique nor did they merely signify the disappearance of old values and traditions. It is also worth pointing out that traditional patriarchal industrial communities such as the Inha Ironworks were not static and harmonious communities. On the contrary, industrial communities have always existed in a process of transformation, development and uncertainty, depending on the economic situation and technological development (see Ahvenisto 2008; Kortelainen 2008, 25).

However, change is perceived differently when we look back at the past from the vantage point of the present. A life story, a retrospective evaluation of a life lived, is one means of constructing continuity and dealing with the changes that have affected one's life, identity and subjectivity (see Mullen 1992, 269; Löyttyniemi 2004, 49). My intention in this research is to analyze narrated experiences and to draw attention to the process of personal meaning making and the negotiation of cultural norms and ideals. The narrator narrating her/his life produces many different versions of her/him self in relation to other people and to the world. These selves and their relations to others may manifest in internal contradictions. However, recurrent themes and key narratives or key dialogues reveal something important about the ways in which life is made meaningful, as Elsa Koskinen's narrative repertoire makes clear.

The research questions I seek to answer in this study are:
1) How have gender, class and work shaped the narrator's subjectivity? How does she narrate the changes that occurred with respect to these areas of her life? What are the things that create continuity in her life narrative, and what are the ambiguities that need to be renegotiated in the course of the telling? Why do they need to be renegotiated?
2) How does Elsa position herself in relation to shifting cultural ideals, and what kinds of narrative means and strategies does she employ?
3) How can the study of an individual life narrative contribute to our general understanding of the power dynamics related to social change and to the role that narratives play in interpreting life experiences?

Examining Elsa's life narrative opens up a continuous process of dealing with past experiences that are not merely discursive but are also rooted in her *physical* and *material* life as a working-class girl, a young woman, a mother, a homemaker, an active worker and a retired worker in the context of the present. This negotiation is an on-going process of positioning in which the narrator engages in dialogic relations as much with the self as with the other (in this case me), as well as with other persons narrated within the story and the potential readers of the finished work. My intimate relationship with Elsa produced rich data in which Elsa reflects on confusing and painful experiences in her life. This research material, coupled with my knowledge of Elsa's life and personality offers insights into the complex positioning process of the individual in social transformations and the uncertainties created by social mobility, women's emancipation and technological progress – in other words, the process of looking for one's place in a changing world. The end product is a written version, my version, of Elsa's life narrative as I have interpreted it through the lenses of my scholarship.

Studying the Life of an "Ordinary" Individual

Folklorists have long studied individual storytellers, so-called "tradition bearers", talented performers and expert narrators living in villages and communities with rich oral traditions.[6] My research, on the other hand, deals with a person who was not an extraordinary personality or a well-known *expert storyteller* with skills recognized by her/his community. This is not to say that Elsa is not able to weave a colourful story or captivate her listener.[7] On the contrary, she is a good storyteller and has narrative competence (Hymes 1973, 47–49; also Pöysä 2012, 29). However, only a few people in her closest circle have been able to enjoy her talent and repertoire, which focus mostly on personal narratives, anecdotes and humour.

Everyday life, the perspective from below, has long been the focus of ethnological studies examining people as cultural beings.[8] The discipline of ethnology was established to document the surviving features of the agrarian tradition and life style, in a word, *folk* culture.[9] It was not until after the

Second World War that the field came to include the everyday life of industrial workers and their culture.[10] Since the 1970s, Nordic ethnologists have been analysing forms and expressions of cultural identities: nation, gender, age, class, ethnicity and place (Arvidsson 2001, 9–12; Frykman & Gilje 2003, 9). In the 1970s and 1980s, Finnish folklore scholars studied local communities and their storytellers, examining local identities and the relationship between the individual and tradition.[11] In the 1980s and 1990s, many folklorists were interested in the expressive traditions of women and the ways in which gender shapes culture and tradition.[12] Moreover, folklore scholarship, which had earlier focused on a seemingly homogenous *common folk* and ignored class relations and antagonisms, began to pay attention to class relations and the oral traditions and oral history of the working class (see, for example, Knuuttila 1992; Peltonen 1996; Pöysä 1997).[13]

Studies of workers, working-class culture and factory communities tend to treat working-class people as a more or less homogeneous group with access to similar possibilities, whose experiences gave rise to shared cultural significance. Many studies started as oral history projects aimed at representing the history of a professional group or a worker community (e.g., Ukkonen 2000; Kortelainen 2008). There are very few studies that explore the individual lives and understandings of ordinary female labourers who were not activists of any kind and who had no special role in the community.[14] My aim in this study is to understand the broader historical changes in society from the perspective of an individual female worker. My assumption is that, by studying a so-called "ordinary individual" and everyday life experiences of ethnological interest such as changes in working life, mechanization, gendered dynamics and social hierarchies, I can enhance understanding of what it means (and has meant) to be a subject, and in this case a worker, in a changing society and how social dynamics shaped the life of an individual in 20th century Finland. Consequently, I hope to shed light on the everyday life experiences of a female worker, and her experience of belonging to the category of workers, a category that was defined differently from the outside than from the inside, and was based on individual and collective identities.

Elsa's Life Context

THE LIFE OF ELSA KOSKINEN

Elsa Sanelma Kiikkala (later Koskinen) was born on the 26th of April 1927, the seventh of twelve children in a factory worker's family living in the factory community of Inha Ironworks *(Inhan Tehtaat)* in the municipality of Ähtäri, in Southern Ostrobothnia in western Finland. At the time of Elsa's birth, the family had temporarily moved to the centre of the municipality as a result of a lengthy strike and lockout of metalworkers that directly affected her father. Later in the same year, her family, the Kiikkalas, returned to their home, a small one-bedroom flat in a large wooden building owned by the Ironworks that was situated in the shadow of a tall smokestack next

Multi-dwelling houses in Hamarimäki, the residential area where Elsa's family lived in her childhood. Photo taken in the 1920s by Gustav Welin. Courtesy of the Archives of Fiskars Inhantehtaat Ltd.

to the factory yard. The village of Inha Ironworks consisted of several housing areas and some farmland owned by the factory. Elsa tells me how, in her childhood, people gathered on the steps of the factory workers' multi-dwelling buildings to chat and exchange the latest news and gossip, and to listen to the tales told by the elderly people. This is how Elsa heard many stories and learned about the lives of older women and other worker families in her community.

In early-20th-century Finland, it was usually the fathers of worker families who were the wage-earners, while the mothers stayed at home to rear the children. Besides working in the factory, Elsa's father had to do various side jobs to support his family, and her mother was kept busy maintaining the household and rearing the growing number of children. All of the children, including Elsa, went to school, but owing to the outbreak of the Second World War in 1939, when Elsa was 12 years old, her class did not complete even the six years of elementary education that were compulsory at the time. Instead, Elsa had to start earning money. First she worked as a maid servant in local middle-class families, and then, at the age of fifteen, she began working on the horseshoe line at the Inha Ironworks (see Appendix 2). Unlike her siblings, she ended up staying in the Ironworks community after the war, and married a workman named Eino Koskinen. Elsa and Eino had four children, one of whom died in infancy. Thus Elsa was born into a family of workers. She learned about physical work at an early age, performing household chores, carrying firewood and water, cooking and cleaning, assisting her father at logging sites, biking long distances to buy food on the black market during the war, and finally taking up factory work as a low-level assistant, or as she called it *sällin sälli* (a "dogsbody's dogsbody"). In this way she assumed not only the social but also the physical identity of a worker, dressing in dirty overalls and performing hard physical labour carrying boxes of horseshoes and later operating the machines that formed, cut, and stamped iron products. However, times gradually changed, and so did her social position as the wife of a man who had climbed the social ladder when, in the late 1960s, the factory invested in new technologies. Machines replaced physical work, and new professionals were needed to design and use them. Elsa's husband, Eino, educated himself through correspondence courses and became first a foreman and then a production manager. This meant that Elsa could have claimed the relatively high status as a manager's wife who did not need to work. After the children reached adolescence, however, she made the decision to go back to the low-status physical work of the production line, working at first only in the summer but later full-time again. This corresponds to the prevailing situation: by the end of the 1960s the majority of married women had found their way to wage labour (Haavio-Mannila 1968). I focus in my analysis on how Elsa represented her life in retrospect, how she viewed her life trajectory and possibilities, and how she justified the different choices she made.

Today, Elsa is a widow and continues to live in the municipality of Ähtäri in her own one-bedroom flat in the municipal centre, far away from the old ironworks. She told me how she reminiscences about the old factory village almost every day. She is a skilled narrator, and she tells colourful stories about her life at the ironworks, mostly to members of her own family, but if given a chance, she also shares them with other audiences such as doctors, nurses and home-care staff or visiting friends. She told me that she began telling stories when she was no longer able to write. This happened when she was in her 70s and was diagnosed with breast cancer. Surgery and radiology left her right arm too sore to handle a pen. Up until then Elsa had exchanged letters with her sisters, recounting her life experiences and sharing various memorable events, strange situations, humorous accounts and high spots in her life. When writing became difficult she began talking about her life to me, her only female grandchild. I have been her main audience since 2001, when I decided to record her stories to use in my academic studies.

INHA IRONWORKS – THE FACTORY VILLAGE
Industrialization began fairly late in Finland, in the latter half of the 19th century. A new era of political liberalism begin when Emperor Alexander II ascended the throne in 1855, bringing about many reforms that paved the way for industrialism: the restrictions on sawmills were lifted (1857), craftsmen no longer needed to belong to a guild (1859), and workers were given freedom of movement (1865), for instance (Talve 1997, 316–317). The sawmill industry, and timber cutting, expanded significantly in the 1870s. At the turn of the century the majority of Finns lived off the forest and the land. Thus, Finland was an industrialized but predominantly agrarian nation in the first half of the 20th century (Soikkanen 1981, 445; Haapala 1986, 12–15).[15]

Agrarian Finland transformed into an industrial country in the course of about 70 years (1870–1940), with independent small farmers, a moderate employment situation and sufficient subsistence (Talve 1997, 325). Unlike in certain other countries in which industrialization caused rapid urbanization and impoverishment, in Finland industrial labour offered – albeit inadequately – a stable living for some landless rural inhabitants whose numbers had been growing owing to a population increase that continued throughout the 19th century, and which the capacity of agriculture was unable to sustain.[16] Along with the five largest industrial centres (Helsinki, Turku, Tampere, Kymijoki and Ylä-Vuoksi) and smaller industrial foci and towns, there also existed numerous small factory communities in the Finnish countryside, and Inha Ironworks was one such rural industrial unit. (Haapala 1995, 62–65.)

Inha Ironworks *(Inha Bruk)* was founded in 1851 on the shores of the River Inha.[17] It started out as a small rural factory producing raw iron from scrap metal and lake ore. In addition to the ironworks, there was also a sawmill nearby. All this was typical for the industrial communities of the 19th century.[18] A railway stop was created in the nearby Inha village in 1883, and the railway station was opened in 1887 (Viertola 1991, 23). The factories and the village increased in size at the end of the 19th century, and drew people from surrounding areas. From 1884 on, both the ironworks and the sawmill were owned and run by a Swedish engineer named August Nilsson Keirkner, locally known as the *Patruuna*.[19] The *Patruuna* invested in new technology such as steam engines, and the factory started to process iron into bolts, spikes and horseshoes mainly for domestic markets.[20]

In addition to developing the industry, Keirkner also contributed to the life of the workers by founding a school in 1889 and constructing a generator for the village (*Rautainen tarina* 1991, 15, 30). The factory built several multi-dwelling houses for the workers around the turn of the century. These houses formed two residential areas on either side of the River Inha: Hamarimäki, which was adjacent to the factory yard, and Inhan puoli, which lay on the other side of the river. The workers had the opportunity to cultivate land and keep farm animals such as cows and pigs. Firewood for cooking and heating was cut directly from the factory-owned forest. The workers could do their shopping in the factory's shop (ibid. 31–32). Next to the factory yard was a common baking house and two separate saunas for workers and members of the managerial classes. The workers could go to the sauna and bathe at the end of the working week, before Sunday. The saunas at Inha were used collectively, and there were separate sauna days for women (Fridays) and men (Saturdays). Managerial-class families had a private bathing time scheduled for each family. The official written history of Inha Ironworks, as well as popular historical writings by local amateur historians,[21] describe the old Inha Ironworks factory community and its activities nostalgically, painting a picture of a harmonious and well-organized village. As in other industrial communities, the Inha Ironworks factory community was organized around a hierarchy that placed people in different categories. From top to bottom they would be: the *Patruuna*, the upper management and office staff, teachers, storekeepers and shop assistants, blacksmiths, carpenters, foremen, workers, stockmen and their handymen. In 1910, the number of residents in the area was the highest in its history, almost 900, of which approximately 450 worked at the ironworks (Hahne 1994, 16).[22]

During the first decade and a half of the 20th century, when the semi-autonomous Grand Duchy of Finland was still part of the Russian Empire, the Finnish political system was passing through an unstable phase of democratization and modernization. The Finnish people had experienced a rapid growth in population, industrialization, improvements to the economy, and a rising standard of living. These changes caused growing economic divisions, which led to the rise of a widespread labour movement. At the beginning of the 20th century, the workers of Inha, too, organized and started to engage in various labour-movement-related activities in the fields of culture and politics. A worker's association (*Inhan Työväenyhdistys*) was founded in 1904, and a workers' hall (*Inhan Työväentalo*), often referred to as just "*talo*", ("the Hall"), was built in 1907. The Inha Branch of the Metalworkers' Union (*Inhan metallityöväen ammattiosasto*) was founded in 1909, and was at that time the eighth oldest unionized sector in Finland (*Rautainen tarina*, 30; IMA, 5).

The national awakening of the 19th century still resonated in Finland at the beginning of the 20th century. However, economic, social and political divisions, mainly between the Whites (conservative nationalists, mainly landowners) and the Reds (socialists and communists, mainly crofters and agrarian and industrial workers) were deepening.[23] The February and October Revolutions of 1917 led to the collapse of the Russian Empire during the last years of the First World War. Russia withdrew from the war, and the chaos that ensued in Russia itself brought about the end of the Grand Duchy of Finland and the collapse of the Finnish government, the armed forces, the economy and the social order (Haapala 1995, 151–156). Finland declared its independence from Russia in 1917. The Whites and the Reds fell into disagreement and competed for leadership of the Finnish state. Both sides began forming paramilitary, armed groups, the White Guards and the Red Guards. Finally, the turmoil led to a bloody civil war in the early months of 1918. The Whites won the war three months later, but not before approximately 40,000 people had perished. Most of the victims of the war died far from the battlefields, in mass executions or in detainment camps. Three quarters of the dead were Red combatants and sympathizers. I have not been able to obtain a clear picture of what happened at Inha in 1918. No military action took place in Ähtäri, but because of their ideological views some workers at Inha Ironworks lost their jobs, and approximately ten worker activists were sent to prison camps.[24]

Deep division marked social relations over the next decade; there was bitterness on both sides, and the position of the losers, the Reds, was especially difficult. The boundaries between the Whites and the Reds were visible in everyday life: the workers representing the Reds, for example, bought groceries in consumer co-ops rather than white-owned shops, had their own cultural and sports activities and their own halls for cultural activities (see, for example, Peltonen 1996, 17–19; Peltonen 2003, 308). *Inhan Taimi*, the Inha workers' sports club, was established in 1923. The members consisted of workers of different ages, from young working-class athletes to older union activists. The early years of the sports club were unstable: it was suspected of training Red Guards, one of the paramilitary units that earlier, during the Civil War, had engaged in military action on the side of the Reds.[25] Trade unions were abolished immediately after the war, and their activities were prohibited. In their place, "industrial councils" *(teollisuusneuvosto)* were established to negotiate terms between workers and employers.[26]

Patruuna Keirkner fell ill during the First World War, and in 1917 he sold the factory to Albert Lindsey von Julin (1871–1944), the Managing Director of the Fiskars group. The ironworks was turned into a corporation named "Inhan Tehtaat". Keirkner and his wife moved to Helsinki and devoted themselves to collecting art. He died soon afterwards in 1918 (*Rautainen tarina*, 34). Julin never resided in Inha. The era of the local factory *patruuna* had come to an end. Reinhold Amberg, Kreirkner's former technical manager, managed the factory after 1917. At the end of the 1920s there were approximately 120 homes and 600 residents in the Inha Ironworks village (IMA 2009, 15).[27] The cultural life there was particularly active in the 1920s. Villagers could enjoy plays put on at the Inha Workers' Theatre (*Inhan työväennäyttämö*), where the amateur actors and actresses were young factory workers. Other free-time activities included sewing bees, sports competitions (cycling, skiing), a male-voice choir and children's parties (Hahne 1994, 138–139).

Politically and economically, the 1920s was a difficult time for most of the workers and their families. A lockout followed a strike by the Metalworkers' Union in 1927 lasted over six months, and as a result production was halted for 30 weeks. More than 9,000 workers had joined the strike across 53 factories. Sixteen factories evicted 1,289 workers and their family members from their homes (Koivisto 1963) during the lockout, and 59 families were evicted from Inha (IMA 51 2009, 15). The first signs of the Great Depression began to appear in Finland at the end of the 1920s. The demand for timber decreased, and Inha Sawmill was closed in 1930. Workers at Inha Ironworks worked only four days a week in 1930 and 1931, then production began to recover in 1932 (*Rautainen tarina*, 39, 41–42). The sudden outbreak of the Second World War at the end of the 1930s brought changes to production in the factory as well as to the everyday life of the people living in the ironworks village. The village school closed in 1938 due to war mobilization. Young men were called up to serve in the Finnish Army on the Russian frontier, and women replaced them in the factory. Inha Ironworks served the war industry, producing horseshoes and sled runners for the Finnish Army. The factory area was guarded, and its buildings, especially the foundry, were camouflaged with tree branches on the roofs so they could not be detected by hostile aircraft. A significant number of the factory's young male workers died at the front in both the Winter War (1939–40) and the Continuation War (1941–44) (*Rautainen tarina* 39, 41; Hahne 1994, 86).

In 1943, the factory was absorbed into the Fiskars group, a large industrial corporation owned by A.L. von Julin. Inha Ironworks had celebrated its centenary in 1942, but owing to the on-going Continuation War the celebration did not take place until a year later. The festivities were held in the yard of Corps de logis, a manor house built by the former *Patruuna* Keirkner. A. L. von Julin was present, and workers who had served the factory for a long time were rewarded with medals of honour. Manufacturing continued at Inha after the war. Scrap metal was abundantly available at a low price. When the older methods of producing iron became unprofitable the Fiskars Corporation decided to invest in new technology at Inha, and to transfer the whole production line from the Kellokoski factory in Tuusula. Modern steel and aluminium production lines were installed in the 1960s (*Rautainen tarina* 1991, 34; 41–43). New items produced at the Inha factory included hinges and thin metal products such as radiators and lockers. The Fiskars Corporation moved the production of aluminium boats from the Kellokoski factory in Tuusula to Inha in the 1970s (ibid. 45). Along with the technological advances and automation, more women began to work not only on the production lines of *Inhan Tehtaat* but also in managerial positions.

Factory Workers' Families

Histories of ironworks and other factories are family histories. Factory companies provided many Finnish industrial communities of the 19th and early 20th centuries not only with income but also with dwellings and other necessities for the entire families, including the children, of their workers.[28] This was also the case with the worker families of Inha in the early 20th century, including the childhood families of both Elsa and her husband Eino. Their fathers worked in the factory and their mothers were homemakers. The families lived in dwellings owned by the factory. Elsa's father Kaarle (Kalle) Kiikkala (1883–1948) was born on a small farm in a village near the factory. His family had a large number of children, and the farm could not support all of them. Thus at an early age, Kaarle went to work at Inha Ironworks. In 1916 he married Hilda (Hilta) Hauta-aho (1892), the daughter of a landowning peasant from the village of Ähtärinranta about 30 kilometres from the Ironworks village. By the time Elsa was born, Kaarle and Hilda already had six children. Kalle Kiikkala worked in the foundry of the Ironworks in the 1920s. [29] In order to support his growing family he also had to do side jobs, working as a cobbler mending shoes and harnesses, for example.

The father of Elsa's husband Eino was Vihtori Koskinen (1888–1964). He, too, had worked at the Inha factory since his early youth. He had five children, three of whom, including Eino (1926–1989), were from his third marriage to Rauha Paananen (1891–1866). His previous wives had died in epidemics. Vihtori was known to be a knowledgeable man. He had travelled to America for example, and was actively involved in the local Workers' Association *(työväenyhdistys)* and the trade union branch *(ammattiosasto).*[30] He was also well known and highly respected in the worker community for his diplomacy and negotiation skills, and was chairman of the Inha Industrial

Vihtori Koskinen gives a speech in 1942 at the centenary celebrations of the Inha Ironworks. Courtesy of the Archives of Fiskars Inhantehtaat Ltd.

Council (*Inhan teollisuusneuvosto*), the institution that replaced the prohibited trade unions after the Civil War of 1918. He served as chairman of the Inha branch of the Metalworkers' Union from 1936 to 1944, and later became the first shop steward at Inha Ironworks (IMA 2009, 15). He made a speech at the centenary celebrations of Inha Ironworks in 1942, and received a medal of honour for his service at the factory. Vihtori also received a gold medal from the Central Organization of Finnish Trade Unions *(Suomen ammattijärjestöjen keskusliitto, SAK)* in 1960.

Despite the fact that both Elsa and Eino were born into factory workers' families, they differed in background, especially with regard to their fathers' positions and the sizes of their families. Elsa's father was an ordinary worker, whereas Eino's father was an activist and a man who occupied positions of trust. Both Elsa and Eino started working in the factory at a young age and continued to live in the ironworks village. Together they started a family, but their careers took different directions owing to gender roles, societal changes and personal choices. As already mentioned, worker's families typically lived close to the factories. This spatial intimacy continued until the phase of structural change in the 1950s and the 1960s, when many communities were deindustrialized. Technology and society developed quickly when the economy recovered after the Second World War, and population growth, the increasing use of new technologies in agriculture and forestry, and rapid urbanization affected the rural factory communities and the countryside in general. The change was driven by the demands of the global economy and capitalism. Soon, many former industrial communities deindustrialized or were transformed into modern suburbs without a homogeneous social composition and common social activities, and Inha was one of them.[31] Elsa Koskinen, her husband and their children lived through this change. Eino and Elsa worked at *Inhan Tehtaat* until 1984. Their daughter Raija (b. 1948) and their sons Asko (b. 1952), and Simo (b. 1959) moved away from the village to study. Raija was 16 when she started her studies at a commercial college (*Kauppaopisto*) in Vaasa. Asko and Simo went to professional college *(ammattikoulu)* in their hometown Ähtäri, completed military service and then continued their Studies at a technical college in Vaasa. Elsa and Eino, who had thus far lived in dwellings owned by the factory, retired in 1984 and bought an apartment in the municipal centre of Ähtäri. Eino died in 1989.

Concepts and Theoretical Framework

NARRATED LIFE AND PERSONAL EXPERIENCES

> "Narrating constitutes some of the prime ways known to human beings to communicate their experiences" (Klein 2006, 9).

The flow of events in individual lives can be understood, organized, and communicated through narration. In the process of narrating one's life, *lived experiences*[32] become understood, conceptualized and interpreted in and through language, which draws upon historically and culturally specific structures of knowledge.[33] Furthermore, narratives are means of understanding *lived* time and *processes* of change (Abbott 2002, 3–6). Narratives are cognitive instruments that make experience comprehensible, rather than iconic relations between events and storytelling (see Bauman 1986, 5, 7–9).[34] They help us to process and mediate information about the world by establishing a chronological and causal order (Ricoeur 1984; Siikala 1984, 22–23, 28). However, they do more than carry news and information; they reflect on the meanings of events, doings and sayings – in other words, on the morality of people's behaviour (Riessman 1993, 3–4). Narratives are packages that not only inform the listener but also involve (possibly multiple) explanations and interpretations of series of events and personal experiences (Gubrium & Holstein 2011, 6).

Life narratives are larger compositions of personal history and personal experiences. They may be constructed chronologically or built around certain *turning points*, in other words personal milestones in life such as starting school, getting married or entering working life (see Linde 1993, 52–56; Arvidsson 1998, 61), or *periodizations* based on changes in the historico-political environment or working life (see, for example, Snellman 1996, 15; Paaskoski 2008, 149). Life narratives may be oral or written.[35] The concepts and definitions (which are often confusing) vary from one field and researcher to another (see Bertaux 1981; Arvidsson 1998, 8). *Autobiography* refers primarily to a written text, and *life story* or *life narrative* to orally transmitted material that is often collected in an interview setting (see, for example, Oring 1987; Arvidsson 1998, 8). In contrast to a *life history,* which is often characterized as an objective review by others, a life story and a life narrative emphasize the narrator's own words (see Titon 1980; Watson & Watson-Franke 1985; Gubrium 1993; Chase 2005, 652).[36] In the context of this study, I use the terms life story and life narrative as synonyms when referring to my analysis of orally produced research material.

Specific episodes in one's life and other significant events constitute smaller narrative entities, stories within a story (Linde 1993), which I call *micro-narratives*. These are often dramatic, truth-based accounts of personal experiences, but also include anecdotes and descriptive reports of some phenomena.[37] The epithet *micro-* draws attention to this variety, to the contradictions among smaller narratives embedded in the life narrative, and to the potential for varying interpretation they entail.[38] What is it, exactly, that makes single life narratives and micro-narratives interesting? What can we learn from narratives of personal experience?

The oral historian Luisa Passerini points out that personal histories stimulate "references to the exceptional – to the things that make one individual different from another" (1988, 8). On the other hand, autobiographical accounts encourage subjects to present themselves as unique and irreplaceable, inducing them to reveal their cultural values and hence, paradoxically, throwing light on stereotypes and shared ideas" (ibid.). Telling someone about how one has acted in different situations means portraying oneself as one would like to be perceived by others (Arvidsson 1999, 26). Thus the analysis of personal experience narratives told within a life narrative context may be a fruitful way of looking at how narrators see their lives in relation to cultural norms (Marander-Eklund 2011, 148).

My study is based on the idea that language and narrative not only mediate, but also shape experience.[39] Experience becomes part of the narrator's life history through language and narrative (Tuomaala 2004, 58; Saarikoski 2011, 118). I approach Elsa's life and her narratives ethnographically, exploring *narrated experiences* in their socio-cultural and discursive contexts. These contexts are not static but constantly changing. Each narrative reframes actors, scenes, and events, thus shaping the narrator's understanding of his/her past. We do not have access to lived experiences but can study the process of meaning-making through storytelling by approaching the narrator as a socially constructed and embodied subject with a particular experiential history on the one hand, and as a product of his/her time and culture on the other. Societal changes taking place within the course of her life have made Elsa reflect on her place in the world. Throughout my analysis I will set Elsa Koskinen's experiences within a larger socio-historical framework: the social conditions and circumstances in which she operated. I will analyseze the narrative means and strategies she employs, and thus explore the relationship between cultural meanings and individual understanding.

The Life Narrative as a Negotiation of Subjectivity

A life narrative is a process of reminiscing and interpreting: the formation of explanations regarding a person's past life (Saresma 2007, 100). In this process, the narrator (re)constructs and interprets past experiences for and with the listener, using different narrative elements and devices that are characteristic of his or her culture and social circles (Worthington 1996, 13; Aro

1996, 48; Saastamoinen 2000, 135; Stark 2006c, 84). Oral life narratives are endless, open to constant reformulation, and never complete. They can be told differently to different people and on different occasions (Mullen 1992, 15; see also Linde 1993 and Sawin 2004). However, in order to answer questions about human life, history, culture, and society, for example, researchers capture these stories, interview people and assemble variants of the lives that are being retold. These encapsulated images projected by the narrator show how people see themselves and their lives, and how they want others to see them (Mullen 1992, 7). In other words, life narratives portray us as the agents we want to be (Stark 2006c, 19). Thus, life narratives enable us to scrutinize personal reflections as well as shared mentalities, and help us to better understand the process through which people position themselves in relation to others (see also Ehn 1992, 216).

The role of life narratives in bringing together life experiences from different life phases, and in negotiating the meaning of one's existence is to give the narrator the chance to (re)define the self. This self-reflexivity is considered one of the defining elements of post-modern subjectivity, distinct from earlier predetermined, fixed social identities (Giddens 1991; Hall 2001). The new reflexive self is by no means freed from social forces, but is rather embedded in them in different ways than previously, and is surrounded by a number of potential narrative models and discourses.

I approach the life story as a process of negotiating *subjectivity*[40], the conditions of being a subject formed by a history of lived experiences, varying social contexts and subject positions (Ronkainen 1999, 30). I am interested in the ways in which lived experience, time and space construct the self and enable certain kinds of agency[41]. The concept of subjectivity draws attention to the performativity of storytelling in constructing the narrator's self and identity.[42] Feminist scholar Sidonie Smith (1998, 108–109) suggests that instead of seeing autobiographical storytelling as expressing an already existing interiority, we should treat it as a means of constructing the self. Subjectivity would thus be understood as situated, momentary and fragmentary (ibid.). In the same vein, when talking about subjectivity or the self, I do not assume a coherent self. Some scholars emphasize the coherent self as an eligible and healthy subject agent (see, for example, McIntyre 1985). This view has been criticized, among other reasons on account of the requirement of closure and oneness that it entails (see, for example, Löyttyniemi 2004, 69). It is commonly agreed among researchers, however, that the narrative form tends to construct coherence and offers an arena for negotiating contradicting life experiences and/or major changes, and the passing of time (Ricoeur 1992). In doing so, telling a life story helps the narrator to accept the chaos and fragmentariness of life (Löyttyniemi 2004, 68–70; Stark 2006c, 84–85). Many life stories deal with some unresolved conflicts in the person's life, and help her/him to negotiate new meanings for her/his existence (see Mullen 1992, 16; Frank 1997; Shuman 2005, 9).

This study thus sets out to explore *the dialogic self* as opposed to the coherent self.[43] The self undergoes an internal division in the act of telling: the current narrating self and the past selves enter into a dialogue with each other.⁴⁴ At the same time, life story telling is integrative; it brings together the different selves establishing a continuum between life experiences. The narration of childhood experiences, for example, enables the current adult self to meet the childhood self. The concept of *narrative identity* has been created to express more precisely the aspect of the self as constructed in storytelling.⁴⁵ It is about building a sense of self and personhood by means of narratives: in other words, "an adequate understanding of our own identity requires a narrative account of who we are and how we came to be that way" (Stark 2006c, 83). In my view, this narrative identity consists of different voices that at times may contradict each other (see also Hynninen 2004). I pay attention to the varying narrative strategies and agencies of Elsa's narrated selves in my analysis.

Intersections of Gender, Class and Work
My aim in this study is to scrutinize Elsa's life and experience in the realms of gender, class and work. Gender and class are social and cultural categories that, along with other markers of difference such as age, ethnicity and sexuality, intersect in people's lives and form complex divisions and identities. They both represent socio-economic, cultural and historical divisions. Thus the inequalities and hierarchies based on these categorizations are produced socially and culturally, are maintained in everyday life practices, and are learned through cultural imagery, roles and symbols (Nenola 1990, 11; Moore 1993). Work, on the other hand, is a sphere of life that structures one's time usage, financial situation and social relations. In addition to these practical dimensions, it also shapes people's identities and forms specific cultures.

All three realms concern questions related to power. Gender can be defined as a range of social and cultural characteristics used to *distinguish* between males and females, men and women, masculinities and femininities, and between the attributes assigned to these categories (see, for example, Scott 1986). Social class, on the other hand, could be characterized as a set of hierarchical divisions that *divide* groups of people into hierarchical categories (see, for example, Skeggs 2004, 12; Williams 1976, 62–66).⁴⁶ Work, too, puts people into different categories. It includes the performance of physical or mental labour, household chores and also other tasks and duties. All forms of work tie individuals to society. *Wage labour* refers to a situation in which the worker sells her/his labour and the employer buys it on the basis of a contractual agreement between the parties. The work and labour that persons are expected to do, or which is available to them, is often gendered and connected to socio-economic status. In the context of this research, the social dimension of work is of particular interest.

In the context of this research, gender, class and work function not as conceptual tools, but rather as topics of inquiry and objects of analysis. In other words, I do not take them as points of departure but problematize them as semantic concepts whose content must be re-examined in each new context. It is not my aim or motivation here to focus on subordination, or to deconstruct or challenge categorizations: I simply wish to broaden the scope through which we look at the power dynamics played out in everyday life. I approach gender and class as lived and experience-based, relational and intertwined. My analysis of gender, class and work is thus empirical. I am interested in the ways in which the narrator, Elsa, understands her social position in relation to other people, how she describes different social groups and the ideals attached to them, and how she identifies and defines herself. On the level of narration, the significances of gender, class, and work are produced through discourses and rhetorical moves (see, for example, Valtonen 2004). Gender is connected to ideals, which are often bound to class differences. In my analysis, I consider how a female worker strives to fulfil divergent social ideals (good mother and homemaker, hard worker, for example). Class, on the other hand, always exists in relation to others: to one's peers, social superiors and those deemed inferior. It is an expression of forms of exchange and production (wage labour) but it also determines the resources available.[47] Thus class is both a relation *and* a position. Gender, class and work are also tied to the *physical* reality of the narrator's experiences. The corporeality of work, its routines and conditions, the dirt, and noise of the factory workshops and other sensory factors have left their marks on the autobiographical memory. Everyday-life bodily practices such as dressing mediate the ideals related to gender and class.

I approach these issues of gender, class and work from an *experiential* and *relational* perspective, paying attention to *intersubjective* relations between individuals and between individual and society. I am interested in how gendered cultural ideals and norms of femininity and masculinity, gendered family roles, and the gendered identities of female labourers are dealt with in the context of a life narrative. I look at gender, class and work as subjective and experiential, but I also consider the *discursive* power of social relationships and subject formations that are learned in socialization, played out publicly both consciously and unconsciously, attached and defined from outside and constantly negotiated.

My analysis is based on the notion of the *intersectionality* of multiple dimensions and modalities of social relationships and subject formations (McCall 2005). The theory of intersectionality derives from women's studies, especially from black feminism in the United States. The basic argument is that forms of differentiation are interrelated and create complex systems of oppression (Brah & Phoenix 2004, 78–79; Brah & Pattynama 2006, 187–188).[48] This idea is not, of course, entirely new. In considering the concept of gender in historical analysis and discussing the theories of patriarchy in relation to history, gender historians have long discussed gender in relation to other forms of social difference such as race and class.[49] Feminist anthropologists have also acknowledged the complexity of the category of "woman": Western/non-Western, working-class/middle-class, and so on (see, for example, Moore 1993). It has also been noted that different social divisions have different ontological bases and organizing logics (Yuval-Davis 2006, 200–201), and that each prioritizes different spheres of social relations. For example, class divisions are grounded in relation to the economic processes of production and consumption, whereas gender is a discourse that relates to groups of subjects whose social roles are defined by their biological sexual difference (ibid. 201). The endless list of potential intersecting differences has also been criticized as rendering intersectional theory vague (see Butler 1990; Yuval-Davis 2006, 202–203). In my opinion, however, the concept of intersectionality summarizes what I find crucial to studying subjects and their experiences of social divisions and identities: that different dimensions of social life are not separated but intertwined, that they intersect in historically specific contexts and a variety of social situations, and that different combinations and intersections of identities produce unique and socially relevant experiences. The multiple axes of differentiation are processes constituted in and through power relations, and in particular social realms, and at certain stages of life some divisions may become more important or relevant than others.[50] On the other hand, certain social divisions such as gender, class and age tend to shape the lives of most people (Brah & Phoenix 2004, 76; Yuval-Davis 2006, 203).

The conceptual models of the gender system (*genussystemet*) and the gender contract (*genuskontraktet*) introduced by the Swedish historian Yvonne Hirdman (1988, 1990) have been influential in Nordic gender studies. Hirdman's stance was that gender positions are not only dichotomous but also constitute a hierarchical system of oppression in which men and the male are seen as the norm. Although Hirdman's model has been criticized for being static and overgeneralizing, her original idea was that these systems are historically and culturally specific (Liljeström 1996, 121–122, 126). The theory of intersectionality presents gender as multifaceted and interrelated, even situational, and encourages the study of different femininities and masculinities in historical and culturally specific situations. In my view, it offers a more flexible alternative than Hirdman's gender system, and may be fruitful in the analysis of an individual's varying experiences in changing social circumstances over the course of one lifetime.

Outline of this Book

Chapter Two introduces the process of data collection, the research material and my analytical tools. I also reflect upon my research setting, studying a close relative, and the ethical challenges I faced during the research process. In Chapters Three (A Working Woman: The Negotiation of Gendered Ideals) and Four (Social Class: Identification and Distinction) I seek to illustrate how the dynamics of class and gender within the family, the working community and the factory village appear in Elsa's life. What did Elsa say about family and gender roles, women's place, the opportunities for education and her choice of career? How did she narrate the social dynamics of the factory community and position herself within its hierarchies and divisions? In Chapter 3 I also reflect on sexuality and femininity and their relation to classed position and age, all of which play a central role in negotiating gendered ideals. Chapter 4 on the other hand, which focuses primarily on class dynamics and differences within the worker community, addresses questions related to social identities.

The focus in Chapter Five (Change and Continuity in a Life Narrative) is on the abstract issues of change and continuity. I explore Elsa's reactions and reflect on changes that occurred within the social environment, the working community and everyday life. I also analyze the transformation in her narrated self: the different selves at different ages, all of whom, interestingly, emerged in the context of narratives related to travel. Both of these seemingly different topics illuminate the use of narrative strategies in negotiating subjectivity and agency in the course of social change. Furthermore, they provide insights into the layers of spatiality and temporality in life narratives.

Throughout the following chapters I use examples from the interview material, both the narratives that Elsa rendered, which I identified as micro-narratives, as well as parts of other interview dialogue that included interesting exchanges. I transcribed them as a dialogue, including all my reactions, questions and comments, even the encouraging repetitive ones such as yes, yes/OK/I see or utterances such as hmh. I have not emphasized any tones or pauses, however, so as to make the dialogue readable and the lengthy excerpts shorter. My strategy in translating the excerpts from the interview transcriptions was not to give a literal, word-for-word rendering of the original speech but to normalize and streamline the text in order to render what I interpreted to be the gist of Elsa's words in linguistically correct, comprehensible and readable English. This means that many of the hesitations, false starts, non-sequiturs and the like that are characteristic of natural speech are omitted in the translation, although I have tried to preserve the colloquial and vernacular tone of the participants' speech.

2. The Dialogic Research Process and Analysis

> "No more elegant tool exists to describe the human condition than the personal narrative. Ordinary people living ordinary and not-so-ordinary lives weave from their memories and experiences the meaning life has for them. These stories are complex, telling of worlds sometimes foreign to us, worlds that sometimes no longer exist. They express modes of thought and culture often different from our own, a challenge to easy understanding. Yet, these stories are also familiar. It is just this tension, the identifiable in endless transformation – that is the currency of personal narratives, as they reveal the complexities and paradoxes of human life." (Shostak 1989, 239.)

My research draws from *dialogic anthropology* and *hermeneutics,* in which knowledge production is seen as a process involving the interpreter, the text and the context. Dialogic anthropology as a research field derives from the critical discussion of ethnographic practices and representations of the other that arose in the 1980s, the so-called reflexive turn (see Marcus & Fischer 1986; Turner & Bruner 1986; Crapanzano 1990). Anthropologists, reflecting on the central problem of representing social reality in a rapidly changing world, wanted to make ethnographic description more sensitive to its broader political, historical and philosophical implications (Clifford 1986; Crapanzano 1990; Vasenkari 1996; Vasenkari & Pekkala 2000, 245–248). Dialogic anthropology treats dialogue as more than a conversation occurring between two partners, acknowledging the ontological, functional and ethical/political dimensions of this encounter (Mannheim & Tedlock 1995, 4; Maranhao 1995, 1–24). From the perspective of hermeneutics, knowledge production is a continuous process rooted in history and tradition, but taking place in the present (Verde 2011). Both the researcher and the informant have their own respective preconceptions of the world that they bring to the encounter (i.e. the interview), during which both participants reflect on their understandings. The researcher's understanding of the research topic sharpens and is transformed during the process of interpretation, which would ideally lead to a fusion of the researcher's and the interviewee's conceptions (Gadamer 2006[1975]). The researcher processes her/his knowledge on the basis of her/his intellectual and cultural preconceptions (Maranhão 1986, 299). The result of this dialogic knowledge production thus reflects particular epistemologies and methodologies, as well as culture and history.

My dialogic research process involved two stages, which I describe in this chapter: 1) collecting research data by engaging in a long-standing dialogic interview process, and 2) analysing the interview material based on the *reflexivity* of the dialogic nature of the research material and its *contextualization*. The aim was to produce a detailed description of one individual life as it enfolds in the social, historical and cultural context. My sources of inspiration include *narrative ethnography*[1], which focuses on situational storytelling, and the *ethnography of narration*[2], which aims at a holistic analysis of narratives and narration. My analysis emphasizes the dialogic and socio-cultural context of narration. I wish to mirror Elsa's life and narratives against social dynamics and cultural ideals, the local socio-historical and cultural context, as well as the life world of "the people of today", the audience of this research. My starting point is that the research material, which consists largely of life story interviews with Elsa Koskinen, was created in a dialogue between representatives of two different generations, namely Elsa and me, and involves many voices. Each of us speaks with several voices, addressing other dialogic partners including family members and people of the Inha Ironworks community, members of academia, and even some distant outsiders such as municipal doctors and acquaintances. The cultural ideals that shape Elsa's narratives and understanding of the world and of herself are thus a mixed set of ideas and models stemming from different times and contexts. In sum, I see Elsa's narratives and our interview dialogue as multi-voiced and multi-faceted exchanges between the two of us and our cultural contexts.

The Interviews and Intimacy

Interviews are one of the most common ways of approaching subjective experience in qualitative research. The interview process itself, however, is often portrayed as straightforward and self-evident. In recent decades, however, growing sensitivity to agency, authority, reflexivity and representation in social inquiry have drawn attention to the ways in which knowledge is constructed (Gubrium & Holstein 2003, 3–4). Interviews are now seen as inter-subjective encounters in which information is in the process of being created and both parties influence its production.

INTERVIEWS WITH ELSA

Interviews in which the researcher asks the interviewee to talk about her/his life are called *life story interviews*. They tend to be non-structured (or semi-structured), and aim at giving space to the interviewee's understanding of the world as well as to the dialogue that is conducted between informants and researchers (on the differences between the different emphases see Hyvärinen & Löyttyniemi 2005). Life story interviews are used as a data-collecting method in a number of different disciplines. A common feature of most studies of life narratives is that the analyst carries out a series of in-depth interviews.[3] The revelation of self-exploration to others, even to someone with whom the interviewee already has an earlier trusted relationship, becomes possible only in a longstanding, in-depth interview process. Repeated interviews allow the narrator to present different versions of the same stories and to introduce multiple points of view (see e.g., Sykäri 2012).[4] This process makes the researcher more sensitive both to the interviewee's points and to her/his own assumptions (Chase 2005, 661; see also Polkinghorne 2007, 481).

It has been argued that, in some cases, writing can offer people a means of reflecting on personal and sensitive issues that they would not normally share in interviews (see, for example, Helsti 2000, 31–32; Silvasti 2001, 51–52). This may be true of certain topics and intimate experiences related to realms of private life or taboo matters.[5] However, writing a life story requires special effort and motivation. Most people never write about their lives. Those who do could therefore be considered special cases, and thus constitute a minority (see Roos 1987, 30). Writing about her life experiences is not foreign to Elsa. I know that she wrote letters, poems and a diary frequently before writing became difficult for her. However, at the time I started my research process she could no longer write a lengthy autobiography. I also doubt that she would have responded to any request from archival or other institutions, or would have shared with someone unfamiliar to her as much of her life as she shared with me.

I conducted all my interviews between the years 2001 and 2004 as an undergraduate student (see Appendix 1: Interviews). This means that the 'here and now' of my research material is the beginning of the millennium, not the present time. All of the interviews except the last one were conducted over a period of two years (2001–2002). Only the last interview took place in 2004, significantly later than the others. I had not yet narrowed down my specific research interests during the earliest interviews, which concentrated on life and the oral traditions of the *old* factory community. This encouraged Elsa to talk especially about her childhood and her youth, as well as about the collective oral traditions. The first interview (105 minutes) was longer than most of the others, but contained less reflection on her personal experiences. At the beginning of the interview Elsa told me about the conditions in which she was born. After that she clearly did not know how to continue, so I asked her numerous questions, some of which specifically concerned things that I expected to hear about. I had an intuitive sense of the topics she might have been eager to talk about, but I did not really know how to elicit these topics or give her space to formulate her thoughts.

Interviews 2 and 3 addressed topics of everyday life that were of general ethnological interest: Interview 2 concerned food traditions and Interview 3 shopping and the era of scarcity. In both them Elsa soon started discussing other matters: experiences of factory work and the humour of her coworkers (Interview 2) and memories of wartime (Interview 3). Interview 4 was the first one that primarily concerned Elsa's personal experiences, and began with an open request to her to tell me about higher-class families and her work experiences as a maid servant.[6] These three interviews were relatively short (30 minutes, 45 minutes and 60 minutes, respectively), and involved a large number of questions and much discussion. In Interview 5 I asked Elsa to tell me her life narrative. This interview was longer (90 minutes), and was more of a monologue because my intention was to let her narrate freely without interruptions. She recounted memories of her childhood and youth in the old ironworks community but provided very little information about her later adult life. After the interview had been going on for more than an hour I asked Elsa about the time after her youth when the ironworks community changed (5/12, p. 12). At this point the interview turned from a monologue into a dialogue, and included fewer narratives.

The impetus for Interviews 6 and 7 came from hearing Elsa recount some narratives in an everyday setting, such as when meeting an old friend at the grocery store and reminiscing about shared experiences. In addition to stories about her youth and the companionship of other young ironworkers, Interview 6 involved narratives about her supernatural experiences and matters related to illness, health and healthcare. Elsa discussed the regional dialect (the initial subject), her childhood family and childhood memories in Interview 7, at the end of which we engaged in a long conversation about social class. Interview 8 touched on Elsa's life as an adult and an elderly woman, and the changes that had taken place at Inha and in her life. In this interview, she moved towards her present-day situation. At the time she was in her mid-70s and in relatively good health. She had just survived breast cancer. I, in turn, was in my early 20s, the same age as Elsa was when she married Eino Koskinen (see Appendix 2: Key events and milestones of Elsa's life). My life as a student was thus very different from the life Elsa had lived.

In Interview 9, Elsa again talked about her dreams and supernatural experiences, some of which had taken place recently. Interview 10 began with Elsa's reminiscence about her childhood family life, and continued with recollections of her youth. This interview is a good example of temporal movements between the past and present as Elsa suddenly jumped from describing her childhood experiences to the present day, to talk about her health and attitudes to life, and then went back to recalling the leisure time activities of her youth. Elsa again recalled her childhood memories in Interview 11, describing the dynamics of her childhood family. Later she narrated her experiences during the Second World War. In the last interview (12), Elsa addressed a topic that had earlier aroused my interest: gender relations and sexual humour in the factory community.

Together the 12 interviews form the material of this study, which represents only a partial, temporary and by no means complete picture of Elsa's narrative repertoire. On the other hand, they include certain key experiences and so-called *crystallized narratives* that are told several times in pretty much the same way. The 12 interviews contain 276 micro-narratives, some of which are series of narratives on the same theme.[7] Approximately one third of the micro-narratives are told more than once (see the figures above). Interestingly enough, some interviews are full of these variant narratives (such as Interview 5), whereas others, such as Interviews 8 and 10, lack them almost entirely. These two last-mentioned interviews deal with very different matters. The topic of Interview 8, the *transformation* of the worker community, had not been discussed previously. I decided to bring up the subject because Elsa had already briefly referred to these changes in previous interviews. In Interview 11, on the other hand, she touched upon her favourite topics in her repertoire of life experiences: being young, enjoying leisure-time activities with other young workers and performing with a gymnastics group at evening entertainments. The number of variant narratives is also relatively low in Interview 11, in which Elsa dealt with her childhood family and a key experience of her generation, the Second World War. The low number of variants in Interviews 10 and 11 may imply that Elsa remembered, at least to some extent, what stories or topics she had narrated in the earlier interviews.[8] The fact that I was a young woman who took part in the activities of student organizations and enjoyed the company of fellow students could also have encouraged her to tell me about that particular life stage.

All the interviews except one (Interview 11) were conducted at Elsa's home. The sessions included casual talk, the exchange of news, and chatting about daily routines and other people. Typically, I visited her at the weekend, and for the interview we sat down at her kitchen table, the place where we would have sat anyway. Some interview settings differed from others because of the presence of other people. My mother, Anneli [Elsa's daughter-in-law], also took part in the discussion in Interview 2, and my husband Ilja [who was my boyfriend at the time] was present in the same room in Interview 12, but did not participate in it. Interestingly enough, on this particular occasion Elsa and I discussed gender relations and sexual humour in the ironworks community but the presence of a male listener did not seem to bother her. One interview (Interview 11) was conducted at my parents' home during a visit by my other grandmother Saima Kilponen (née Setälä, 1915–2009). Saima and five other family members were present during the interview. Elsa interacted with the other listeners in the interviews that feature other persons in addition to Elsa and myself, sharing her experiences openly and trying to find a common basis and topic of interest for the discussion. Other family members and Elsa often confirmed each other's lines of thought, and most times the dialogue flowed like a natural conversation.[9]

According to Gadamerian hermeneutics, speech partners should share an agreement concerning the relevance of some questions in coming to an understanding (Verde 2011). As mentioned earlier, in the first interviews I asked Elsa many question instead of leaving room for a flow of talk that follows from a storyteller's associations and reminiscences. Many of my questions addressed the hierarchies of the worker community, the gentlefolk of the factory community, the activities of the workers' associations, and even the year 1918. My questions did not always lead to a fruitful discussion. I also noticed that I did not participate in the first interviews by sharing any of my own experiences, as I did in some of the later ones, which were more dialogical. The change in my behaviour was not due to a conscious attitude shift, but rather reflects the fact that I was an inexperienced interviewer and in a new situation. Folklorist Venla Sykäri (2012) notes how, in the first interview, many interviewees aim at giving expected answers in full, coherent narratives, whereas in later interviews they tend to provide the interviewer with less formulated answers and engage in reflexive dialogue. This was also the case in my interviews with Elsa, even though we knew each other and had engaged in discussion about her life before the interview process started. Our pre-existing close relationship produced unique research material, but also has its restrictions.

STUDYING A RELATIVE – SUBJECTIVE KNOWLEDGE AND VALIDITY

Along with the linguistic and narrative turn in the humanities and social sciences, and the emergence and development of reflexive methodologies in anthropology, studies of one's own cultural background and even one's own family have become more common in folklore studies, anthropology, ethnology and cultural studies.[10] When the researcher is closely related to the informant, the research process necessarily involves self-reflection, which is one aspect of reflexive positioning, the realization and articulation of the partiality and subjectivity of all research.[11] Self-reflection often concerns questions related to the researcher's role and responsibilities: the pre-existing "silent" knowledge that shapes the researcher's understandings of the research subject, the researcher's role in the interview situation and the expectations of the researched community or individuals. All these questions affect interpretation (see Ruotsala 1998 and 2002; Haanpää 2008, 79). The setting of this research, the study of a close relative, has challenged me to reflect on what subjective knowledge and a pre-existing close relationship has meant for my research, the roles and perspectives both Elsa and I assumed during the research process and the motives that drove us in communicating with each other.

Carolyn Steedman's study of the lives of two working-class women from two different generations (1994, orig. 1986) is a good example of subjectivity, in the sense of being close to research subject, can serve to produce knowledge about neglected but significant areas of the human condition. In *Landscape for a Good Woman*, Steedman analyzed two stories of working-class childhood: that of her mother, a weaver's daughter born in Lancashire, and her own. From the time she was a small child, Steedman learned that she and her younger sister were regarded as a burden by their mother, who blamed them for not having achieved a better material living conditions, modern commodities and pretty clothes. Steedman later found out why she blamed her children for her low position. After her mother's death, Steedman found out the reason for all this: her parents had never married but nevertheless, lived together.[12] Her father was married to another woman and had another family. Because of this, Steedman's mother could not obtain a legitimate social status as a married woman, the wife of an engineer. Steedman's autobiographical writing reflects on how she learned and became aware of her mother's working-class background, her family's illegitimate status, her mothers' ideas of a good life and how her mother's social envy was transferred to her daughters in the form of passive and bitter consciousness. Through studying her mother's stories and her own memories and emotions, Steedman demonstrates how personal and material inequality shaped the lives of her family.

In her study, Steedman revealed her mother's story, and in doing so challenged the conventional ways of thinking about gender and class, about working-class families with strong father figures and about collective or individual activism as the basis of class consciousness. In my view, Steedman's study showed the relevance of subjective knowledge in academic research on working-class culture and its social history. Experiences of intimate relations such as those relevant to family life do not necessarily ever enter public documents. Steedman's story was one of children who earlier had been the potential key to a happy family life and who were then taught that they had failed to accomplish this task and had become a burden. In view of the power of cultural myths such as the idealized figure of the good mother who sacrifices herself for the well-being of her children, I doubt whether a story like this would ever have entered public knowledge in earlier times except possibly in the realm of fiction. Extending the boundaries of conventional sociological and historical inquiry, Steedman explored her mother's story by making use of her own memories and emotions to guide her analysis. In her research, subjectivity constituted the only valid means to reach an unresearched subject and to create new knowledge.

Steedman reminds her readers that her study is not about history, "a search for a past or for what really happened" (1994, 8). Instead, she argues, "it is about how people *use* the past to tell the stories of their lives" (ibid. my emphasis). In the same vein, this study examines how Elsa shaped the narrative of her past and performed it to me, and I argue that my close relationship with her and my subjective knowledge of her life and personality constitute an essential condition and strength of this research, although I had to make an unusual decision regarding research ethics. Elsa was unlikely to have been "found" by anybody else, nor would she have talked about her life – her childhood and youth, the work she did, or her ambivalent experiences of upward social mobility – in a similar way to anybody else. The interpretations I present in this study result from our relationship, in which both of us have embodied multiple roles: two experts (narrator and interviewer/researcher), two relatives (grandmother and granddaughter), representatives of different generations and social positions, an uneducated female worker and a university student. These roles have directed her to tell about certain topics and to represent herself in specific ways: sometimes critical, sometimes nostalgic, sometimes in the role of educator.

In assessing the validity of the research it is also important to take into consideration the dual roles Elsa and I had. Both of us acquired new roles during the process: I became a representative of the academic audience and Elsa turned into an expert who was responsible for giving an accurate picture of life at the ironworks. At the same time, however, we continued to be relatives who shared mutual experiences and were connected on the emotional level. I had to ask myself if the close and intimate relationship between us might have a negative influence on the research process, and if it might prevent me (or the readers of this book) from obtaining certain kinds of information. These are difficult questions. How does one become aware of the influences of one's cultural background, social position and generation, or of the questions and issues that are ignored in social interaction? How can one recognize hidden agendas and blind spots? How could I maintain this kind of analytical distance? First of all, I am sure that both of us left some things out: Elsa did not talk to me about certain experiences, and I ignored some perspectives that either presented her (or me and my family) in a negative light or were not in line with my intentions. Furthermore, we were both, consciously and unconsciously, pursuing somewhat different agendas. My aim in the following pages is to analyze the blind spots in our communication and understanding, and to justify the choices I made related to research ethics and the representation of the research material.

Blind Spots and Reflexivity

The advantages and disadvantages of insider/outsider views have been widely discussed in ethnographic research.[13] Both the insider and the outsider statuses affect the power dynamics of the research and open up different perspectives on the material. Is a researcher who studies his/her own people and kin automatically on their side, and does the research setting allow critical questions or contradictions to emerge? The insider status, which is often inherited, is no longer seen as something that would prevent the ethnographer from taking an analytical and critical stance towards her/his topic, or from assuming a researcher's role in the field. The expectations of a research subject with whom the researcher shares a common background and history may nevertheless be heavy, or even restrictive. The outsider status may thus sometimes allow for more freedom and the asking of "stupid questions". (See e.g., Ruotsala 1998; Haanpää 2005.)

Although it could be argued that my kinship and close relationship with Elsa makes me an insider, I would claim that in many ways I am an outsider who explores an "other", a person who has lived in a different culture, at a different time and under very different circumstances. It is important to note that even the use of categorizing concepts such as class can easily set the researcher outside the studied group and lead her/him to romanticize the *folkness* of the studied person. In his book *The Man Who Adores the Negro* (2008), folklorist Patrick B. Mullen reflects on race relations and the practice of folklore research. Analyzing his own experiences and attempts to carry out collaborative research with Jesse Truvillion, a son of the African-American folk singer Henry Truvillion, Mullen came to notice some crucial differences between himself and his informant. Both men, Mullen and Truvillion, grew up in southern Texas, came from working-class backgrounds and had moved upwards in the social hierarchy through higher education. However, their racial positions and different intentions towards the studied subject, the songs of Jesse's father, placed them in almost opposite positions and led to the end of their collaborative relations and friendship. Analyzing the reasons that led to the unresolved conflict, Mullen realized that they both shared a common attitude towards what he refers to as working-class "folkness": admiration, appreciation and a romanticizing search for authenticity, as well as a sort of identity crisis resulting from their upward mobility (Mullen 2008, 178–192). However, Jesse Truvillion felt that Mullen did not have a right to the legacy of the Truvillion family's tradition and to the culture of black people in general.

I never had to struggle with a similar kind of question concerning whether I could claim any rights in relation to the subject of my research. Nevertheless, Mullen's reflexive attitude reminds me of the danger of romanticizing the research subject's cultural background, the working-class, which is, as I have noticed, also embedded in both Elsa and me. Although we are representatives of different times and generations we tend to romanticize our backgrounds from a very different basis. Especially at the beginning of the research process, I had a black-and-white view of the class differences and divisions within the ironworks community of Elsa's childhood and youth. In the first interviews, I exaggerated the class differences between the worker community and the ironworks' upper classes through my questions and comments, as in the following excerpt in which Elsa describes her routines and duties as a maid servant in a higher-class family:

> E: I had to clean and take care of it so that I could serve the lunch at noon when the master came to eat. He came for lunch, and I had to prepare it. The lady of the house helped me. They always had potatoes and sauce for lunch. Sometimes it was lard source, sometimes mushroom sauce. And there were the side dishes…
> I: Yes. Did they cook fancy food?
> E: Well…just ordinary food. But when they organized a dinner-party and invited the doctors and nurses and pharmacists…
> I: Invited?
> E: Yes, they were invited, and also Mister Illman and his wife were there. They were exciting events for me. I was only a girl from a poor family. I was so nervous, I had to stay in the kitchen until they called me, change the plates when I heard the bell ringing.
> I: Yes.
> E: But it went fine.
> I: *Were they friendly to you?*
> E: Yes, they were really friendly, especially the lady of the house… (4/12, pp. 2.)[14]

I asked Elsa questions that clearly emphasized the social distinctions and distance between Elsa and the higher-class family. Why did I do so? Was I seeking a distinct, *authentic* working-class experience, a strong self-identification and even a politicized worker identity? Certainly, I had not expected that social class would be such a complicated and contradictory matter. Another example of my one-sided thinking has to do with women's roles, a subject that particularly interested me during the interview process. In addition to asking leading questions, I also offered Elsa feminist interpretations:

> I: Did women tell any stories, or was it men who told them?
> E: Men mostly, women didn't…
> I: Elderly women, did they tell stories? Any narratives?
> E: They had their own problems, and they told about their own lives. People of today could not live like they did.
> I: How?
> E: How they lived. Men in those days, they did not do anything for women, women were only…

I: *Servants?*
E: Servants. Yes, men would not do women's jobs.
I: No.
E: Men went their own ways (1/12, p. 16.)

In this case she seemed to accept my suggested value-laden word ("servants") and my interpretation. In later interviews, however, she put forward other, somewhat contradictory views on gender relations, which I discuss in more detail in the analytical chapters. I should point out, however, that both issues, class and gender, were of special interest to me, and that I took part in constructing Elsa's life and experiences particularly around these themes.

Earlier I gave an example of the ways in which my presumptions and interaction influenced the interview dialogue. What about the knowledge and perspectives that guided my interpretations? Where did they come from, and how did my interpretations and perspectives change over the course of time? In my view, reflexivity could also be conceptualized as reflexive *distancing*, which allows the researcher to see the research material, the interaction, and interpretation from a new perspective (see also Ojanen 2008, 3). I found new perspectives from the research literature and from spending time in a different cultural environment that emphasised different values and mentalities with regard to the issues I was analysing.

Folklorist Katherine Borland's (1991) analysis of her grandmother's narrative offers an illuminating example of divergent views on women's role and place in society. Borland interpreted her grandmother's narrative from a feminist perspective. When she asked her grandmother to comment on the text, Borland found that her views regarding the narrated event differed significantly from her own interpretation. In Borland's interpretation, the narratives of her grandmother concerning incidents that happened at a horse race reflected a struggle for autonomy in a hostile male environment and presented her grandmother's father as a representative of the patriarchal order. Her grandmother expressed strong disagreement in a letter she wrote commenting on the interpretations. Explaining that "the female struggle" had never bothered her and emphasizing that she had grown up in a loving family with a strong but warm father figure, the grandmother claimed that the narrative was no longer her own. Borland's article made a deep impression on me and influenced the ways in which I began to look at my own research material and my interpretations. Representatives of a different generation tend to view things from a different perspective, even if they agree on certain interpretations. Experiences related to gendered identities and practices and their interpretation are one example of such potentially varying views (see also Erdmans 2004). It is worth noting that in some cases the perspectives chosen by the researcher may force the research material in directions other than those the narrator desired, or may end up simplifying the complexity of the narrated experience.

THE CHALLENGES OF INTERGENERATIONAL DIALOGUE

Many people have told me how they regret not having taped the stories their grandparents told them. Elderly people's stories of their own lives describe worlds that are in many ways foreign and even exotic to us, yet many of their experiences are familiar to us, fun, touching and human. In addition to reflecting on life in general, these stories can teach us about traditions, changes and continuities in personal, family, local and national history, while at the same time offering us subjective views of the past. Like other types of folklore, the life stories and the personal narratives of people close to us are part of dining-table conversations, everyday life and social interaction. However, life narrative told in an interview setting, even to a person one knows, differs from regular narrative interaction.

Telling stories about one's life is not characteristic only of elderly people (Saarenheimo 1997; Mullen 1992, 3; Wallace 1992),[15] although older people have accumulated a vast knowledge of traditions, professional experience and experiences of universal life events such as human relationships, births, deaths, etc. (Mullen 1992, 3; Reinharz 1992, 141).[16] In addition, elderly people who have already experienced their major life events and are approaching the end of their lives possess the material for *a life review,* a process of returning in their minds to past experiences (Mullen 1992, 16; Arvidsson 1998, 21).[17] However, not all older people like to talk about their past or feel any need to reflect upon their lives. In her research on elderly people's reminiscing, the psychologist Marja Saarenheimo (1997, 43, 46) found that many of her informants did not share the idea of reminiscence as a therapeutic healing practice. Instead, some of them regarded it unfavourably, explaining that they did not want to awaken any memories or reminisce. Often, however, they simply could not help memories of the past popping up to bother them. Some of these elderly people felt that in the middle of their lonely and featureless daily lives, they had too much time to think (ibid. 90–91).

Like oral life narratives and life itself, a person's identity is not fixed, not even in case of elderly people (Mullen 1992, 277–278). In her study of a community of elderly Jewish people in an urban ghetto in California (1978), anthropologist Barbara Myerhoff draws attention to the constant process of identity formation. The elderly Jews were continually engaged with the question of what it meant to be a Jew. Myerhoff notes that being a Jew also works as a metaphor for being human (ibid. 20). Her elderly informants, who immigrated to the United States around the turn of the 20th century, had lived through hardships such as immigration, poverty and alienation, but had avoided the Holocaust. These elderly people needed an audience for their stories, but could not find anybody other than their peers to listen to their experiences of their past lives and to bear witness to their life as Jews. Most of them were from very poor backgrounds. The cost of their rapid social ascent and the freedom they could offer to their children in the New World created social and cultural barriers between them and their children (ibid. 17).

In Myerhoff's case, she, the researcher, who shared the same ethnic background but represented a different generation, offered her informants the audience that they were longing for, someone who would make their story heard (see also Skultans 1998, 51). Elsa's life history does not involve losses as dramatic as leaving behind one's own home and culture. However, Elsa's social and physical environment changed significantly during the course of her life. The old iron industry gave way to more modern steel and aluminium production, education replaced family background as the factor directing people's lives, the standard of living rose, and more and more women found their way into working life. At the same time, these changes also affected small villages like that of Inha Ironworks: workers who were made redundant moved to urban areas or to Sweden to find jobs; new office staff were recruited, but their families moved to municipal centres and in consequence services disappeared from the villages and from the countryside. One by one, the old multi-family dwellings of the factory workers, including Elsa's former homes, were demolished. In the end, Elsa too, left the factory village. She builds bridges between her experiences in the old ironworks community and today's world in her narratives, and seeks to make these experiences understandable to me. Elsa's narration is thus motivated by her willingness to engage with subsequent generations and today's world.

Some researchers have pointed out that the dialogue between grandparents and grandchildren can be easier, less charged and less complicated than that between the two sequential generations of parents and their children owing to the fact that grandchildren cannot claim authority over the experiences of a period when they were not yet born (see for example E. Peltonen 1997).[18] I am thus less likely to challenge the way Elsa tells about past events than, for example, my father, whose version could be different and who could challenge his mother's truth. I have noticed that talking about social class, for example, is much more difficult for the members of my father's generation, who – unlike me – spent their childhood in what was still a very hierarchical factory community and who themselves experienced social mobility. In many cases, this generation has had to struggle to make its way upwards and in doing so has needed to distance itself from its past.

One of the challenges of intergenerational dialogue is indeed the fear of being misunderstood or ignored. The psychologist Marja Saarenheimo (1997, 100–101), who studied the reminiscences of elderly Finnish men and women, noted that her female informants suspected that representatives of younger generations would not understand them or believe them when they told about their life experiences (see also Virkkunen 2010, 31). Saarenheimo suggests that this kind of assumption reflects elderly persons' fear of being neglected and of marginalized in our current future-oriented and rapidly changing society. Elsa, too, thinks that people of today would not believe what life was once like. She often emphasizes the differences between the past and the present by referring to "the people of today", whose lives are easier, who would not have coped in the kinds of circumstances she has had to face, and who never seem to be satisfied with anything. In Elsa's view, the people of today are not capable of understanding the conditions of her childhood and youth and the kind of work she has done, since the world they live in is so different, so full of material goods and unlimited choices. In my view, however, this is not a personal criticism of any actual individuals. The category "the people of today" rather functions as *a rhetorical other*, serving to underline the uniqueness and authenticity of the narrated experience:

> E: *People of today* don't understand these things at all. When the shops are full of all kinds of shoes…
> SK: [Saima Kilponen, my other, maternal, grandmother]: I think that people of today, they can't understand what it was like. And when they can't understand it, they think it isn't true, just stories.
> E: They don't *believe*, they think these things didn't exist to start with.
> I: They do believe.
> E: Who believes?
> I: I do, for example.
> E: Well, you're a different matter (11/12, p. 17.)

Excluding me from the category puts me in a special role and could thus be seen as a sign of trust. This trust in me derives from our close relationship as a grandmother and granddaughter, but also from the scholarly interest I have shown in listening to her stories of the past.

Despite the rapport and mutual interests, there were also moments when Elsa and I did not reach an understanding, but talked pass each other. The nostalgic tone of many of her narratives irritated me. Occasionally, they took on an idealized nostalgic tone, as in the following example when a little earlier we had been talking about class dynamics and how they bothered Elsa:

> E: I don't know, but I miss those times. Everybody misses those times we had. Many people who left to go somewhere, and who I've met at the cemetery, they ask if I remember what a wonderful time it was. *Everybody was like a sister and a brother to each other.*
> I: Yes, it was…
> E: We sat on a rock and talked late into the night. In the summertime… the summers were warm, not like these days. It was always warm, but it was not hot.
> I: Hm.
> E: And when it rained, it was warm, too. [Laughs, and seems to understand the obvious nostalgia] It was so nice, so warm. I don't know why it seemed so. Barefoot, we would run across the streams.
> I: Yes.
> E: The water [of the streams] was not cold. But now, when it rains, it is so cold. But when you are a child, it's all so different.
> I: Hm.
> E: Of course, the life there [at the ironworks village] changed little by little (7/12, p. 16.)

Here, Elsa seems to be aware of the nostalgic character of her childhood memories. There were also situations, in which I pointed this out and challenged her nostalgic recollections, as in the following dialogue:

E: There were a lot of us, there was a nice group of us there. It was like that all the time, we had fun. We joked and…told jokes. It's not like that for young people anymore, I think.
I: Yes it is.
E: I don't think it is.
I: Well, you should come with us and see how we spend time together. If we have nothing else to do, we go to somebody's place, we go to sauna and then we sit at the table after that and…
E: Yes.
I: And we tell jokes and talk and just sit there at the table.
E: Yes, yes.
I: We are not doing something special all the time either.
E: But we did. We would find a warm place, like the guard's shed, the old men were so friendly, they would let us in. They said we could come in to get warm again. We had no other place to go. (6/12, pp. 4–5.)

I doubt if I could challenge somebody else's views in the same way I challenged Elsa's. In my opinion, the close relationship between us and my position and role as a grandchild, and not a researcher, allowed me to juxtapose Elsa's nostalgic remembrance against my own experiences. Later, however, I came to realize that we were actually talking about different things. When I analysed this particular dialogue, I realized that what Elsa was trying to say here was not that she believed that young people of today are incapable of having fun outside the realm of organized activities and mass culture but that she appreciated and longed for the communality that existed between the young people – and the older ones – of the ironworks of her youth. Situations in which the past is clearly romanticized or in which we challenged each other's views are interesting and important in the analysis of the narration and presentation of the self. In my analysis, I have tried to point out these conflicts or misunderstandings and to reflect on the deep underlying assumptions that guided my interaction and initial interpretation in the interview situation.

Research Ethics

According to feminist scholar and oral historian Daphne Patai (1987), the possibility of the interviewer's exploitation of the narrator is built into every research project. Indeed, going deep into another person's life raises a difficult question: Do I have the right to do that? According to the ethical statement of the American Folklore Society and the ethical code of the American Anthropological Association, informants should be informed about the aims and also the anticipated consequences of the research (A Statement of Ethics for the American Folklore Society 1988). The ethical starting point for the present study was that Elsa was willing to talk about her life to me and gave me permission to study her life narrative. By doing so, she exposed herself and her life story to the interpretations of me and other people who would read my text. We might ask and wonder whether she knew what she was doing when she started to tell me her life story. The answer is perhaps both "Yes" and "No". At the time when I started my fieldwork, I had a somewhat idealized vision of conducting ethnographic research. I wanted to make Elsa my co-researcher (see Honko 1992; Reinharz 1992, 33) and engage her in the research process. Elsa, too, was very excited about recalling her past. She started writing down memories of her life at Inha Ironworks as they came to her and told me about new things she had remembered whenever I visited her. I asked her to read some studies such as *Marina Takalon uskonto* by Juha Pentikäinen (1971; English version *Oral Repertoire and World View*, 1978) to see how folklore scholars have used and analysed different kinds of oral materials. After reading Pentikäinen's work, Elsa told me she had skipped the theoretical parts but had been drawn to read the informant's own descriptions of her life. Elsa felt that she could easily identify with the informant (Marina Takalo), who like herself had performed hard physical labour.

Elsa knew from the beginning that she was telling her story to a wider audience.[19] At first she hesitated to talk in the presence of a tape recorder. I had to ask various questions, none of which she ever really answered. Moreover, she spoke more formally than usual. She became used to the recorder surprisingly quickly, however. Nevertheless, she was always aware of its presence, which becomes obvious because all the interviews contained some additional information, mostly in the form of asides that were often self-evident to me. This differs from the notions of Sandra Dolby Stahl (1989), who studied her mother's narratives and reflected on the influence of their close relationship on the content and interpretation of the narratives. Stahl pointed out that narratives and the meanings embedded in them can be understood on the basis of shared contextual information. The closer the relationship between the interviewee and the interviewer, the more allusions – references to shared contextual knowledge – can be found, and the more opaque the narratives are to outsiders (ibid.8–9). Throughout our interviews, Elsa continued to make comments and provide additional information, which, in my view, demonstrated that she was always aware of the presence of the tape recorder and thus of the on-going production of research material (see also Pöysä 2012, 231). She would not talk about matters that she did not want other people to hear about and avoided mentioning the names of some people who were still alive at the time of narration.[20]

I made one important decision with regard to the limits of the research process and my close relationship with Elsa, which pre-dated this research and continues as it ends: I have only analysed the taped material. Consequently, I did not use any of the narratives I had heard at some point but had not recorded as research material. Nevertheless, I could not stop these narratives and all the other confidential information that I had gained, as a relative, outside of the research context having an effect on how I interpreted Elsa's narratives. Although I tried to bring out the contextual information whenever necessary and relevant, on many occasions I suspected that Elsa did not want to share her experiences or mention certain names in the presence of a tape recorder. For the most part I tried to respect her wishes, but because I was not able to consult her during and especially at the end of the research process, I had to rely on my own views and considerations. One of the major ethical choices I made was to leave out information concerning the marriage between Elsa and Eino. In my view, bringing this issue into the open would have caused discomfort not only to Elsa but also to her children.

This research project began as a joint dialogical endeavour. Elsa commented on my texts and interpretations at the beginning of the process when I was writing my Master's thesis,. She read the paper I presented at a Master's thesis seminar in January 2003, and wrote me a letter with her comments (see Appendix 3). In it she explained her motives for narrating her experiences. First and foremost, she wanted to use her experiences to educate me (and other people). Folklorist Patrick B. Mullen (1992, 25–42), who studied the life stories of elderly American people, noted that one of the roles available to the elderly who wanted to be recognized and respected in their own communities and in a rapidly changing world – a role that could be seen as a norm in the folklore interview – was that of a teacher. Most of his informants viewed the past as a golden age characterized by moral uprightness, communality and hard work and wanted to pass on these values to the following generations. Elsa's commentary ("*aika kultaa muistot*" [Memories grow sweeter with time]) demonstrated that she was aware of the nostalgic power of reminiscence and the retrospective point of view of the life narrative. At the time, I was relieved by her commentary not only because she expressed her acceptance of my work in general but also because it demonstrated that she had understood my role as the researcher who interprets her words.

To write in another language, a language other than the informant's native tongue is part of the larger issue of the ethics of representation and interpretation. In analysing the research material, I have operated in two languages, Finnish and English. However, most of my scholarly works are published in English, and so is this final account of this research. There were several factors supporting this decision. At the very beginning of the research process, Elsa gave me permission to study her life story. Later on when I told her about my plans to write a PhD dissertation based on the material, she told me that she hoped the study would not be "easily accessible to her neighbours to read". I suggested to her that I could write it in English, which she thought was a good idea. Writing in English, therefore, was a compromise, a way of respecting Elsa's wishes and bringing the research results into the scholarly discussion. It does not resolve all the ethical dilemmas, and in many ways it creates new ones: because this text is written in English, a language Elsa does not know, it is now impossible for her to read the final result. Continuing the interaction and including the informant in the process of interpretation is a principle of *reciprocal ethnography*, evolved and recommended by folklorist Elaine J. Lawless as a more ethical research strategy (1992).[21] Unfortunately, due to Elsa's desire to protect her life story from the scrutiny of her peers and contemporaries, I am not able to fulfil the requirements of reciprocal ethnography.

In addition to the language barrier, there is yet another problem hindering Elsa's active participation in the research process. Over the last couple of years, her health and other faculties, especially her memory, have deteriorated. In June 2010, she was diagnosed with Alzheimer's disease. Sad as it is, she does not remember that I am writing this study of her life story. For this reason, I have not asked her for any additional information or negotiated with her about my interpretations since the first clear symptoms appeared in 2008. Despite the tragedy of memory loss, dementia has also brought along new perspectives to the whole issue of life story telling. I have noticed, for example, that certain key narratives continue to be important or even crucial to Elsa's self-representation and communication with other people. In addition to using some of the narratives I have taped and analysed, she continues to create new narratives. In addition, she has still kept her humorous attitude to life. As a result of her illness, I am no longer able to discuss ethical problems or interpretations with her. This is very unfortunate in many respects. In many cases, other family members provided me with valuable contextual information, but I did not include them in the process of interpretation by asking them to read and comment upon my text, nor did I ask them for their opinions. My reasoning was that I wanted to grant Elsa autonomy over her personal narrative, and this is a study of the narrative she shared with me. None of my relatives have expressed any dissatisfaction or discomfort with my project, or wished to get more involved in it.

The choice of language has naturally played a role in the process of interpreting the research data and writing this text. Translating the narrative material was not easy, and during the process the texts has lost the colourfulness of spoken language and all its nuances: the regional dialect of the Ähtäri area that Elsa used (as did I on occasions), the wittiness of her spoken word, her humour, irony and many other features such as hesitation, repetition and voiced sounds. The process of translation nevertheless allowed me to take distance from the research material, perhaps even too much. In the process of translating and formulating my thoughts I omitted parts of primary analysis in which I perceived my own role in the interview dialogues. I also lost the track of the original version and emphasis.

Writing in a foreign language is not only about research ethics, but also about wider issues such as the politics of representation and sustainable research practice. My work is accessible to a foreign scholarly audience, but not to any people from my own community. This does create a bias, but on the other hand it makes it possible for a larger academic community to comment on my work. As anthropologist Ruth Behar (1993) states, the academic examination of intimate material such as life stories is hard to justify: to take away somebody's story, to analyse it and to twist it, is an act of violence. Behar doubts whether her informant, a Mexican woman called Esperanza, would have wanted to have anything to do with the book she finally published. Remembering and telling about the past is always a selective process. In this research process, I have further selected and left out many parts of Elsa's life story. Over the years, I have forced Elsa's stories of her life into chronological order, transcribed her oral expressions into textual form and translated them into another language. I would like to believe, that, as in childbirth, something constructive and beautiful has emerged out of this seemingly violent and painful process.

Tools of Analysis

Micro-narratives and Key Dialogues

The main analytical tool of this study is the micro-narrative. Micro-narratives are dense formulations, which express and dramatize important matters in the narrator's life (Marander-Eklund 2011, 148). Like narratives in general they involve *structural components*, sequential segments or episodes (beginning, middle and end, or set-up, conflict and resolution), which build up *narrative tensions* of cause and effect, problem and solution (Arvidsson 1998, 29). They also contain *narrative keys*, markers that point to important meanings such as signs of emotion, emotive or value-loaded words, or silence, metaphors, quotations (reported speech), humour and irony (Marander-Eklund 2002, 113 and 2011, 148).

Narrative performances often begin with an opening expression. Examples of such opening expressions used by Elsa are "I always remember how..." as "Yes, and once...". Markers of this kind indicate the beginning of a narrative, shifting the authority and power (if only temporarily) into the hands of the narrator and forcing the interviewer to listen (Arvidsson 1998, 25).[22] Other narrative keys used by Elsa in her storytelling included shifting the tense of the narrative from past to present form, varying her tone of voice (changing the timbre, whispering, shouting) and the use of short words that indicate turning points in the narrative ("then", "you see", "Oh my God", and so on).

Sometimes micro-narratives manifest themselves as *small narratives*, stories which are familiar to the listeners and thus need not be recounted in their full length and detail. According to narrative scholars Michael Bamberg and Alexandra Georgekapoulou (2008), these stories occur in everyday life communication and are important in identity formation, a dynamic process in which both narratives and identities are 'in-the-making' or 'coming-into-being'. Arguing that the smallness of everyday talk is ignored by autobiographical methodologies which study "fully-fledged stories", Bamberg and Georgekapoulou suggest that, rather than seeking to recognize narratives by their structural/textual features, researchers should concentrate on their interactional functions, the "narrative orientation to the world" (ibid.). The concept of the small narrative may be useful in analysing oral narration within a larger narrative frame, such as the life narrative. Short narratives in-the-making also draw attention to the fact that narratives may have different cycles: they may be being told for the first time, have a crystallized, established form or exist in a large number of variants (Abrahams 2005, 78; Heimo 2010, 54–55). The focus of my analysis is not on structural issues, however, but rather on the content of the micro-narratives and their relation to the life-narrative context, in other words, the meanings given to the narrated subject or event in Elsa's life. Therefore, other narrative components such as the actors and their positioning assume a central position.

I identified and *named* the micro-narratives of Elsa's life narrative in the first phase of my analysis (see Appendix 4).[23] In naming them I considered their significance: how did the narrated event or episode relate to

Elsa's life and experiences? In the context of the life narrative, it is crucial to analyze single micro-narratives not only in relation to each other but also for their significance and meanings with regard to the larger life narrative framework. This is because within the life narrative context, certain narratives receive more emphasis than others (see Arvidsson 1998, 62; Johansson 2005). These narratives can be called *key narratives*. Some of these narratives are repeated in various different situations, but their message and form remain the same. Some key narratives may be told only once, but they summarize something that was said earlier and clearly emphasize meanings important for the narrator and her/his life trajectory and identity. By this, I do not mean only dramatic turning points in life, or *epiphanies* as Denzin (1989) calls them, but rather key dialogues or *core episodes* that draw together certain experiences of different times and life stages (see McAdams 1993; 1993; Hyvärinen 1994). Interestingly enough, the key narratives do not always create coherence or build bridges between different experiences; rather they often point to unresolved ambiguities and contradictions between past experiences (and past selves) and the contemporary narrating self. Narrative scholar Varpu Löyttyniemi calls such narrative entities *core dialogues* (2004, 100). Key dialogues, especially if they discussed contradictory experience, are interesting with regard to narrative positionings to cultural ideals. They helped me to consider why certain experiences caused a need to reflect over social dynamics, societal change and the sense of self.

Narrative Positioning

The basic elements of narrative comprise the actors, events, time and space (Bal 2009, 3–13). These elements can be presented from various points of view. Life story interviews produce narratives recounted mainly in the first person "I". However, people often narrate other people's experiences, use their points of view to highlight important issues in their own lives and incorporate narratives from the collective oral traditions to their life narrative repertoire. Portrayals of other people and social groupings and categorizations are important for my analysis because the experiences and points of view of other people can shed light on how the narrator sees herself in relation to others.

In her life narrative, Elsa tells numerous stories about central figures of the village of Inha Ironworks, her family members, older workers and her female colleagues. I am interested in her relation to *significant others*[24] and also to seemingly random other persons and stereotypical figures whose roles seem to be of minor importance, but who might represent a group that is significant for some aspect of her identity or collective identification (*'us'*). Sometimes, of course, these other persons simply represent outsiders, *others* or *them*. In my analysis, I have identified the actors of the narratives in order to gain an understanding of Elsa's social world and its different social roles and relations (see the appendix 5).

The narrative scholar Susan Chase states that "rather than locating distinct themes *across* interviews, narrative researchers listen first to the voices *within* each narrative" (Chase 2005, 663, original emphasis). According to

Chase (ibid.), that can be done by identifying different narrative strategies such as the use of the first-person voice or other forms, the positioning of the self and others, juxtaposing contrapuntal voices and navigating the disjunctions between discourses. Interestingly enough, the first person plural form "we" commonly occurs in Elsa's life narrative especially with regard to her childhood and youth. Adult Elsa, on the other hand, often stands out as an individual. It is interesting to see how the categorizations, identifications, and distinctions are shaped and negotiated in different contexts and life stages.

Patricia Sawin characterizes the role of others in Bessie Eldreth's storytelling by assuming: "The often-heard or feared voice of local social criticism sounds more loudly in her ears than my recent questions" (2004, 58). According to her, many of Eldreth's remarks make more sense in the past historical, social and moral context than in the interview situation. Indeed, it is important to note that narratives cross boundaries between different times and transport lived experiences into a new context, into the present communicative interview situation. The folklorist Katherine Young (1987) has studied the phenomenology of narratives and distinguished between three realms that narratives draw upon: the conversational realm (in this case, the interview dialogue between Elsa and me), the story realm (the narratives and Elsa's narrating "I" in the interviews) and a tale realm (the world of the narratives and Elsa's experiencing "I").

The folklorist Ulf Palmenfelt has developed Young's analysis on narrative realms. Palmenfelt calls these realms "narrative dimensions" and adds emotional and spatial (geographical) dimensions to them. This allows him to analyze the temporal-spatial patterns and mental/emotional landscapes of personal narratives and thereby obtain fruitful perspectives on teller-listener interaction and the creation of meaning in the narrative performance. Palmenfelt points out that the analytical strength of Young's model lies in its ability to provide links between text-centred and performance-centred analyses, especially with regard to the roles taken by participants during different phases of the narrative event: "While talking, participants in any conversation perform a complicated game of positioning themselves, as well as trying to determinate the position of others, in relation to these fields" (Palmenfelt 2006b, 105). This positioning includes movements between different times, locations and emotions, creating narrative orientations and strategies such as idealization, nostalgia, distancing, and humour (irony, parody etc). Analysis of the spatial and emotional dimensions of the narratives could thus indicate how the narrator negotiates meanings within the interview dialogue.

Elsa's movement between different times and spatio-emotional narrative orientations was particularly clear when she talked about different life stages. She described her childhood and youth colourfully, emphasizing the collective nature of her working-class childhood and community, and engaging in nostalgia. She described the work and the factory environment from a close distance, including many embodied memories and bodily expressions and metaphors. Interestingly, another narrative tendency/

strategy, humour, enabled her to distance herself from the harsh factory environment and physical work, as well as from her later experiences of illness and pain in her old age.

Cultural Ideals

Narrating one's life can be seen as *emplotment*, which means the organizing of life experiences according to different but conventional dramatic schemas (see Ricoeur 1984, 64–66; 1991). In other words, we adjust ourselves to the plots we have received from our culture while trying out the different roles assumed by the favourite characters of the stories. Thus life stories have a close relationship with narrative models, with culturally specific *grand narratives*, which are normative cultural patterns and ideas, available to the storyteller to accept, to reject, to approve, to adjust or to transform (Gergen 1991 and 1999, 68–70; Hänninen 1999, 50–51). Here, I do not refer to grand meta-narratives[25] but rather to so-called dominant *master narratives* (see Andrews 2002; Shuman 2005, 12; Bamberg & Georgakopoulou 2008) or cultural narratives (Phelan 2005, 8) which emphasize common interpretations of historical developments or shared values. They are thus collectively rendered by a society or a significant subgroup of society and often become formulas which underlie the personal narratives and storyplots of literature and films (Phelan 2005, 8). These master narratives come close to *cultural ideals*, such as national myths that larger groups and whole societies adhere to: for example, perseverance and guts (*sisu*) in Finland or the archetypal strong Finnish woman (see e.g. Markkola 2002a). Different cultural master narratives often exist simultaneously and parallel to each other. They are connected to collective ways of remembering and can appear, for example, through rhetorical positioning such as the *we*-form.

The relationship between an individual's narrative and cultural master narrative may be supportive, ambivalent or even critical. Individual life narratives may contain stories that contest the model narratives, and which can then be called counter-narratives (see Andrews 2002; Hynninen 2004). These narratives are articulated by an individual and from her or his point of view, but they may also have common intentions, for example, that of laying claim to a marginal position. The grand narratives that I analyze in the context of Elsa's life narrative have to do with the modernizing developments that shaped the lives of 20th-century people, and they are closely tied to the intertwined categories of gender, class and work. They include ideas and trajectories such as women's emancipation through paid labour, and social climbing as a way to personal success and technological progress as a way to an easier life.

Cultural ideals and model narratives tend not to be explicitly or fully articulated by any one narrator: they are cultural constructions that direct narration, ideas that are referred to or are *shared* by narrators. How, then, can they be identified? Cultural ideals may be manifest in *narrative frames* such as a survival or quest narrative, which are connected to a historical situation, a collective identity and ideas of good and bad, right and wrong. They are not fixed truths, but are rather resources and models that can be applied and transformed. In order to recognize these cultural ideals and models researchers need to familiarize themselves with the cultural context and the collective memory. Collective cultural ideals assume particular significance in times of crisis, such as in wartime, in the aftermath of a personal tragedy or in a challenging life situation, when they may help in building a positive sense of self and a sense of community. It is therefore highly necessary to contextualize the narrative within a historical and social framework, as well as a personal life situation. Here I have used plenty of research literature on Finnish history, as well as in fields such as (narrative) psychology. To a certain extent, however, cultural ideals exist in the researcher's mind and are (re)constructed by her/him. For example, the ideal of a strong Finnish woman who has worked alongside men, undertaken many physically demanding tasks in both agricultural and industrial work, and has been active in politics is reconstructed and maintained by researchers who are interested in gender history and studies, women's organizations or female's work (see Markkola 2002a).

Life narratives aimed at representing the self, situations and choices of earlier life in a favourable (legitimate) way mirror personal experiences against the cultural ideals that should be (or made to be) understandable to the listener. An analysis of micro-narratives, their contents, actors, spatiality, roles in the interview dialogue and their mutual relations can shed light on how narrators position their narratives in relation to other people and other narratives, including dominant master narratives. Any conflicts and ambiguities between actors or between different narratives are interesting from the point of view of master narratives. They reveal the creative strategies deployed by narrators in fitting their own lives within the larger frameworks of cultural ideals. In addition, instead of studying life narrative as an attempt to build coherence, the analysis of micro-narratives can provide us with new information about the ambiguity of different life experiences as well as confusing and even painful aspects of social change.

3. A Working Woman:
The Negotiation of Gendered Ideals

The period between the First and the Second World War brought changes and developments that carried far-reaching implications for the lives of working-class women. In Finland, the number of married female industrial workers grew significantly during the 1920s and 1930s (Lähteenmäki 1995).[1] At the same time, the nation-building and national unity policy of these two decades emphasized gendered ideals of female citizenship that were based on motherhood and new ideologies of homemaking.[2] These ideologies promoted the importance of a balanced family life and the mother's role as a homemaker by appealing to the physical, social and emotional wellbeing of the children; women were to function as the moral and emotional foundation of the family (Sulkunen 1989b; Markkola 1994, 229). Female labourers, especially those who had to contribute to the family income, were in a disadvantaged situation, and numerous women's associations discussed the question of working mothers during this period (e.g. Ollila 1993, 271; Markkola 1994, Nätkin 1997).[3] Different women's organizations had differing opinions regarding social policy, but all of them agreed on the important role of the mother and supported the idea that a woman's place was in the home (Nätkin 1997; Ollila 1993, 53).[4]

At the beginning of the 20th century, health and morality were closely intertwined and connected to social class. It was thought that the lower classes, especially working-class people, had to be controlled and "civilized" by the upper classes. Working-class women were advised to improve their living conditions, hygiene and diet (Helén & Jauho 2003, 19). A new international image of the modern woman appeared during this time: independent, fashionable and urban, a flapper who smoked, drove cars, and sought entertainment (Vehkalahti 2000). These new ideas tended to gain ground only among the upper-class elite and the urban population, however. Most young females in the Finnish middle and working classes in the 1920s and 1930s were still expected to embody moral purity and to orient themselves towards motherhood: the qualities ascribed to modern independent women were considered dangerous for young, unmarried working-class girls employed in factories who had free time and money to spend on entertainment.

In this chapter, I address the question of how Elsa narrated her experiences of gendered practices, norms and ideals at different stages in her life:

her childhood in the 1930s and her youth and early adulthood in the 1940s. What kind of behaviour was expected from a Finnish working-class girl living in an agrarian factory community in the 1930s and 1940s? What models did Elsa follow or reject, and what choices could she make? How did she view her past life in relation to the roles and ideals of her youth juxtaposed against new ideas about emancipated women? In the first part of the chapter, I analyze how Elsa reflects on gender roles, good motherhood and the normative expectations concerning the proper behaviour of female labourers. In other words, I am interested in examining her reflections concerning the place of women. In the second part, I concentrate on exploring gender roles in Elsa's working environment. How did young girls who were not yet adults cope with the masculine factory environment and working culture? My intention is to study narration about both factory work and workplace culture as it is portrayed in Elsa's narratives.

In this chapter I also scrutinize different types of narratives: namely 1) true-life experience-based narratives and 2) humorous narratives, some of which can be characterized as jokes. In both types of narrative, Elsa evaluates her own life and contrasts her situation with that of with other women such as her own mother and fellow workers. The humorous narratives touch upon sensitive issues and taboos that are not addressed in personal experience narratives, including male-female relations and the sexual norms that prevailed at the work place. The humour, in which these matters are exaggerated, parodied and turned upside down, calls into question some of the most obvious aspects of social dynamics which might otherwise be taken for granted.

Family Dynamics, Generations and Gendered Ideals

THE MODEL OF THE HEROIC MOTHER

Parents often belong to the significant others whose meaning and importance is discussed in life narratives.[5] The mother and the father can be given the role of either good characters, with whom the narrator identifies, or bad ones, from whom s/he seeks to distance him-/herself. Elsa grew up in a large family of twelve children. Gender roles in the family were clear and sharp: Elsa's father worked outside the home, earning an income for the big family, while her mother stayed at home to rear the children, cook food and do the laundry. Elsa respected her parents, especially her mother Hilda, whom she described as a silent and industrious woman. Elsa's father Kalle was an authoritarian figure who often aroused fear among his children.[6] He raised the children of the family through intimidation and discipline and required that his orders be followed without questioning. Elsa's descriptions of her father portrayed him as ruling over the home with an iron hand:

Stuck in the Arm with an Awl

So our father was strict. He often did side jobs, he was a shoemaker, so he repaired shoes that neighbours or somebody else brought round. And we were not supposed to go anywhere near his corner, especially when he was sewing the bottom of a shoe with tar thread. He pulled it a long way back, and he had an awl in one hand and he had one in the other. So he had two awls. He made a hole with one and then pushed the end of the tar thread through it, the same way as a sewing machine. And I happened to pass by him right then, I didn't watch out. And the awl came towards me like this when he pulled on it. And so when I went by, I got stuck in my arm. They didn't comfort me; I cried, but I wasn't even supposed to cry. My father was so strict, he said "You won't ever come here again; remember you're not allowed to." [...] He stood up and had to interrupt his work. And it was my fault that I had gone there even though I was told not to. (11/12, 3, p. 1.)

Compared to her strict father, Elsa's mother's character was different. According to Elsa, her mother was quiet and calm, although she was always busy. When I inquired whether Elsa's mother had told the children stories or played with them, Elsa laughed at my question and explained that her mother had been too busy feeding the large family:

Mum's Discipline

I: Was she the kind of mother who would tell you stories and play with you?
E: Well, she [laughs] kind of bustled around, and we children played around her legs...
I: She must have had work to do...
E: ... she did all the household work. Yes. There was a huge tub for dough when it was baking day and ...
I: Yes.
E: And we had big saucepans, a pot for boiling potatoes on the stove. And the sauce was prepared, not in small portions like we make it.
I: No.
E: So, she had no time. We could play there, and sometimes we played pretty wildly. We, that is Aino, Aili and me – Helena was small at that time. So she didn't play with us, but she was under our feet. Sometimes we made hats, fine hats for our heads.
I: From what?
E: Whatever we could find. We wrapped it around our heads...
I: Yes.
E: And we laughed. She [mother] was tired then, of course. All she did was come over to us and clap her hands over our heads [Elsa demonstrates this by clapping her hands] and said *"lits, läts"*. We knew we had to stop. We had to be quiet. She never hit us. She just did this [claps her hands]. It was funny, I still remember how she did it, she came to me and clapped her hands over my head.
I: Yes.
E: And she went back to her household chores. We didn't say anything.
I: Hm.
E: We accepted it. We knew it [the game] was over. We didn't insist. We just went quietly to another room and stayed there thinking to ourselves. (7/12, 7, p. 11.)

Parents whose hands were full with work did not have time to play with children (see also Korkiakangas 1996, 243). As becomes clear from Elsa's response, the children understood their mother's situation: she constantly had a baby to nurse, and her hands were full trying to feed the big family, keep the house clean and do the laundry in a flat which lacked running water. She could not rest even when she would have desperately needed to, nor did she ask others for help under such circumstances. For instance, Elsa recounted one story in which Hilda went to the outhouse without assistance just a few hours after giving birth:

The Heroic Mother

E: My parents were both over 30 years old when they got married.[7]
I: Over thirty?
E: Yes,
I: OK.
E: And every one-and-a-half years they had [laughing] a child.
I: Yes.
E: Well, I couldn't follow in her footsteps like that. No way.
I: No.
E: She was pregnant all the time. I never saw her having periods.
I: No,
E: You see, they never had time to start.
I: No.
E: And the old workers of the ironworks once said to me that my mother was brave, since she had just had a child [...], and there was the world's biggest outhouse. *Yes.*
E: So they saw her out there [going to the outhouse],[8] and asked how come Hilda is here, and she having just given birth. She just told them that she's going now, when her stomach is empty [when she was no longer pregnant]. She'd been pregnant all the time. So, so when her stomach is empty, off she goes [to the outhouse].
I: That was pretty tough.
E: It was.
I: Certainly brazen, but sort of [I + E together:] gutsy.
E: Yes, it was. And then because the river was close by, you see, she didn't have time to lie around on her confinement bed.
I: No.
E: She went and washed the laundry there.
I: Goodness.
E: The old people were really as tough as old tree stumps.
I: True.
E: People of today couldn't do that sort of thing. No way. The office staff also saw her, because the office was by the river bank. They wondered why Hilda was washing the laundry when she'd just given birth. And nothing happened to her.
(7/12, 5, p.8–9, variant 11/12, 2, p.1.)

The communal outhouse that served the worker's families who lived next to the factory in the residential area called Hamarimäki was a red building beautifully decorated with white wooden ceilings. It was variously called the Worlds' Biggest (maailman suurin), Europe's Biggest (Euroopan suurin) or the World's Most Beautiful (maailman kaunein) outhouse. Year unknown.]

During the interview I commented on Elsa's narrative with murmurs of wonder and admiration, thereby encouraging her interpretation. Elsa, for her part, simply underlined her mother's strength by describing how *other* people had commented to her about her mother's situation. These other people, who were "old workers of the ironworks" and members of the white-collar office staff, admired her mother's strength but also worried over her health. In my view, Elsa used these mixed reactions to portray her mother as a heroine of everyday life.

Heroic narratives about overcoming difficulties, so-called survival narratives, dominate cultural narratives in presenting oneself or the people one admires. Elsa's narratives about her mother do not describe overtly difficult or exceptional experiences, however. In discussing the concept of heroism in everyday life, historian Ilona Kemppainen (2010) wonders whether an uneventful life can offer any opportunities for heroic deeds. Kemppainen, who analysed written responses to a questionnaire regarding Finnish people's perceptions of heroes and heroines commissioned by the Finnish Literature Society's Folklore Archives in 2002 and 2003, found that the heroines mentioned by the Finns who answered the questionnaire were often the respondents' own mothers (ibid. 199). According to Kemppainen, one way of becoming a hero was to cope under harsh conditions, to persevere, to overcome the odds. This kind of heroism was not seen as a choice but rather as the result of circumstances that left a person no option but to carry on. In this sense, designating someone as a hero may hide other, less admirable, sides of the person, may draw attention away from the question of why s/

he ended up in a particular situation in the first place, or may help to highlight and understand the circumstances under which the person lived (ibid. 203–204). Elsa felt respect but also pity for her mother. In the preceding narrative, she states that people living today, including herself, could not have lived like her mother. Elsa's mother Hilda had no choice but to take care of her numerous children and do all of the household work herself. She had no means of controlling the number of children she had, nor did she have enough help available to be able to rest sufficiently.

Kemppainen also points out another interesting reason for celebrating heroic female figures: the sacrifices of women are often underlined by contrasting them with the less heroic behaviour of men (2010, 210–213). This is also true in Elsa's narratives, which portray a strict and cranky father and a calm, hard-working mother. Elsa's narratives include some references to the severe tensions in her family caused by her father's drinking problem, which affected both the family's economic situation and their emotional well-being. For example, in the narrative I have entitled *Real Santas* (1/12, 35, p. 23, quoted in Chapter 5, p. 146), Elsa told about one Christmas during which her father had been away from home drinking heavily with other men. Interestingly enough, she never recalled in detail in the presence of the tape recorder any of the instances in which her drunken father came back from a gathering of male workers who had just been paid and began to behave aggressively: she only referred to them briefly. On these occasions she mentioned that her mother and the children had to escape from the house into the dark night, but none of these horrific experiences ended up being recorded even though I and other members of the family had frequently heard such stories from her. Elsa, for example, had told me how her mother advised the children to put on warm clothes when they went to bed in order to be able to make a quick getaway from the house if their father returned home and became aggressive.

The overconsumption of alcohol among adult males was a typical and serious problem in working-class families, which according to ethnologist Orvar Löfgren (1987) adversely affected their well-being. Using the term "working-class respectability", coined by historian J. Robert Wegs (1982), Löfgren argues that workers fought a two-front battle "against the middle class and against the lowest proletariat".[9] Thus there were "good worker families", whose fathers did not drink on a daily basis and whose mothers took good care of the family. But even if the home was tidy and safe, working-class children could get themselves into trouble, drink alcohol and engage in criminal or other morally suspicious activities. Worker families lived in a constant fear of losing their footing in society (Löfgren 1987, 84). Although Elsa's father had various side jobs and was the major breadwinner of the family, he was also the one who wasted money on drinking and playing cards. The drunken, and unpredictable and sometimes aggressive father stands in sharp contrast to the heroic and calm mother, who was constantly pregnant and had to take care of the needs of a large family.

Whereas Elsa's narratives do not offer any direct moral judgments on her father's drinking, she represented her mother as a stable and admirable figure who managed to remain stoic and calm in the face of her struggles to maintain a large household despite the threat posed by her husband's alcoholism. But what purpose did these stories about her mother (and father) serve in Elsa's life narrative? How did her model and family background affect her life? By depicting someone as a hero we not only show respect for that person but also construct ideals and set standards against which we can compare other people's achievements (Kemppainen 2010, 209). In telling about her mother's constant pregnancies, Elsa identified her mother with the older generation of persons whose lives were difficult and full of toil but who were nevertheless strong and persevering (see E. Stark 2011, 253–254). Celebrating the endurance and strength of women in the past is one way in which the stereotype of the hard-working Finnish woman is constructed. Ethnologist Hilkka Helsti (2000) has studied cultural knowledge and experiences related to childbirth in early 20th-century Finland and particularly the image of the hardworking Finnish superwoman who gave birth without assistance in the midst of her agrarian and household chores and shortly thereafter returned to work. Helsti points out that these stories of heroic mothers in the agrarian communities of 19th-century and early-20th-century Finland are understandable in a culture that extolled the virtues of the hard worker.

In my view, Elsa's narratives about her mother can be interpreted as both supporting and contesting this idea of the strong and hard-working Finnish woman. Her narratives discussed the ideals and harsh reality of the women of her mothers' generation, but Elsa's life was different and easier compared to the circumstances of these women. Nevertheless, Elsa, too, had to find a balance between her own desires and the ideals of the hard-working woman and the sacrificing mother, albeit in different ways. Her life trajectory included other kinds of work, paid labour in a factory and home-making. Despite the challenges presented by these different kinds of work, Elsa acquired the necessary skills for both.

The Working Mother as Homemaker

Elsa's school career, which began in 1934, was brief. In 1939, military mobilization closed the school at Inha Ironworks. One morning, Elsa woke up and looked out of the window in her white nightdress and saw a soldier staring her in the face. Terrified, Elsa called her mother, who told her to close the curtains and be quiet. Troops had arrived during the night. There were more soldiers in the yard; they had come to ask if they could buy some coffee.[10] The school building began to be used as a training camp for non-commissioned officers of the Finnish Army. When the school was closed, Elsa, like other children, had to contribute to the family income. She began working part-time as a maid servant in the family of a teacher who lived and worked at the nearby Tuomarniemi Forestry Institute, and she later took up employment in a family whose head, Ove Amberg, the son of Reinhold Amberg, the former general manager of Inha Ironworks, worked as a technical engineer in the ironworks.[11] While she was serving in these families, Elsa became familiar with middle-class ways of doing household work and rearing children.[12] Elsa's work as a maid servant was a position of apprenticeship that gave her many skills that turned out to be necessary in her future life as a married woman. She told about both the positive and the negative experiences that she encountered in these jobs, which will be the subject of a later analysis. Here, however, I highlight Elsa's narrative about one of her employers, the lady of the house Mrs. Amberg, who advised Elsa in her tasks and whom Elsa clearly admired. The ideas of Mrs. Amberg provide insights into the attitudes and expectations regarding the future of a working-class girl:

The Perfect Household

E: So, yes, it was quite a nice place. The lady was really nice, she gave me friendly advice and they had a perfect household. She always said to me: "Elsa will remember that we have a perfect household, and Elsa will bear in mind how to do things so when she has her own home, she can keep it in order." So, that's how right from the start there I got guidelines for a slightly better life.
I: Wasn't that a great thing?
E: Yes, that was indeed a great thing. (4/12, 3, p. 3.)

Earlier in the interview I asked Elsa if the Ambergs were friendly to her (see Chapter 2, p. 40 for an excerpt of our dialogue). In response, she explained how nice both Mrs and Mr Amberg were and how she never received any complains, not even when she accidentally did something wrong. My questions and comments highlight Elsa's otherness in comparison to the Amberg family. At the beginning of the 20th century, the upper classes saw it as their duty to teach and civilize the lower-classes.[13] Middle-class housewives were expected to provide a model for working-class women such as maids from working-class backgrounds. The working classes admired the upper-class life style, the "better life". In order to obtain this better life for herself, Elsa needed to learn how a middle-class household was organized. She assisted in cooking, cleaning and ironing, carried firewood, served meals and washed dishes. At the same time, she learned about table manners, proper dress, and socializing.

When Elsa worked as a maid servant, she was still a child. Confirmation classes were considered to mark the boundary between childhood and youth and were understood to be a clear step towards full adulthood with its concomitant rights and responsibilities (Järvinen 1993, 117; Ruoppila 1954; Tuomaala 2009b, 61).[14] After completing confirmation classes at the age of fifteen, Elsa began full-time work at Inha Ironworks in 1942. This was due to a war-time law passed that year, which obliged all citizens above the age of fifteen to perform productive work.[15] Girls could also sign up for voluntary work camps (Saraste 1990; Sysiharju 1997).

Inha Ironworks served the war industry, and workers were sorely needed.[16] Elsa related: "we, the girls of the ironworks were lucky, because we got work at the factory. If we had not received that, they would have taken us somewhere, to work on the wetlands or on logging sites cutting firewood"

(5/12, p. 2). Here, Elsa was referring to the duty of providing the state with a certain amount of firewood *(mottivelvollisuus)*, an obligation which concerned all adult citizens (Saraste 1990). Elsa was happy to have a chance to stay at home in a familiar environment, despite the fact that it meant harsh physical labour in rather unpleasant circumstances:

> Then I went to work [at the factory]. I got more money there. But it was the kind of work that *today's people* wouldn't do. You know, they burned coal there. We heated the furnaces and… It wasn't a clean job. It was heavy. (4/12, p. 7.)

This illustrates how Elsa used the rhetorical category "today's people" to underline the uniqueness of her past experience. She highlighted the dirt and arduousness of the work but at the same time celebrated the fact that she managed to cope with it.

In the 1930s and 1940s, work in factories was divided into men's and women's jobs. Men carried out the most physically demanding tasks, but also those that required the most training and professional knowledge. Mechanization and the lightening of the workload opened up more opportunities for women (Lähteenmäki 1995, 55). At the ironworks, women worked as handymen, packers and production line workers, while men operated and repaired the machines, rolled iron, and fed the coal furnaces. The gendered division of labour changed during the war when women had to replace men in the factories. Statistically, however, the proportion of Finnish women in the industrial work force during the Second World War did not radically increase (Hytönen & Koskinen-Koivisto 2009, 142). The significant change was that women, including young women, now had to do – or had a chance to do – more demanding tasks, in other words, *men's work*. Through this work, many women gained self-esteem and valuable working experience during the war.[17] Although some women gave up their wartime jobs and returned home to rear the children and to take care of the household after the men came back from the war, many women continued working. Elsa was among these women who were able to stay on at work – at least until she married in 1948.

Social policy historian Ritva Nätkin reminds us that the discourse pertaining to the double burden of working women and their need to juggle between work and family was introduced only very recently. Motherhood was long considered to be a straightforward matter, a natural part of the life of female citizens, and it was portrayed as the mission of all women (Nätkin 1993, 165–166). Elsa did not question the period in which she stayed at home to rear her children. Her repertoire of narratives nonetheless includes very few narratives dealing with her role as a mother and a homemaker or her experiences of being at home with her children. When I asked her directly about her daily life at home with her children, her answer was interesting:

> I: What was daily life with the kids like at the ironworks?
> E: Well, I wasn't working then. I kind of filled in as a sort of replacement during the summer holidays. They asked me then because there were some things still running there. (5/12, p. 15.)

Thus, instead of reminiscing about the years when her children were small, Elsa told me she was not working full-time but was a summer replacement worker. It seems to have been her choice to portray herself in these interviews as a worker and not primarily as a mother. She might also have thought that I was interested in learning about factory work and life in a factory community rather than childrearing, a sphere of life potentially too mundane to be worth telling about. However, I was able to find some narratives that touched upon her experiences of childrearing and some controversies of everyday life.

On two different occasions (Interviews 5 and 6), Elsa told about encounters with health care professionals in which she disagreed with them on issues related to childcare and family size. One of the narratives concerned a situation in which a district nurse who had recently begun to hold appointments at Inha Ironworks paid a visit to her house to see how she was doing with her first child:

Inconsiderate Advice

Then, you see, this nurse appeared. She had an office, an empty room out of the way, and she started to hold [appointments] every day for a short while. And she came to see me and asked me whether I should start thinking about having another child. I said "Listen, if I could just first get this one raised till it's big enough to walk." So she apologized. Yes. (6/12, 23, p. 15.)

Elsa told me how rude she felt the behaviour of the nurse was and how she defended herself. The nurse, however, was only expressing the concerns of the time. At the beginning of the 1930s, birth rates decreased in Finland, which alarmed population policy-makers (Nätkin 1993, 167; 170–171; Helsti 2000, 225). The state began a major promotion of childbearing. Motherhood continued to be a central issue in policies that were pursued during the Second World War and the period of post-war reconstruction.[18] In the wartime and post-war periods, the Finnish state and many women's organizations were worried over the welfare of families, children and mothers. In 1941, the Family Federation (*Väestöliitto*) was founded to improve the living conditions of families with children. In its early years, the Federation promoted a family model of at least four and ideally six children per family (Satka 1993, 60; Nätkin, 1997, 82–83, 89).

The general atmosphere of Elsa's youth during the wartime and the post-war period encouraged young women at all levels of society to become mothers and homemakers. The wartime period taught young Elsa household management skills through her work as a maid servant, but it also gave her access to men's work at the ironworks. Thus during her lifetime, Elsa experienced both homemaking and factory work, but not simultaneously. She stayed at home to rear her children during the period of post-war reconstruction, and went back to work when her children were older. Engaging in factory work or staying home to rear her children were not choices that Elsa questioned in her narration of her life. Rather, she presented these two life stages as representative of her generation. However, going back to factory work and thereby avoiding the life of a middle-class housewife was a conscious choice that Elsa made – or at least it was how she wanted to represent herself to me. In my view these became the crucial themes of her narrative, and through them she renegotiated her role as a woman and her own place in the world.

It should be remembered that Elsa made her choice at the time when married women, including middle-class women, made their way into wage labour, and when wage labour became the norm for *modern* women. This was in the late 1950s and during the 1960s: in 1950, 29.4 per cent of wage earners were women; by 1960, the percentage was 38.5, and in 1964 it was 39.8 (Haavio-Mannila 1968, 57–58). It could thus be argued that Elsa's choice followed this trend.

The Woman I Want (You) to Be

The following narrative, which I have titled *Back to Work*, is, in my opinion, one of the key dialogues that feature in Elsa's life story, although it is not repeated in any other of the interviews, and has no crystallized form (see Chapter 2). The narrative is full of meanings and emotions and of contradictions. At the beginning of this long narrative, Elsa describes the situation in which she ended up after raising her children at home for several years:

> Back to Work
>
> They studied at the same time, Raija [Elsa's daughter, the eldest of her three children] in Vaasa, and Eino [Elsa's husband] studied at home and took his exams. So I had to go back to work. I worked, and my life was kind of, well, Raija studied upstairs and the old man downstairs. [...] I had to be quiet. Simo and Asko [Elsa's sons] were doing their own things outside [playing and practising sports]. Many times I went outside crying. [...] I couldn't do anything, no household work or anything. So my life was like that. But on the other hand, our financial situation became better when he [Eino] graduated. (8/12, 1, p. 1.)

Elsa's husband Eino took a correspondence course in the 1960s in order to get a technician's diploma. At the same time, Elsa's eldest child, her daughter Raija, had started her studies at a vocational college. It is most likely that Elsa and her husband were paying for their children's studies and financially supporting them since their children – unlike working-class children in their parents' youth – could receive and were expected to undergo secondary vocational education after primary school. By continuing to work in the factory and thereby securing the possibility for her children and husband to study, Elsa gave up her space and her activities in the home, at least temporarily. However, Elsa, who acknowledges that these arrangements contributed to the welfare and income of the family, describes herself as feeling subordinated and powerless in the face of these changes, which affected her life at a social, personal and emotional level.

> E: [...] It was so that I shouldn't even have worked after Eino graduated. And I've always been a "greasy-skinned worker", as they used to call people who did dirty

work. I was one of those. And then my husband was there among the white-collar staff. So I suffered from this, too.
I: So, was it so that the grandpa [Eino] didn't want you to work?
E: No, he didn't. (8/12, 1, p. 2.)

Having educated himself, Elsa's husband had obtained a better position at work and had risen in the social hierarchy. At this point, he would have wanted Elsa to stay at home. Through this narrative, Elsa touched upon issues that were central to her sense of self, expressing her worker identity with a colourful expression, which I will analyse in more detail in Chapter 4. The following episode was a turning point in which Elsa's feelings culminate in emancipatory action:

(Back to work continues)

I: So *he was better than you*?
E: Yes, and we talked about it constantly, because I wanted to [go back to work], as our sons were already studying. They went to Vaasa, both of them, Simo and Asko. They were at the technical college. At the same time. They were there at the same time, although Asko was already married, he had a family, or not a family, but a wife. They were, they lived there. And Simo went there as well; he was staying in a student flat. And think about it, we needed money, and it was difficult for me at home alone. So I talked about it. I said I would go to Tuomarniemi [the Forestry Institute] to ask for a job. My husband forbade it strictly. "You won't go there." And I said nothing to him, when I heard that some other women had got jobs [at the factory] when their husbands were taking courses. I thought that since my husband had been studying and was still studying, I could go and ask. So I went to the engineer, and I told him who I was, and I told him that I'd thought about this, and that I'd heard that women whose husbands were studying or went taking courses could get a job. So I asked if I had a chance. He said "yes" right away. So I got work, and we didn't discuss it anymore. I just plucked up courage and went there.
I: All by yourself, without permission?
E: Yes, without permission. (8/12, 1, p. 2.)

At first I interpreted this narrative as being told by "an emancipated working woman claiming her rights". As my questions reveal, this is how I interpreted Elsa at the moment of narration. This had something to do with some of her narratives about her husband and their marriage that I had heard outside of the taped interviews, and that left me with the impression that Elsa's husband was dominating ignoring her wishes and following his own will. My interest in studying women's experiences of paid labour, class and agency from the perspective of feminist epistemology also affected my first reading (cf. Markkola 2002a). Later, however, when I listened through the tape and analysed our interaction, I noticed that what Elsa had actually said was that she had followed the example of other women in similar circumstances. Furthermore, her narrative contains a contradictory follow-up:

E: Yes, I did, without permission. *But at that time, a wife was almost like a man. Men were men in those days, in my opinion. Compared to nowadays.* They [people of the past] lived according to what men decided. There were the old folks, I followed them, they were at home. Men earned the money, and very few women worked. Then it started to change, the factory expanded. It started producing hinges and lots of other things, so the workers were no longer the same, they said, and since hinge production was suitable for women…
I: Yes, steel.
E: Yes, all the steel objects. So there were many other wives of white-collar workers there. But the fact is that they [the other workers] looked down on us a bit, they didn't talk about everything when we were there.
I: Hm.
E: And I suffered from that. I thought I was still the same working woman as the others were. I hadn't been to school. I just had the skills to do the hard work. (8/12, 1, pp. 2–3.)

What exactly did Elsa mean by stating that back in the old days, men were men? The man's role as the breadwinner was the norm in most ironworks and steel industry communities of the mid-20th century.[19] If a man could not meet his responsibilities and his wife had to work outside the home he felt shame (Modell & Hinshaw 1996; Lappalainen 2008, 71). This norm might explain why Elsa's husband did not want her to work.[20] However, it does not explain Elsa's confusion and feelings of ambivalence about being proud of her independence on the one hand, and being nostalgic about the days of *real* men on the other. As I interpret it, the issues of social climbing and class identity are keys to understanding Elsa's situation and her later reflections. Her choice of going back to work and this narrative could be viewed as a class issue: she wanted to distance herself from the higher-class status her husband was about to achieve. Through studying and obtaining a higher position, he had delivered on the expectations of a male breadwinner who was the responsible head of his household. Perhaps Elsa's nostalgic longing for real men and traditional masculinity expresses her feelings about the *real* manual labour of the genuine working class? Even if she does not express that her husband's abandonment of manual labour and a working-class identity caused her to lose respect for him?

Folklorist Patricia Sawin has emphasized the fact that changes in gender roles – even when these roles are flexible – require negotiation (2004, 59). Sawin's informant, Bessie Eldreth lived in a hierarchical and patriarchal Appalachian mountain community. Her husband did not fulfil his responsibilities as the breadwinner of the family, and in addition to rearing eleven children, Eldreth had to work outside the home in various low-status and physically demanding jobs. Sawin notes that in representing herself, Eldreth often used reported speech, especially men's authoritative arguments and positive evaluations of her actions. During the several years of dialogic ethnography between Sawin and Eldreth, the narrator seemed to develop and become emancipated as a speaker. This, according to Sawin, enabled Eldreth talk back to her unsupportive husband although after he had passed away (2004, 25). Following Sawin's logic, it could be argued that when recounting the critical moments of her own life Elsa, too, moves closer to today's values of female emancipation, a development I think she, for the most part, supports and appreciates. Interestingly, however, she does not use reported speech or anybody else's voice, but talks from her own perspective. Perhaps the process of reflecting on her experiences enabled – or even forced – her to present a more emancipated narrated self. However, it is important to note that Elsa also expressed ambivalent feelings about her experience of this change. By educating himself, Elsa's husband had lived up to the new ideals and possibilities of individual improvement. Elsa – like many other women of her time – did not get a chance to change her life in the same way. By going back to work, Elsa chose from among the few possibilities available to her, and in doing so she undermined the patriarchal power within the family and acted according to new gendered ideals of equality, albeit not necessarily consciously. Decades later, when recounting her life to her female grandchild, Elsa was aware of this shift in expectations and of all the opportunities open to today's women: education, work and economic independence. Despite her emancipatory experiences, she partly longed for the good old days, when social divisions were clear and she was treated with respect as the worker she felt herself to be.

Gender and Humour in the Factory Environment

Along with reflexive first-person narratives Elsa used strategies such as humour to communicate her experiences and connection to the work she did, and to the working environment. Humour is used for a variety of purposes in everyday social interaction. It serves, for example, to express solidarity and friendliness, thereby creating a sense of community (see, for example, Pöysä 2012), although divisive humour may accentuate power differences and give rise to exclusion (see, for example, Lappalainen 2008). The narrator can gain distance from the narrated event through humour, and address the power dynamics of everyday life. Humour plays a central role in Elsa's life narrative. She learned to appreciate joking during the monotonous labour at the production line, to experience relief in the absurd jokes that poked fun at the hierarchies and the toil of everyday life, and which indirectly derided the ridiculous expectations of the social environment. As an elderly woman, she often views her past experiences as funny, and makes fun of her own current situation. Humour has come to characterize Elsa's attitude to life.

Dirty Work, Dirty Talk

During the era of modernization, Finnish women were regarded as having a crucial role as the moral heart of the family and the nation.[21] According to Löfgren, gender roles in everyday life practices such as drinking patterns and forms of socializing were often quite rigidly defined among the working classes (1987, 86).[22] Men went to work and participated in public activities such as politics, sport and cultural events. Drinking and playing cards were also common male pursuits (cf. Anttila 2000; Salmi-Niklander 2004, 241–242). Women, for their part, not only took care of the household and reared children, they also kept up the family's reputation by staying at home, keeping the house clean, teaching the children good manners and dressing them well. And even when they did take part in public events and worked outside the home, they were still were expected to perform their domestic duties. Expectations regarding the behaviour of young working-class girls, future mothers, and housewives, were accordingly rigorous and somewhat contradictory. As working-class girls, they worked in the male-dominated factory spaces and were given some freedom to move outside the home, but the morality of their behaviour was nonetheless carefully monitored.[23] Elsa's narratives of erotic joking among men and women shed light on the ways through which both older and younger workers, male and female, communicated their ideas about sexual morals and respectability in the working environment.

Young girls in the factory environment were the targets of sexual jokes on the part of elderly men and women. This became clear when Elsa talked about her experiences as an insecure young woman who did not know the double meanings of the factory jargon and could not appreciate the verbal arts of the elderly workers. Through their teasing the experienced workers taught the younger women to cope with the less pleasant and less ordered aspects of working life – dirty work and dirty talk – with humour and amusement. It was important to be able to talk back and fight fire with fire. All this reveals the ambiguity of female sexuality and women's role in working-class culture (see also Weggs 1980; Skeggs 1997).

Humour, since it is closely tied to situational as well as to cultural contexts, is not readily intelligible to everyone. In studying occupational folklore and working-class culture, folklorists have emphasized that worker communities such as lumberjacks and metal workers have their own rules and specific cultural codes for regulating gendered and sexual relations and that some of these codes are expressed through humour and joking (Lappalainen 2008, 60; Pöysä 1997, 69). Newcomers joining these occupational groups have to learn the relevant hidden and double meanings in order to be able to react in a socially acceptable manner. Many of Elsa's humorous narratives are difficult to translate into English. A good example of this is a story of a man who worked at the rolling mill of Inha Ironworks. This place was known as *valsvärkki* or simply *värkki* (the name originates from the Swedish word for rolling mill, *valsvärk*). In Elsa's anecdote, when the rolling mill stopped running for some reason owing to problems with the machinery or the furnace, the man decided to go to see his wife, who was washing laundry in a nearby building. The man told her that the rolling mill had stopped functioning by saying: "I came because the mill is at a standstill" *(Tulin tänne kun värkki seisoo).* Since the word *värkki* can also refer to male genitalia and the verb *seisoa* has the double meaning of to "be at a standstill" and to "be erect, to stand straight", the man's statement had a sexual connotation that could be immediately understood by Finnish-speaking listeners. According to Elsa, the other women who heard the announcement burst into laughter, and the man left. Later, Elsa and other members of the community often used this same line within the factory community.

Elsa's repertoire of narratives confirms what has been written about female workers who, generally speaking, did not remain a passive audience in the face of male humour. In the factory environment, especially older female workers indulged in sexual joking, for example when trying to embarrass their male co-workers.[24] Folklorist Niina Lappalainen, who has studied the humour of Tikkakoski factory workers (2008), claims that in small industrial communities and within the factory work environment, women were expected to take part in and to be able to respond to crude sexual jokes. Another strategy was to learn to put up with the dirty talk, to let it go and not take it seriously. Most of the women interviewed by Lappalainen, as well as she herself, who had lived and worked in the community, did not suffer from their exposure to sexually-oriented jokes. On the contrary, female workers not only accepted the joking culture of sexual innuendo but also felt that it created a sense of group affiliation. Age, however, is a significant factor in the joking culture. Young people, due to their inexperience, were easy targets for teasing and practical jokes (see Lappalainen 2008; also Kaivola-Bregenhøj 1998.) In the factory where Elsa worked, humour played an important role in socializing new workers into the working culture. By teasing the young girls, the older workers, both men and women, taught them not only the factory work but also how to cope in an adult world and in the masculine working environment. In addition to learning how to run the machines, young girls needed to know the meanings embedded in the humour that was typical of the worker community.[25] On the other hand, Elsa's narratives illustrate how a young woman might also have felt extreme discomfort when confronted with sexual innuendo:

You've Been Getting Some

E: I knew nothing about those things [sexual relationships].
I: Hm.
E: And after some weekends, there were several holidays in a row, the furnace men started teasing me and said, "You've been getting some." And I said that I hadn't got anything. They said that they could see it from my nose and my eyes. [Interviewer laughs.] My God. I got angry, and I said: "You're lying. I haven't got anything on my nose."
I: So?
E: So, they just laughed so much, the stokers. They also said that it's obvious that you've had some. So I asked the other women what they meant. And they told me not to mind their talk. Let them just gabble on. We don't care. And Annikki [name changed] had been there all the time that I was there. And then some men came there and started to argue about something. I understand it now, but at that time I had no idea. [She laughs.] It was about hard-ons – how men's tools are so funny when they're up.
I: [Laughs] What did Annikki say, she just laughed?
E: She argued with them.
I: About that?

E: Yes. The men said it wasn't like that and that she didn't know anything. But Annikki said "I know. I'm engaged." [Interviewer laughs.] And I wasn't then. Tiina said to me "Isn't that so, Elsa?" And I said, "I don't know. I expect men know about their own things best." (12/12, 3, p. 2.)

This narrative occurred in Interview 12, which was the very last interview in the long process. At the beginning of the session I had to urge her to talk, and asked additional questions to clarify what the narrated events meant and how people reacted to it., It was embarrassing for young girls to display total ignorance of the sexual world, but also dangerous to express any knowledge of it. In this example, the possibility of responding properly to her male co-workers' teasing was very limited. If Elsa had shown any knowledge of the matter, her reputation as a morally respectable young woman could have been compromised. From this perspective, her response reveals some quick thinking.

In addition to direct questions, there were other humiliating ways to test a young girl's knowledge of sexual matters. For example, Elsa described how she ended up in a difficult situation as a result of one of these "tests". Elsa was told to ask her father if he had seen the "black fox" the previous night (12/12, 7, 4–5). Without knowing the erotic connotation related to the expression, she went and asked her father, who lost his temper, almost beat her and shouted: "You need to learn what they mean…!" In the old Finnish folk tradition the fox, the bear and the wolf were all associated with the creation of the female genitalia (see L. Stark 2001, 6–7).

This teasing and joking sometimes approached what we might call today sexual harassment. However, it is important not to anachronistically apply modern interpretations to phenomena existing in the narrator's lifetime. For example, the following practical joke did not seem to bother Elsa very much:

Handprints on Your Backside

…when we had done the laundry over the weekend [and had clean light-coloured overalls on us], on Monday morning we went with [the older men's] greasy hand prints all over our arses [laughing]. You see, they patted our tight bums as they went past. They were all greasy from mending the machinery.
I: Yes.
E: It really made you furious, since they [the stains] were difficult to get out.
I: I'm sure they were.
E: Yes, but there was nothing you could do about it, except ask them if they really had to mess them [the overalls] up again. (12/12, 8, p. 5; *variant 2/12, 6, p. 10.*)

Laughter, in this case, is not necessarily a sign of humorous pleasure, but is a reaction to a confusing situation that violates social conventions (see Thomas 1997; Tuomaala 2004, 333–338). In addition to the obvious sexual dimension, this anecdote is also about the boundary between "dirty" and "clean" in the work context, and the tensions surrounding this boundary. According to ethnologist Gösta Arvastson (1987, 19), dirt is a symbolic marker that characterizes the working class. In his view, it is not exclusively a negative marker, but is also a sign of belonging to a respectable group that performed hard work. Perhaps the older men were trying to embarrass the girls not only sexually, but also because the girls were trying to remain clean in a working environment that celebrated dirt in a carnivalistic fashion?

According to Elsa, the adults she knew rarely explained or spoke directly of anything related to sexuality. They did, however, make fun of it openly and did not hesitate to tell sexual jokes in front of children, which appears to have been characteristic not only of Finnish folk tradition but also of Finnish working-class culture more broadly.[26] Sexual jokes and teasing were common in Finnish agrarian communities, especially among older women (Kaivola-Bregenhoj 1998). Having heard many sexual jokes as a child and young woman, Elsa was used to dirty talk. Despite this, she was hesitant at first to talk about the sexual humour, and on some occasions, as in Interview 4/12, mentioned that the men talked dirty, so dirty that "one ought not to tell about it". I often tried to encourage her, as in the following dialogue, to provide me with some examples, but she did not do so and changed the subject:

Jesus, It's a Whore

I: Did they [the older workers of the Ironworks] tell stories?
E: Well, they were kind of dirty.
I: So it was OK to tell them?
E: Oh yes.
I: That's a kind of folklore genre.
E: You know, I didn't always get them then…
I: Hm.
E: But now I understand them fully.
I: And you remember them all?
E: Yes, I do. For example, there was a long house just next to our home. There were flats for seven or eight families there, and the building had two floors. And there were funny old men who called out all kinds of things…
I: Yeah?
E: And there was one man… Can I say his name?
I: Yes, you can say his name.
E: He was Ville [name changed]. One of his legs was shorter [than the other]. It had been like that since childhood. And he took snuff a lot – at that time they did – and we always sat on the steps, like on the handrail. And he did too, and it was Saturday night, and there was dancing at the Workers' Hall. And young people came there from the nearby villages and from the centre of Ähtäri in those days [sighs], when all that was there was the church village and the railway station. And they had electric lights there when the sawmill came. And we were curious and wondered what it meant when this old man looked at the women who passed by on their way to the dance and shouted: "Jesus, who's this?" [Interviewer laughs.] And if they didn't answer, he shouted: "Jesus, it's a whore!" [Interviewer laughs again]
I: He shouted at them…
E: Yes, I don't know if they heard. They just walked on. (1/12, 2, p. 2.)

Women of Inha factory outside of the factory hall in 1962. Courtesy of the archives of Inha Metalworkers' Union 51.

It is evident that the man looked down on the women who were dressed up for the dance. The man's shouting could also be seen as a kind of warning: if you are not known to me, if you do not greet and introduce yourself to me, and especially, if you are a woman going alone to a dance, there is a reason to suspect your moral behaviour.[27] By narrating her experience and giving examples of the sexual morals of her childhood and youth to a younger woman like me, Elsa was, in turn, acting as an educator. The education related to gender roles and ideals that she offered was subtle and indirect, and she did not explicitly talk to me about chastity or the ideal of motherhood, for example. However, she educated me about the conditions in which she grew up and in so doing, addressed sensitive issues such as sexual morals and taboos.

Absurd Ideals: Working, Resting and Taking Care of the Home

Work-related, collectively shared humour is often performed by a few active jokers, talented raconteurs of the group, who specialize in certain types of stories and humour (Lappalainen 2008, 63). This also seems to have been the case at the factory in which Elsa worked. Even if she told many jokes related to her own life, it often became clear that she was not the person who had originally told the jokes. In her narratives, Elsa often mentioned two female co-workers, cheerful women who constantly joked with their female colleagues and thereby created a relaxed atmosphere. These two women are often mentioned by name in different stories and described as persons with a sense of humour. Both of them were good friends of Elsa. One was the same age as Elsa, while the other was much older.[28]

Eeva-Liisa Kinnunen noted that women's humour, particularly humour performed at work places, often takes the form of *parody* and *self-irony*, in which women make fun of themselves and their own lives (1996; 1998, 424–425.) Self-irony plays with the possibility of misunderstanding: only insiders can always interpret it as it is intended to be understood (Hutcheon 1994, 43; Salmi-Niklander 2004, 154 and 2007). In Elsa's stories, the female workers make fun of the middle-class ideals attached to housewives, who, in addition to cleaning and decorating their homes, were supposed to even have time to enjoy themselves and relax during the day. The following parodies were performed by Elsa's older fellow worker, a single mother of several children. Elsa enjoyed the ironic comments she made at work to entertain her co-workers. Elsa recounts (2/12, 8–10, p. 11) how her colleague Maija (name changed) came back to work one day, ironically announcing that she had just had a light lunch – with wine and music. She said she had left her mentally disabled daughter to tidy the hallway. She said that all the work had been done except the flower arrangements. This narrative indicates how ironic inside humour works. The woman did not express her concerns to her co-workers directly, but rather made fun of her difficult situation. Ethnologist Tytti Steel, who has studied female longshoremen, states that working women who had small children felt not only worried but also ashamed when they had to leave the children at home alone (Steel 2011, 125). In some cases, however, they did not have any choice but to play their part in earning the family income, and to fall back on other people's help in looking after the children (ibid. 110).

The series of absurdly humorous comments by Elsa's co-worker continued with another piquant anecdote:

Pickled Gingerbread

When the women were talking about [all the things they had to do before] Christmas and what they'd been baking, gingerbread and so on, she came in saying: "That's nothing. I've already pickled my gingerbread." She would make fun of everything. She was hilarious. It would have been much harder without her. (2/12, 11, p. 11; *variant* 6/12, 3, pp. 3–4.)

I interpret the purpose of these ironic comments as both entertainment and criticism of the prevailing ideals and expectations related to, for example, the role of wives and mothers in preparing for seasonal festivities and holidays such as Christmas: working mothers did not have much time to spend on their homes and households.

In a later interview, Elsa relates a funny story by the same woman about her visit to a doctor. The doctor, who had started to visit the factory once a month, examined the woman and told her that she had to take it easy and that she should eat well and rest. But her co-workers knew that she could never rest; she had children, and she had to work all the time. But after a while she went to see the doctor again. He commented that she seemed well and asked why she was so cheerful. She told him that she had rested, eaten well and led a peaceful life as she had been told to. The doctor started laughing. He, too, realised that this had never happened. She had to go to work and look after the children. The other workers laughed when she told them this story because they knew what her life was really like. (6/12, 23 p.15.)

Elsa narrated this story about her co-worker after describing her own experiences with health-care workers. The narrative poked fun at the middle-class doctor while presenting the workers as agents of their own lives. Doctors and health-care workers were expected to help and cure factory labourers but not to advise them, since the workers thought that such medical staff knew nothing about their lives and backgrounds (see also the narrative titled *Inconsiderate Advice* earlier in this Chapter, pp. 69–70). The doctor had expressed a naïve ideal of a worker's wellbeing that was far from the everyday reality of a poor single mother. The fact that the doctor also laughed made him look less ridiculous in the eyes of the quick-witted female worker.

Parody, self-irony and absurd remarks can be interpreted as a way of negotiating the conflicting ideals encountered in the everyday lives of working women. But why did these women simply not hide their weaknesses instead of openly making fun of their situation? Gary Alan Fine (2009) has stated that the unspeakable is dangerous. Humour addresses taboos and other issues that are too complex to articulate. The social hierarchy is one such issue about which people avoid talking directly (see for example Lappalainen, 2008, 60; Lappalainen 2010). In my view, by making fun of themselves and participating in the rough joking culture, female labourers took away the weapons of moral judgment that might possibly have been wielded against them by others. Self-deprecating and absurd black humour also created a group identity among female labourers of different ages.

A FEMALE-REBEL OR YOUNG PEOPLE HAVING FUN?
According to sociologist Gary Alan Fine (2009), the experience of humour often depends on two elements: the perception of a normal pattern and the perception of a violation of such a pattern.[29] Humour thus plays with the boundaries of normativity and their violation. In such cases it can serve as a way of negotiating power within the social structure (Fine & DeSoucey 2005, 6, 11; see also Tuomaala 2004, 335). My own view, however, is that the lines between normality and abnormality, respectful and disrespectful behaviour, are often very unclear in the context of humour – at least for the listener. Nevertheless, the thin dividing line seems to provide a fruitful ground for humorous narratives. One of Elsa's co-workers was also known to be an excellent actor who often imitated other workers and mimed their comical features. In the following narrative Elsa described how this worker made fun of the traditional expectations of decent mourning:

If I Became a Widow

Sometimes we just talked nonsense and laughed so much. Once she started by saying, if she became a widow, she would dress in black during the day and grieve. She'd go to church, but when night came she'd dress up in her finery. She showed us how she would move and said she'd go to parties, and we laughed our heads off at her antics. (2/12, 12, p. 12.)

This parody carries some elements of humorous fantasy in which a fanciful image with comic overtones is constructed on some theme from real life, in this case the ritual of mourning and gendered norms of behaviour (see Kinnunen 1998, 412, 416–421).[30] After talking about her friend's behaviour, Elsa said that this episode deriding the virtuous widow was also heard by the male workers nearby, who thought it was shameful that these women talked "nonsense" and laughed loudly. But why should these women, who were expected to take part in dirty talk and other humorous social practices of the working culture, not have been allowed to make fun of traditional (gendered) practices such as mourning? If women were seen as the moral heads of the community, perhaps this sort of humour was perceived as threatening to fundamental norms. Perhaps the men who overheard the women talking were afraid that some of the foremen would hear them, misconstrue their dark humour and accuse them of immorality.

In some cases, humour was shared by female workers and the foremen, and arose from their very interaction. In the following narrative, Elsa describes a funny incident that happened to her just after she began working at the factory:

Asking for a Raise

E: Once, I'd only been working there for two weeks, and I'll never forget what happened. We were working, and one girl who'd been there a long time, said that we should go and ask for a raise in wages. To the laboratory. And there he was, Amberg [the head engineer] and Suutela, in that laboratory, and we went there. The men at work said it wasn't going to work, but we went there to ask. I was there in the front row since I was one of the smallest and skinniest, and there were some big girls. There were a lot of us, and the tallest were at the back, and the girl who had spoken was next to me. And Amberg asked what we girls wanted. And she said that we thought we might get a small raise [laughing].
I: How did he take it?
E: [laughing] It was so funny, we all laughed.
I: Well?
E: There was one tall woman at the back, in the back row. She whispered something. And he said "You should get back to work". He thought that our salary was enough. There was complete silence for a moment, and then we heard a whisper from the back row: "Fuck you."[31] Everybody burst out laughing, Amberg laughed too, and we others started laughing and we ran out. And the men were curious to find out what had happened. We told them, and they were angry. They said that they were always having to feel ashamed of us [laughing].

I: Was it a prank going there in the first place?
E: Going there?
I: Asking for a raise?
E: It turned into a joke. You know, she was just whispering, no-one was meant to hear it. But everybody heard it because it was so quiet in the laboratory. I'll never forget it, my goodness. And I'd had only been there two weeks [laughs].
I: It wasn't a serious atmosphere then?
E: No, it wasn't. (4/12, 17, p. 10–11, *variant* 12/12, 13, p. 7.)

For Elsa, this account was both funny and absurd. She told the narrative twice in a very similar way, the other time in Interview 12 (12/12, 13, p. 7). I was not sure how to interpret this anecdote in the storytelling situation. Was Elsa telling me a funny story? Were the girls seriously trying to get a wage raise, or were they only joking in the first place? Was it appropriate or even possible for them to express such a request?

In my view, the narrated scene was a parody of some sort. Elsa's narratives involve other comic situations built around the workers' use of vulgar language before their social superiors. Similar kinds of story plots can be found in the oral tradition of the working classes (see for example E. Stark 2005, 39–40). The gender aspect is also interesting. According to Elsa, the *male* co-workers were angry and ashamed of the behaviour of the young girls. Could it be that the girls were poking fun at the patriarchal labour union's wage negotiation practices? According to Lauri Koski, a former activist of the Inha Metal Workers Union who was interviewed for the publication of the union's 100th anniversary, the engineer mentioned in Elsa's story, Amberg, also swore and used profane language when he sat down to negotiate with the union (*Inhan metallityöväen ammattiosasto 100 vuotta* 2009, 42). The colourful and rude language could have been a way to create a more equal encounter between the classes but it can also be seen as a performance of masculinity.

According to historian Kari Teräs (2001), who has studied metal workers' occupational culture and organizational activities in the early 20th century, the practices related to the wages of industrial workers varied according the field of industry and the factory concerned. Foremen typically set the starting wage, but later it was possible to negotiate one's wage personally with the management (ibid. 69). Teräs also analyzed the occupational culture of male metal workers in the early 20th century, emphasizing that ironwork units often had their own rules and norms of solidarity and their own forms of carnivalistic behaviour. *Eigensinn* is a term coined by historian Alf Lüdtke (1989) to describe the workers' own culture, their relation to the labour they performed and the conditions under which the labour was performed. The word can be translated as the *self-will* or *stubbornness* of the workers, and is it manifested in the creative ways through which they individually or collectively managed to stake out a space for themselves in working life, to handle things their own way and to assign their own meanings to employer-defined norms of discipline and power relations (Teräs 2001, 84, 87).[32]

Other forms of exhibiting *Eigensinn* in the factory environment included the open contestation of rules and orders. In the following event narrated by Elsa, the girls did not go back to work when their co-workers called them:

Hiding at Work and the Big, Big Boss

E: The men didn't mind [us singing]. They enjoyed it when we had a chance to sing. And sometimes we went a little bit too far away, so they had to come and find us. And once we were there when they'd built a box, for the horse [to pull the sludge out of the outhouse], and they'd made a new box for the purpose [of collecting the sludge], from new wood. It was Saturday night and they were repairing a machine, and we went into the box, lay there and closed the lid. There were a lot of us girls but we all fit in that box, it was so big. And we sang there, all the songs, dance pieces. It was wartime, so wartime songs like *Eldankajärven jää* and *Iltatähdet* and all the songs they used to sing then. And some big bosses were coming. The big bosses were coming and the fitters of that time, I don't remember what we called them, they were fitters…
[The tape ends, and the story continues on another cassette] Well, the men couldn't find us but they could hear us singing. [Interviewer laughs.] And they walked back and forth and they shouted "God damn it, women, where are you?" We just sang louder and louder, and they didn't realise that we were in that box in the yard.
I: No
E: So finally they found us, and they said: "Hurry up and get to your machines, there are some big bosses coming." And the big bosses came and they were really big. One of them was so fat that the others had to carry a chair for him so he could sit down once in a while. He was so fat.
I: Hm.
E: It [his appearance] was striking. Yes, [sighs]. But we got back to the machines before those bosses arrived in the workshop. (1/12, 14, p. 11.)

The girls' absence didn't matter until the higher managers and guests appeared.

In another story that was narrated twice, the foreman tried to chase the girls back to work but did not succeed:

Different Levels of Authority: Cutting Firewood

Once, they were repairing some machine again. And one girl started singing alone. She sang *Punertaa marjat pihlajan*, and she sang loud. And our foreman came there and asked if the girls would please get to work. She just raised her voice and sang louder. None of us looked at him, and then the technical engineer, Amberg, comes, and he asks: "Girls, don't you fancy working? Would you rather go into the forest to chop wood?" We would have had to go and do logging work. Well, we got a move on then (1/12, 16, p.11; variant 4/12, 15, p. 10.)

Niina Lappalainen has pointed out that defying orders and talking back to the foremen were often accepted behaviour in the factory environment, especially in relation to work (Lappalainen 2010, 236). The work and roles at the factory could be seen as a form of play that included a competitive dialogue between the workers, who could openly mock the bosses. The foremen were expected to tolerate this banter (ibid. s. 237). In this narrative, the girls did not stop singing until they confronted a higher authority, the engineer Amberg. The girls' behaviour towards their foreman could be described as passive resistance, a form of subtle contestation (see also Kortelainen 2008, 172). It also included an activity that was typically performed in their free time outside work: singing. This resistance inverted the hierarchical order between the experienced older male foreman and the inexperienced young female workers.

In her analysis of the behaviour of working-class girls in the classroom of an agrarian state school, Saara Tuomaala has drawn attention to the performativity of their acts (2004, 337). One of the female narrators she interviewed described her school memories of a classroom where the girls created a coffee table, their own space, in the classroom, and joked about only missing a coffee pot. Tuomaala noted that even if the girls' behaviour, an attempt to take over the classroom space defined by middle-class professional adults, were to be interpreted as agency, they were also performing and thereby reinforcing gendered ideas about female activities and female spheres (ibid. 337 ff.).

Elsa also recounted many situations in which the young girls of the ironworks escaped, hid or somehow tried to fool the foremen so that they could take advantage of all possibilities to get a few moments to rest, relax and have fun.

Rude Names for Places

I: Did you then have breaks during the working day? What did you do then? Did you have a good chat?
E: Yes we did. Those breaks were such fun. They don't have those breaks anymore. […]
I: So what did you do during those breaks?
E: The old men taught us to work, and when a machine broke down and it had to be fixed, we went somewhere to sit down far away, and I tell you straight, that it was difficult to get cigarettes, but somebody always found some. We took deep puffs. [We found] a place where it was warm, there was no heating anywhere. But the backs of the furnaces were warm. So we sat behind the furnace of the rolling mill, but that place had a rude name… [Laughs.]
I: What was it called then?
E: It was called the "arsehole".
I: Ah.
E: You see, there was a hole for cleaning the furnace.
I: Yes.
E: Yes, there we sat until the mechanic came to get us. (1/12, 13, pp. 10–11; *variant* 4/12, 14, p. 10.)

In the first interview I asked about these breaks, moments of free time in the middle of the working day, that Elsa had often talked about. She called them *hitsinväli,* a word that is awkward to translate into English and even somewhat difficult to understand in Finnish.[33] According to Elsa, they took place every hour or 45 minutes depending on the cycle of certain machines and furnaces.[34] Everyone could take a break when a machine broke down, which allowed the machinists to stop work. This gave everybody, including the lowest dogsbodies, a moment to take a short rest. Allowing workers time during the working day for their own personal activities is a tactic philosopher Michel de Certeau (1984, 25–26) calls *la perroque*, and which "re-introduces 'popular' techniques of other times and other places into the industrial space".[35]

Elsa described what the girls did during these breaks, how they violated the boundaries of expected behaviour in behaving like male workers, smoking and using vulgar physical language, for example.[36] In so doing, they pushed the limits of normative behaviour and challenged the ideal of sober and innocent girls. I wondered whether this kind of behaviour was allowed because these girls were still considered children, or because their presence in the factory was a result of the exceptional circumstance of the wartime obligation to work: or did the factory environment and the long-standing (masculine) traditions encourage them to behave like other real (male) workers? What is interesting in these performative acts is that the girls also challenged the ideal of girlish behaviour: instead of being silent and obedient, modest and innocent, they laughed, smoked, talked dirty and were loud-mouthed.[37] To some extent, the factory environment seemed to offer them some form of agency, and encouraged them to find ways of making the working day easier and more enjoyable, despite the hard work and exceptional wartime circumstances.

Women in Manual Labour

Women have worked in factories since the early years of industrialization. However, men and women have typically worked at different tasks and in different areas of industry. In Finland, as in other countries, the textile industry was one of the major branches that offered work for women in the 19th and early 20th centuries. Women also found jobs in the foodstuffs industry, sawmills and plywood production, the paper industry and construction work (Lähteenmäki 1995, 49–61). The traditional metal industry, ironworks and steel manufacture had long been regarded as a male-dominated and hierarchical sector. Blue-collar working culture has also been known for its masculine orientation and masculine customs.[38] At the beginning of the 20th century, all the skilled labour force of the metal industry was male (Teräs 2001, 45). Most female workers in the industry did unskilled jobs or non-productive tasks: they worked as assistants, porters, cleaners, packers, and only later on the production line, which was regarded as providing suitable work for women who were deft with their fingers (Arvastson 1987, 111–115; Alho 2011, 85–86). Even if the most physically demanding tasks were usually performed by men, many of the auxiliary jobs were also heavy, dirty, and monotonous.

Strength and Self-control

Elsa recalled how she experienced demanding tasks and heavy working conditions with a mixture of bitterness and pride. Young girls who took over men's work during wartime were expected to have good physical health, stamina and humility:

You've Eaten, Haven't You?

> And it was a demanding job gathering the horseshoes. [...], you would just throw a horseshoe onto a pile on the floor when it was ready. So [at the end of the day] there was a huge pile a horseshoes on the floor. Two people at a time took care of them. There were four of us, so every other morning we had to go to work early to weigh the shoes. And you can't imagine, the box where we put them was so full, nearly fifty kilos. One of us grabbed one end [of the box] and we had to carry the box next to the window and load it on top of another one. And, believe me, it was hard work. But we did it. We had grit. Yes, it had to be done. We couldn't start working before we did it. I often think about this, how on earth we were able to do that. If you didn't feel strong enough and you told the master [the foreman], he would say: "Go on, lift it. You've eaten, haven't you?" He just said that and walked away. So we just had to do it. It was no good saying anything. We built up our strength doing it. (12/12, 15, p. 8.)

Similar qualities, strength and diligence, were also valued in the agrarian settings in which young women were expected to handle the physically demanding farm work (Stark-Arola 1998, 90). In earlier interviews, Elsa had emphasized how the older male workers were generally very friendly, helped the young girls, and taught them how to work in the factory. Elsa had also told how the girls occasionally escaped and hid from the foremen whom Elsa also called "masters."[39] The narrative above differs from these recollections of the workers' own culture and unity and reveals the reality of daily labour and the social order: the girls were paid to work and were expected to be up to it. Foremen were there to ensure that it happened.

Elsa often wonders how she, as a small young girl, managed the heavy workload. She seems to have assumed the cultural ideal of gutsy perseverance, of never giving up. But although Elsa's narratives emphasize the physical challenges encountered by the teenage Elsa, they paint the picture of an adult woman who had a strong nature, whose behaviour was disciplined and who held her head high despite the hardships and subordination she encountered. This self-respecting ideal emerged in the encounters between the workers and the foremen. Elsa twice recounted a situation in which a foreman forced Elsa and her friend to work under intolerable circumstances, in a freezing factory hall. According to Elsa, she and her co-worker were the only ones working on the night shift one Saturday night. Everyone else had gone home. It was winter and very cold. All the furnaces had been put out, so there were no sources of heat. A man who was able to light the furnaces happened to come to where they were working, and they asked if he could light one of the closest furnaces, which he did. As it happened, the foreman came to check up on things, and when he saw that one furnace was lit, he put out the fire and scolded the women. Elsa recounts what happened next:

Working on Saturday Night

My friend Pirkko [name changed] burst out crying. I didn't, not even then. I thought that he can shout and scold us as much as he wants but that was what work was like then, there wasn't any labour welfare officer then, nothing. So he went away when I said to Pirkko: "Shut up. Don't say anything. Let's just be quiet and listen to him." He left when we didn't protest, and I told Pirkko not to give them the satisfaction of crying because that's just what they wanted us to do. You see, she was sensitive, it was cold, and we had to file those heavy long iron bars. (9/12, 23, p. 12; *variant* 2/12, 14, p. 12.)

In this narrative, Elsa describes a situation in which the workers are dependent on their foreman who forces them to work under horrible conditions in a cold factory hall. Elsa and her friend go against his wishes. By ordering the furnaces to be shut down, the foreman, in my interpretation, subordinated the workers' bodies to the interests of the factory and to its patriarchal hierarchy. Interestingly enough, Elsa told her friend not to show her disappointment and exhaustion by crying in front of the foreman but instead to control herself. Anthropologist Lila Abu-Lughod has noted that the socially weak tend to try to protect themselves and avoid confrontations that would emphasize or make explicit their dependent position (1986, 234). Elsa's self-control also involved a gendered aspect. Crying could be interpreted as a sign of emotionality and lack of self-control, a *female* weakness, which women performing manual labour in a masculine working environment might have wished to avoid.

According to my interpretation, by representing herself as the one who stays calm and rational, but also as the one who perseveres and endures harsh conditions and difficult situations, Elsa reconstructs and offers me a model of a being a strong woman. The strength itself does not seem to be as important as the attitude: not giving up but getting by, regardless of the odds.

Embodied Femininity: Pretty Girls in Dirty Overalls

Elsa remembers how she, as a child, wondered why the snowy wintery landscape of the factory yard was divided by black paths that dissected the glistening white snow (Black paths 5/12, 6, p. 4, the interview in which Elsa tells her life story). Soon, she learned that it was due to the dirt, mainly the soot that came from the coal burned in the furnaces, which hung in the air of the factory halls and was tracked there with the shoes of workers. In all the narratives concerning work in the factory, Elsa emphasizes that it was truly *dirty*. She often highlights the dirtiness by stating that *people of today* would never do the kind of work she and many other young girls had to do (4/12, p. 7; 5/12, p. 2; 7/12, p. 23).

From the very few descriptions of the actual work processes at in the handwritten magazines of young people of Högfors Ironworks in Karkkila, folklorist Kirsti Salmi-Niklander discovered that the representations of industrial work and workers of the early 20th century tended to be poetic and even mythical in nature, often employing strong and colourful images of Hellish furnaces and slaves tied to machines, in which the workers' bodies are described as being exposed to awful conditions, becoming permanently marked by dirt and being debilitated by the toil, the heat and the sweat. In these writings, the dirt and the sweat have become part of the workers' personality and identity (2004, 304–205). As discussed earlier, female workers were socialized into the dirty joking culture, learned to handle it and to use it for their own purposes. But how did the masculine imagery of workers and working-class culture shape and influence Elsa's views on femininity and herself as a woman? How does her narration depict (young) women – including herself – as part of the dirty, noisy, dark factory environment?

It is worth pointing out that many other jobs of the time, such as agrarian farm or forest work, were likewise very dirty. However, it seems that, symbolically, the dirtiness of factory labour was also linked to masculinity and the lower class. In the following narrative, Elsa told me how the girls who worked in the dirty factory hall did not want to be seen in their filthy overalls:

How's the Hammer Doing?

E: It was really a nuisance when they had the wrestling competitions at the [Workers'] Hall. We had to work then on Saturdays, we worked long hours at that time, also on Saturday, and if you were not on the day shift, you worked the morning shift from half past six to two o'clock and then the night shift from two or three to eleven o'clock. And the wrestlers, the lads came from all over the country to take part in the competitions.
I: Yes.
E: And they came to the factory to see what the work was like. [Laughing] You can imagine how upset we were when we couldn't get away from the machines. And they recognized us when we went dancing. One lad came to ask me to dance with him. And he asked me how the hammer was doing [laughing]. I asked him: "What hammer?" And he said: "The hammer. I saw you, miss, earlier working with a hammer." You see, it was a press and they thought it was a hammer because it looked like one. I told him that it was a press, not a hammer. They really were a lot of fun. But we were so upset that we would really have liked to run away. They were teasing us. They were good dancers. But we were good too, even if I say so myself. The girls of the Ironworks were beautiful and good dancers. That's what they said. (4/12, 13, p. 9, *variant* 12/12, 11, p. 6.)

The factory yard of Inha Ironworks was an open area which anybody could enter and see how the workers performed their daily labour of processing iron: taking turns at warming up the furnaces, rolling, shaping and pressing the iron into horseshoes, railway spikes and nails, carrying around boxes in the dark factory halls. The working girls, whose faces and hands were sooty and who wore dirty overalls, could not escape this outside gaze. In this case, the gaze was also a *male* gaze. Even though the wrestlers who came to see the girls were also working-class, the young women would rather have appeared to them with their nice, feminine, clean, and maybe even new and fashionable evening outfits, in dresses rather than in trousers. The idea that the men saw them in their dirty overalls made them uncomfortable, even *ashamed* (a word Elsa uses in the variant of the above narrative in Interview 12/12).[40] Elsa's narrative, even if told with irony and self-deprecating laughter, reveals the fear of being despised by the young men, the outsiders, as marked by the dirty work. Clean, feminine clothes were, after all, a sign of a good woman (Aikasalo 2000, 119–120, 157). Therefore, clothing was not only seen as a practical matter for the girls. When outsiders, especially young males, entered the factory environment, the factory worker's uniform became undesirable for young female labourers.

Femininity was especially vulnerable in other people's eyes, especially those who came from outside the small factory village. Elsa emphasized that even if the girls of the ironworks worked under conditions of dirt and sweat, they dressed well in their free time. She once told in an amused way how some men had later confessed to her that they did not dare to invite the girls of the ironworks to dance, since they looked so elegant. She mentioned how difficult it often was to get nice clothes owing to the rationing, and vividly describes how she managed to get some fine fabrics (see Chapter 4, pp. 110–111 in this study). However, she did not like the way the boys of the ironworks made fun of the girls' attempts to look nice. The boys had a saying: "Cotton is cheap, but girls are beautiful" (11/12, 19, p. 19). This hurt Elsa, who tried to avoid looking cheap. Girls who dressed up in fashionable new clothes, put on makeup and went to evening parties easily became the targets of moral admonitions and warnings against the bad influence of sexually active and degenerate women (see, for example, Vehkalahti 2000 and Tiihonen 2000).

In her analysis of the discussion surrounding women wearing of trousers Finnish women's magazines, ethnologist Arja Turunen notes that during the Second World War attitudes towards working-class women's dressing changed (Turunen 2011, 358). Earlier, working-class girls had been accused of bad taste or wearing loud or too fancy clothes, whereas during the war they were used as models of frugality, simplicity and modesty. Turunen suggested that the wartime need for a general feeling of unity might have affected the ways in which these magazines portrayed young working-class women. During the war women's wage work was needed and encouraged. The fact that young women did men's jobs and managed under physically demanding and materially poor conditions might well have inspired this kind of sympathy; in general, the shared struggles of the Finns during the Second World War brought people both of different classes and of different ages closer together. Elsa's narratives of her youth do not indicate any negative attitudes towards young working-class people on the part of the upper classes or older people. The girls, however, wanted to look good in the eyes of their peers, and especially young male workers, whose opinions and admiration they considered most important. In sum, the factory environment was contradictory in many ways for a young female.

4. Social Class: Identification and Distinction

"Kulturella konflikter förekommer inte enbart mellan samhällsklasserna utan också inom varje människan, hennes värderingar av gammalt och nytt, bättre och sämre." (Arvastson 1987, 13–14).

"Cultural conflicts occur not only between social classes, they also occur within every person and her evaluations of the old and the new, the good and the bad."[1]

At the beginning of the 20th century, factory communities were not only hierarchal and patriarchal but also communal and intimate. The members of a factory community grew to learn the dynamics of the social order and acquired a sense of community and belonging. In addition to distinguishing between different groups within the worker community, research into studies of the hierarchies and dynamics of factory communities have shown how different symbolic borders between "us" and "them", workers and their superiors, or between the outsiders and the insiders of various groups of skilled labour are established.[2] Some of these borders were marked by materiality, and the built environment in the hierarchical order of dwellings and everyday life practices and access to objects of wealth such as nice clothing and good shoes. The boundaries and statuses became obvious in encounters between people who belonged to different social categories.

The issue of social class is one of the most prevalent features of Elsa's life experience. Elsa was born into a factory worker's family of many children. As mentioned in the first pages of this study, she started factory work at an early age, married another worker and even went back to work on the production line later in her life. Elsa's worldview is based on a dichotomy between the gentlefolk (*herrat*) and the workers (*työläiset*)[3] which she represents in her narratives about the old factory environment. Her category of gentlefolk is rather broad. In addition to the hierarchical positions of the factory environment (the employer, managers, and foremen), it also includes middle class-professionals such as doctors, pharmacists, teachers, university educated foresters and pastors (see the Appendix 5). Her attitude towards them as well as experiences of social class in general is ambivalent.

This chapter examines the ways in which Elsa narrated the social world of the Inha factory community, as well as her own class-defined self. First, I analyze her relations to different groups of people around her: her peers, upper-class housewives, male workers, other working-class men, upwardly mobile persons, foremen and managers. In my analysis, I will try to elucidate Elsa's understanding of the class dynamics of the ironworks community by analyzing the *language* of and the classifications within her narratives and the construction of *stereotypes*, *idealizations* and *symbols* attached to the class hierarchy. Categories which are expressed through language and metaphor form a local and group-specific cultural grammar (Ehn & Löfgren 2001, 8–11; Frykman 1998; Paaskoski 2008, 80). I will examine how Elsa narrated these hierarchies, built and used class stereotypes in her narratives, how she named different social groups and how she located herself in relation to them. Second, I will scrutinize Elsa's personal experiences of social class. I will pay attention to the symbolic and *emotional* content of the narratives, and consider how class-based and social distinctions as well as factory work and manual labour created and shaped Elsa's sense of self and her narrated identity.

Narrated Worlds: Social Dynamics in the Factory Community

THE DAYS OF THE PATERNALISTIC FACTORY OWNER

The first Finnish ironworks in the 17th and 18th century were owner-oriented, isolated communities. They were characterized by clear occupation-based and socio-economic segregation. The hierarchies of professional and non-professional workers were long maintained by the old guild institution. For a long time, industrial workers were not designated as artisans (smiths, glaziers, etc.) and thus did not have a clear status in Finnish society. The factory owners chiefly belonged to the Burghers' Estate, whereas most industrial workers – especially non-skilled labourers – existed outside the privileged estates (Vilkuna 1996, 43; Marttila 2010).[4]

The ironworks of the late 19th century were characterized by a patriarchal managerial culture. The industrial patriarchy had its roots in the agrarian *ancien régime* (the society of the estates) and was manifested, for example, in the provisions of the law that stipulated that the factory owner must look after the dwellings, food, health, education and morals of his workers.[5] Patriarchal order reminded a family in which the father looked after his children.

The workers' close personal relationship with their paternalistic employers declined with the advent of the capitalist economy. The workers' movement and the trade unions played an important role in this shift. As society modernized, civil associations and the state took responsibility for social matters that earlier had been the responsibility of wealthier privileged people such as the factory owners and other upper-class groups. Little by little, the *ancien régime* and the older patriarchal order turned into a modern capitalist system, and patronal owners gave way to hired managers (Haapala 1986, 33; Karonen 2004, 140; Ahvenisto 2008). This transformation did not, however, immediately change the way workers saw the managers (Alestalo 1985, 170–171; Sappinen 2000, 4; Kortelainen 2008, 167; Ahvenisto 2008). The old distinctions, which were based on deep historical divisions and antagonisms, continued to influence social structures and mentalities. Even though the estates were dismantled in 1906, the status inherently associated with them continued to exert an influence throughout the early 20th century

(Soikkanen 1981, 435–436; Stark 2006a, 24; Mikkola 2009, 308; Stark E. 2011, 147–148).

Elsa's life story contains several narratives about the patriarchal social order of the old factory community led by the *factory owner, Patruuna*. [6] Although Inha Ironworks had many owners, local people associated the title with the owner August Nilsson Keirkner (1856–1918), who ran *Inha bruk* (the Swedish name for Inha Ironworks) during the years 1884–1917. Keirkner died in 1918, about ten years before Elsa was born (in 1927). Nevertheless, Keirkner and his wife, Lydia Ingeborg (née Bremer, 1961–1945), who was called the *Patronessa*, or *Nessa* for short, appear often in Elsa's narratives (in particular, in four interviews 1/12, 2/12, 6/12 and 7/12, the *Patronessa* slightly more often than the *Patruuna*).

Interestingly enough, I brought up the *Patruuna*'s name at the beginning of the first interview, when Elsa told me who she was and where she was born:

I Was Born during a Lockout

E: Well, I was born in the village of Ähtäri in the Tynell house, and I was born there because all through my childhood my childhood home was the Inha factory, and my father had to leave there because there was a lockout. So.
I: What? [Murmurs]
E: A lockout means that the capitalist closed the factory.
I: The *Patruuna*?
E: The *Patruuna*. Hmm. Then, all the workers lived in houses owned by the factory, and everything was part of the upkeep at that time – the house, the heating, the wood. So you didn't pay any rent. And when there was no work, you had to leave your home. I wasn't born yet, but Father took his big family to the village of Ähtäri. (1/12, 1, p. 1.)

In 1927, the Metalworkers' Union started a strike, which was followed by a lockout imposed by the employers.[7] This was why Elsa was not born at home in the Ironworks village. Elsa must have learned this story from other people, presumably her parents. The word "capitalist" reflects the politicized situation of the 1920s and belonged to the political language of agitation, placing the factory owner in the faceless group of the dominant class. The use of this kind of anonymous collective appellation was typical of the activists in the workers' movement. Throughout this language, agitators aimed not only at increasing awareness within the workers' movement but also at forging a working-class identity (see for example Salmi-Niklander 2004, 182, 192).

Elsa's use of the word "capitalist" was successful in provoking me into a response. I reacted by asking whether she meant the *Patruuna*. My question was not well thought out because I should have known that the famous *Patruuna* was no longer alive at the time when the narrated event, the lockout, happened. It should be borne in mind that this exchange took place at the beginning of the very first interview I had with Elsa. We both mixed up our facts, not only because we were ignorant about the circumstances of the event but also because we were somewhat confused by the newness of the situation. I found out later that the only time Elsa used the word "capitalist" in the course of all twelve interviews I conducted with her was in this narrative. In my opinion, it expressed an antagonism that emphasized the difficulties her family faced and the circumstances in which Elsa, together with the other children in the family, grew up: Elsa's family belonged to the group of poor workers, and on the other side of the conflict, there was the wealthy factory owner. The message of the narrative could thus be summarized in one sentence: *this is where I (or we) came from.*

Later in the first interview, Elsa and I engaged in a discussion dealing with the social dynamics of the old factory community. When I asked if there were any stories about the "gentlefolk" *(herrat)*, Elsa told me some stories she had heard from other people. According to her, factory owner Keirkner was proud and known for his irascible nature:[8]

The Factory Owner's Dogs

I: Did the workers have any nicknames or the like for the gentlefolk? Or did they tell stories about them?
E: No. Not any more.
I: Did they dare to?
E: No, not that I know of. The only thing I heard was that the *Patruuna* had two dogs. Those kinds of dogs, from what the old people told me, and I suppose they meant the kind of dogs Kekkonen had. So he had those, how would you call them?
I: Were they sort of …
E: Pedigree dogs.
I: Yes.
E: Yes, so a workman wasn't even allowed to look at them.
I: Ah.
E: Somebody tried to speak to those dogs as he passed by.
I: And?
E: Well, the *Patruuna* said: "Who the hell are you to address my dog?"[9]
I: OK. [Laughs.] Yes.
E: So nobody could talk to the dogs.
I: So, he spoke bad Finnish then?
E: Yes, of course. So, these were the sort of things the old people told me. (1/12, 11, pp. 8–9.)

This narrative was full of symbolic meanings that emphasized the factory owner's distant role and absolute authority as well as the depth of the class divisions. First of all, the factory owner was distinguished from the workers by language:[10] originally from Sweden, he spoke poor Finnish. In addition, in his behaviour, ordering the workers away from his dogs, the *Patruuna* treated the workers like his dogs – as his subordinates. His angry words could even be interpreted as placing his dogs above the ordinary workers, who were not supposed to talk to them. In the beginning, Elsa's explained that she had heard this story from "the older people". As an aside, she explains to me that the dogs of the factory owner were the same breed of dogs that Urho Kaleva Kekkonen, the longest-serving Finnish President (1956–1982),[11] owned. The use of Kekkonen's name in connection with the factory owner is interesting, almost ironic.[12] However, this juxtaposition underlined Keirkner's position as factory owner, and his personal cult within the Inha Ironworks community.

Factory owner Keirkner and his wife also feature in a ghost story related to the manor house, *Corps de Logis*, which they built in 1899. In the first interview I conducted with Elsa, she described her happy childhood memories, which included playing freely around the factory area and the manor house. Before I began the interviewing process, I had several times heard a story about the ghost of the manor house from Elsa. In addition, she had also told me about her personal experiences related to haunting. So I asked her to tell me the story:

The Ghost of the Manor House

E: Well, the old people say that *Nessa*, the *Patronessa*, rode horses there and that there was Vasilev, too, from Russia, who was a cavalry captain.[13] And there were all sorts of rumours, of course. That they were always riding together, around Sara-aho [a farm that belonged to the factory]. Well, I don't know if it was true, but that's what the old people assumed, that they had an affair.
I: Yes.
E: And then Vasili disappeared. Just like that. Nobody knew where he was.
I: No.
E: Well, of course, the old people thought he was haunting the place [the manor house].
I: Yes. Could the *Patruuna* have seen to him?
E: You never know.
I: Could he have got rid of him?
E: [Laughing] You never know. (1/12, 7, pp. 6–7.)

As Elsa would not say so directly, I put forward the suspicion that it was the factory owner who murdered his wife's lover, and that the ghost was the spirit of the Russian captain who had come to the manor house looking for the *Patronessa*. I had heard about this lovers' tragedy that turned into a ghost story many times, as it was part of the living local lore of the Ähtäri region. The ghost story continues to fascinate people in the area, and today, for example, it serves to nurture "legend tripping", the custom of visiting the site of a legend in the hopes of experiencing a supernatural encounter there (see Ellis 2001). It has also inspired local song writers and authors (see for example Ranta 2009).

The oral tradition related to Inha manor house is fuelled by the exceptional nature of the place: the house has long been uninhabited, it is not open to the public, and it is guarded. The architecture and the interior are exceptionally gorgeous, displaying various styles, frescos and paintings as well as imported furniture such as an ivory pool table. The building was long used only for public relations purposes by the Fiskars Inhantehtaat Company.

Elsa, too, becomes part of this regional storytelling tradition by recounting narratives of her own supernatural experiences (memorates) related to the manor house. Local people were rarely let into the building, but one summer, Elsa was asked to clean the building with another person, which must have been a gesture of confidence on the part of the company:

Sound of Footsteps at the Manor House

E: You often ask me about the haunting at the manor house. It is no surprise to me that the haunting appeared. Nobody stayed there. I was there, one summer, we cleaned there, you know.
I: Yes.
E: It was the last day I was cleaning there. We had cleaned all over and we were about to leave. Suddenly, we hear that the front door opens and we hear steps on the stairs. My friend hid behind a door. I thought I would go and have a look to see who was there. But I did not move because I could see the hall from there. I heard a sound similar to spurs. They say you can hear Vasili's spurs there. I thought they were keys jangling. I thought there was somebody with keys there. I heard the steps but I didn't see anybody. I heard the steps going to the other side of the building. I asked my friend if she heard the same. She said yes. I stood there for a while and then I said I would go around the building and have a look. And there was nobody there (6/12, 17, p. 10; variant 9/12, 10, p. 6.)

Elsa told this narrative twice. In both versions she explained how her friend witnessed the event, was scared and hid behind the door. Elsa, for her part, kept calm and checked if there was anybody there. In this and other narratives about supernatural powers, haunting experiences, dreams and premonitions (most of which are also dreams), Elsa represents herself as an active agent and expert who knows what is happening and how to act in such situations. She presents herself as master of both the oral tradition of her own community as well as confusing situations and their interpretation.[14]

It is difficult to ascertain from Elsa's narratives who is supposed to be the morally evil character of the ghost story of the manor house: the *Patruuna*, the Russian captain or the *Patronessa*? Perhaps it was the complicated ethical issue and the social position of the protagonists of the narrative as well as the potential for drama and scandal (the *Patruuna*, too was suspected of having an affair with another woman) that inspired Elsa to narrate this story and to reflect on the morals of her social superiors. According to the ethnologist Anna-Maria Åström, the portrayal of the privileged estates and upper classes in folk narratives is often pejorative. Upper-class people can, for example, be associated with supernatural beings such as evil ghosts or demons (1993, 222). In Elsa's narratives, *factory owner* Keirkner's character was portrayed, if not as evil, at least as distant, rude and authoritarian. His female counterpart, the *Patronessa*, on the other hand, was highly regarded among the workers. Elsa mentioned, for example, that the *Patronessa* looked after the welfare of the workers by starting a sick fund and socializing with the family of a farmer who cultivated lands owned by the factory. According to Elsa, the *Patronessa* also kept in contact with the workers of Inha after the

Patruuna had died. Eino's father Vihtori, whom Elsa often (as in the following narrative) called "Grandpa Koskinen", had been among those workers who had visited the house of the *Patronessa* in Helsinki:

Workers Visiting the *Patronessa*

E: Grandpa, I mean Grandpa Koskinen [Elsa's husband's father] had gone to take care of some business [in Helsinki]. And some other old men had gone to see *Nessa*. It was a long time ago. She was still alive then, but I didn't know about it, nobody spoke about it.
I: About the *Patruuna*?
E: The *Patruuna*, no. I don't know how he died.
I: Ah.
E: So those old men they were there at the glass palace[15]. Grandpa told this.
I: Vihtori?
E: Vihtori, Grandpa. So they were there, and they got to see all the finery, and they were well fed, and there was this uncle of Kalevi Kaukola.
I: OK.
E: Yes and of course they served potatoes, too, and Hemma Kaukola said he couldn't be bothered eating potatoes; he got potatoes at home. [Laughing] He took everything else except the potatoes; he wouldn't touch them. (2/12, 5, p. 10.)

In the Appendix 5, I have placed the Patruuna and Patronessa in the category of "them". This narrative, however, emphasizes the sense of community between the Patronessa and the workers. Elsa had heard the narrative from her father-in-law Grandpa Koskinen, who had emphasized that the *Patronessa* had received the workers and had shown them great hospitality.[16] Folklorist Kaisu Kortelainen (2008, 167–169) has analyzed the ambiguity related to the social distance versus daily interaction between the workers and the management in a small factory community. According to her, narratives of this kind about the intercourse between people from different social backgrounds both constructed and underlined the social distinctions. They revealed that some individuals and families were good enough to associate with their social superiors. By telling about her family member's connections with the legendary factory owners and his wife Elsa, too, connected herself with the history of the ironworks community and its golden age.

In my interpretation, the stories about the era of the *Patruuna* laid the foundations for Elsa's views regarding the social order and the class hierarchy. The title "*Patruuna*" carried both positive and negative connotations. In the stories that Elsa had heard from her family and other local people, the factory owner's power over his workers and their families was represented as absolute and authoritarian and indeed as excessive and unfair. On the other hand, Elsa cherished the symbolic connections that linked her with the factory owner's old manor house. Thus, these narratives of the social hierarchy of the old factory community served two purposes, offering possibilities for both identification and distinction.

The Stereotype of the Rough and Drunken but Genuine Worker

Stereotypes are products of social evaluation attached to a group of persons rather than to individuals. In stereotypical representation, the differences between groups are exaggerated while the diversity within them is downplayed or ignored (Pöysä 1997, 28). Stereotypes thus underline existing symbolic borders and social norms (Taira 2006, 85–86). Oral tradition and popular culture are full of descriptions of antagonistic relations between two male figures such as a farm owner (or a bailiff) and a farmhand or a worker and a foreman (Knuuttila 1992, 152, 198; Teräs 2001, 50). These representations are common in joke scenarios that call into question the hegemonic social order. In the narrated world, oppressed persons can act differently from the way they do in reality, where their social superiors must be respected. They can, for example, prove themselves wiser than their more educated "betters" or humiliate them in some other way.

Ethnologist Anna-Maria Åström (1993, 1995) studied the relation between the upper-class elite and the common folk in the Savo region of Finland, pointing out how the lords of the manor saw their workers as uncivilized, misbehaving children. On the other hand, in the view of the common folk members of the upper class with their fine manners were childish. At the beginning of the research process, I asked Elsa to tell me about the class relations and antagonism in the ironworks community, assuming that lower-class workers both envied and made fun of their social superiors. Elsa, however, did not provide me with funny stories in which violated norms or incongruent elements inverted hierarchical social relations. Nor did she mention any severe tensions between groups of workers and their foremen. Instead, she pointed out that the different social classes often interacted in a distanced but nevertheless friendly way. I have, however, identified stereotypical representations of male workers in Elsa's narratives:

A Drunken Worker

> I: Were there any sayings that come to mind about particular people? Generally, maxims or jokes, the kind that were often repeated?
> E: Well, we had some that we always told. There were some, of course, though I don't really know. Well, they were the kind where we mimicked people and…
> I: Who would you mimic?
> E: Well, there were some who were always a bit tipsy, and they would go up boldly up to speak to the social superiors, like the old engineer, Amberg. One of them often did this, and once when this Aatu [name changed] was about to fall over [because he was so drunk], he told us how the Engineer had said to him: "You Virtanen [name changed] don't fall over." "How can I help it if I stumble?" [Elsa mimics a drunken slur]. He talked like that, and then he got to work. We mimicked him all the time.
> I: So this man had always had a tipple?
> E: Well, he was that kind, I don't know if I ever saw him sober [laughs].
> I: Yes, that kind of worker (*duunari*). (1/12, 24, p. 15.)

It should be pointed out that, again, I provoked this narrative with my questions but did not laugh at Elsa's response. However, I did give some kind of reaction in my comment "that kind of worker", which was meant to be ironic. The word *duunari* (workman) is a colloquial expression referring to a person who does manual labour, and industrial work in particular.[17]

In many cases, alcohol enabled and justified outspoken behaviour and the violation of the boundaries of propriety. However, the intoxication of the worker can be seen as both comic and at the same time tragic (see also Ahvenisto 2008, 158–159). On the one hand, drinking was related to the leisure time activities of individuals and groups of male workers; on the other hand, it was seen to be as one of the reasons for the poor living conditions of working-class families and as a severe threat to the wellbeing and morals of working-class women (Sulkunen 1986; Apo 2001, 202–203). This ambivalence characterizes the history of the culture of drinking in Finland, especially as far as the working classes are concerned (Apo 2001, 200, 202–205).[18]

Although Elsa's narratives represented the drunken older male workers in a positive light and their behaviour as comic, she, too knew the difficulties caused by the consumption of alcohol. This is how Elsa described the situation of her childhood:

E: When I was a child, the work was hard, but so was men's free time carousing…
I: Yes.
E: Yes, they drank most of the time.
I: Always on wage days?
E: Yes, yes, and any time when they didn't have to work.
I: I see. (1/12, p. 13.)

The well-known Finnish saying "Hard work needs hard fun" to which Elsa referred refers to the association between workers and a heavy consumption of alcohol. In the 19th century, drinking was part of the metalworker's culture and the carnivalism of everyday life. Alcohol consumption was also a part of initiation rituals such as the completion of an apprenticeship and reaching the next level in the hierarchy of workers (see Teräs 2001, 52; for the case of glassworkers, see also Nurmi 1989, 66).

After the narratives describing drunken workers, Elsa provided another example of the stereotypical behaviour of the male worker:

Workers Use of Language

E: And sometimes the boys were up to mischief…
I: Yes.
E: There was a house right next to the factory gate. And there was a family that later moved to America, the whole family. They had a lot of children. And the son was called Raineri. And Amberg, the general manager, passed the father of the family on the road and said to him, "Your son's been up to mischief at the factory. So this man yelled, "Jesus Christ, [Raineri], I'll kill him"! [Interviewer laughs]. We would mimic this on suitable occasions.

I: Hm.
E: [Raineri], I'll… Well the master of course said, "Now, now, not like that…"
I: Hmm.
E: But they would speak rough like that there.
I: I bet, among the workers.
E: Exactly.
I: Especially among the men?
E: Yes. (1/12, 25, p. 16.)

The beginning of this narrative suggested that Elsa was going to tell a story about a young boy's prank. But it was his father's reactions and behaviour that was depicted in a humorous light. In addition to unruly cursing and a sudden burst of aggression in front of his social superior, the narrative included a comic element that requires some background information in order to be accessible to an outsider to the community: the old general manager Amberg's first name, Reinhold, is another version of the name of the worker's son Rainer *(Raineri or Raihneri,* as Elsa pronounces it). Thus, ejaculation of this name could have been interpreted as cursing using Amberg's ownname as a curse, which must have sounded droll to the ears of the villagers.

The narratives *A Drunken Worker* and *Worker's Use of Language* present a class stereotype of the *male* worker whose behaviour was juxtaposed with that of a representative of the *civilized* bourgeoisie, this time an engineer (see also Pöysä 1997, 241–243). Folklorist Jyrki Pöysä, who studied Finnish lumberjack lore, has noted that straightforward and genuine behaviour in which workers did not act differently than normal in front of their social superiors than among their peers created a picture of working-class men as *rough* but *true to themselves* (see Pöysä 1997, 241–243; also Kortelainen 2008, 168). This kind of positive stereotype could also be regarded as a form of idealization. Elsa's narratives, told from a female perspective, introduced another stereotype: that of the *drunken, rough* but *authentic* working man. Although she represented their behaviour as amusing, the female perspective and the discussions following the narratives created a sense of realism and introduced a critical tone. In my view, Elsa's narratives about the stereotypical worker neither inverted nor reasserted class differences but rather reflected the ideals and contradictions inherent in working-class masculinity.

Youth, Solidarity and Sense of Community

In her reminiscences, Elsa repeatedly emphasized the solidarity, the symbolic sisterhood and brotherhood among the young people of the Ironworks, and the tight peer groups that were formed especially among those who took part in the activities of the local workers' sports club *Inhan Taimi*. Elsa was one of a group of girls who performed at evening entertainments *(iltamat)* in the local workers' halls. In addition to other programme items (speeches, plays, and sports performances), these parties also featured partner dancing, a popular activity especially among young Finns.[19] The reason why the programme had to be varied and include so-called "educational" elements was at least in part financial: since the 1920s, an event of pure entertainment was taxed more highly than a varied programme. The taxation aimed at directing the activities of all civic organizations towards higher moral goals (Seppänen 2000, 176–177; Salmi-Niklander 2004, 254). During the Second World War, dancing was prohibited for reasons of both security and morality. Large gatherings were easy targets for air bombing raids, and dancing and having fun were not regarded as appropriate at a time when many people were mourning the loss of their loved ones and men were still fighting at the front. Toward the late 1940s, the attitude towards dancing became less critical (Pesola 1996, 254; Laine 2005), and it came to be considered a natural part of the leisure activities of modern urban life and a popular form of amusement (Salmi-Niklander 2004, 258).

The evening entertainments and dances offered young people opportunities to meet each other and to find a marriage partner.[20] Thus they were also important public arenas for negotiating gender and class identities. Tensions often arose between different groups of young people, as the following narrative in response to my questions about the tensions illustrates:

A Bike Hoisted up the Flagpole and Smashed Skis

I: Because it was a tight community would they mock outsiders who came from other villages? Did you joke about them?
E: Well, I don't know about it, really it was that kind of thing, they told me. I wasn't going to dances yet, but the lads from Tuomarniemi [the nearby forestry institute], they were [called] "gum dicks" (*pihkakullit*) and "cone boys" (*käpypojat*) and all sorts of things… Our lads never called them by their real names. They didn't know them either. But they came to the dances anyway. And there were some tensions between them. One lad's bike was hoisted up the school flagpole when he had stayed in the village too long, courting a girl. But they didn't make any big fuss about it.
I: They didn't fight?
E: No they didn't. I don't think they did. Well, they did when the war started, and the Karelian boys [evacuees] came. Then there was a bit of trouble, and there was fighting. But I don't know what they fought about. But we went to the dances on skis. And one time they had a dance at the Ähtäri Workers' Hall, close by the railway station. So we skied there, I and the other girls. We took a short cut straight across Voilampi [a small lake] on the way there. There was a track there, and we put our skis neatly against the wall, and when the dancing was over, some boys came – I don't know who they were – we were still inside, but when we went outside, there was a fight going on, and my skis had been smashed to bits, and I started crying: "oh dear, how can I get home when the others are out skiing?" Well, the boys from the Ironworks, they said that I needn't worry. I'd have new skis when I left there. And I don't know where they got me a pair of skis. [Both laugh.]
I: Did they take someone's skis?
E: Yes, they just said what goes around, comes around.
I: They stood up for you?
E: Sure, we always stuck together. Nobody got left anywhere; when we decided to go to a dance, we always came back together.

I: Yes.
E: Nobody let anybody walk them home. That was for sure. It isn't like that anymore. Nowadays there aren't those kinds of groups, they go in twos or...
I: Yes.
E: There were always a lot of us, all the young people and lads from the village. I think I have beautiful memories of my youth. Even if it was wartime, rationing and all that, and we didn't get things we wanted. We had to work, and it wasn't nice work; it was dirty, and it was disgusting. (1/12, 37–38, pp. 25–26.)

In this situation I could expect some colourful narrative from Elsa. In the first episode, when the bike was hoisted up the flagpole, Elsa described the relations between the young lads of the Inha factory community and the students of the Tuomarniemi Forestry Institute,[21] which was located a few kilometres away from the Ironworks village. Pranks and verbal mocking were part of the local youth culture, fuelled by class distinctions and competition for the attention of the working-class girls. The forestry institute was a boarding institution set away from the larger villages and town centres. The boys of the Ironworks did not like for any outsiders, especially the higher-class forestry students, to socialize with "their girls". And they were ready to defend this view. Sticking together also guaranteed the girls' reputation; leaving the group, especially on the way home, and allowing someone to walk one home would have been regarded as immoral.

In addition to the solidarity of her peers, Elsa often mentioned the friendliness and helpfulness of the railway workers towards the girls of the Ironworks. The railway workers of the nearby train station sometimes, for example, helped the girls with their luggage. The following example depicts the chivalrous behaviour of the railway workers of at closest railway station in Inha:

Silk Stockings and Hemp Leggings

E: Once we were coming back from a dance in Kolho… Can I tell you these kinds of things?
I: Mhm, yes.
E: When we came back from Kolho we had silk stockings on. We didn't have any nylons. We came by train, on the morning train. They knew us there, as we always took the train somewhere, a big group of us. Yes, and the men said to us, "Your legs are going to freeze when you go." And then they went to fetch some hemp from the station. And each of us rolled some hemp around our legs and then we ran across the ice to the Ironworks. And we didn't get frost bite. [Laughs.] They took good care of us. They had some hemp ready, for when the girls came. It wasn't cold yet when we left. They thought that when the girls come back, they'll need to cover their legs. (5/12, 23, p. 11.)

It is interesting how Elsa asks me at the beginning of the narrative whether she can tell me "these kinds of things". She may have hesitated to recall her memories about her leisure-time activities and her contact with the opposite sex under the assumption that I, and the wider academic audience, would be more interested in other more serious matters. Another possibility is that the social criticism of dancing in the post-war period had remained strong in her mind. This may be why she so often underlined the security and togetherness provided by the peer groups, the solidarity and communality which guarded the morals of young females in particular and upheld class boundaries.

SOCIAL MOBILITY: MAKING AND BREAKING BOUNDARIES
Industrial paternalism embodied ideas of the social order as an indispensable, natural hierarchy based on inherited privileges, wealth and social status, which were created and ordained by God.[22] All the members of the industrial community had their own places and purposes in the hierarchical system. (Koivuniemi 2000, 25–31; Ahvenisto 2008, 166). Social climbers threatened this order and its clear distinctions.

In the course of the modernizing process in Finland, the individual and her/his competence rather than the family or the household became the basis for modern society. The individual was given the responsibility for acquiring the skills, education and wealth needed to improve her/his life circumstances (L. Stark 2006b, 56). Education, in particular, epitomized the new values linked with individualism. Through it, individuals could be liberated from the shackles of the position into which they were born by gaining access to social mobility (see for example Komulainen 1998, 36–37; Leino-Kaukiainen & Heikkinen 2011a, 11).[23]

Although upward mobility was not yet common in factory families and worker communities in the 1930s, young girls from working-class families had numerous career opportunities. They could, for example, apply to take continuation courses after the basic primary school, look for better jobs both within and outside of their own communities, in households, shops or post offices, or apply to study in vocational schools (see Kaarninen 1995; Leminen 1996, 167–169; 183). One potential option for young working-class women seeking a better life was to try to find a good post as a maid servant.

Before Elsa entered factory work, she worked as a maid in middle-class families. This period which took place during the Second World War lasted three years: from the age of twelve to fifteen.[24] For the most time of this time, she served in the family of Ove Amberg (the son of the older general manager, Reinhold Amberg), who was the technical manager of the factory at the time. His extended family also included Reinhold Amberg's son-in-law, Birger Illman, the former office manager and subsequently the new general manager of the factory (*Rautainen tarina*, 39).

The lines of social division between Elsa and the members of these middle-class families were drawn in a friendly manner: Elsa used the titles *herra* (Sir) and *rouva* (Madam) for the members of the household, while she was addressed by them in the third person as "Elsa". Elsa pointed out that no one in the Amberg family ever called her a maid servant in front of her (4/12, p. 6). Elsa still switches to a more official and cultivated register when referring to her service in the family. One example of this is her use of the word *hän* (the third person pronoun "she" or "he") instead of the more colloquial *se* ("it") when referring to the masters and ladies of the houses in which she served, which is exceptional in the vernacular language.²⁵ The use of more formal language can be seen as a sign of respect but also as a way of getting closer to her employer's social level and world.

As discussed in the preceding chapter, Elsa's service with the Amberg family taught her many necessary household skills, which she described as "keys to a better life". Elsa said that she admired both of the ladies of the household, Mrs. Amberg and Mrs. Illman. The older lady taught Elsa and was friendly and patient with her even when she once burned her silk underwear with a hot iron (2/12, 2, p. 3). According to Elsa, the younger lady, too, was kind and also very beautiful (7/12, 12, p. 15–16). Despite the advice and friendliness on the part of the ladies, Elsa told me that she often felt uncomfortable and insecure especially when serving guests at dinner parties. She simply had no experience of such events and was afraid of doing something wrong. Elsa was clearly careful about her reputation in the eyes of these ladies. She told about one incident that happened during a party held by the Illmans (2/12, 10, p. 6–7). Elsa had been cooking in the Ambergs' kitchen when a young man climbed in through the kitchen window. Elsa was horrified and ran into the house calling to Mrs. Illman. The lady came into the kitchen and gave a lecture to the young man in Swedish. She was not upset with Elsa but explained to her with a smile that the young man had behaved like that because she looked so pretty.

From Elsa's point of view, Mr. Amberg and Mr. Illman were members of the upper-class in that they held the highest possible positions at the Inha Ironworks. Even so, these men were easy-going and also helped her in her duties:

A Born Gentleman

I: So what was he [the master of the house] like?
E: He was totally ... he was not some social climber; rather, he was a born gentleman
I: Yes?
E: You see, there were these upstarts who had risen in society.
I: From the common people…
E: Yes, from the common people. But he was really nice in that he gave me advice, and when it was time for a house cleaning, and I was carrying big armchairs outside, he noticed and said that I wasn't supposed to carry them by myself. So he came and carried them. (4/12, 6, p. 4.)

By helping Elsa, the master of the house earned her respect and admiration. Elsa, who did not expect this kind of behaviour on the part of an upper-class *male*, explained his behaviour as part of his social background, making a distinction between "the born gentleman" and "social climbers".²⁶

For a long time, it was very difficult in the worker community of the 20th century for persons to cross the boundary between blue-collar and white-collar work (Salmi-Niklander 2004, 303). In his study of the work culture of

Technicians at the office. Elsa's Husband Eino Koskinen is the second man from the left. Elsa Koskinen's family album.

metal workers, historian Kari Teräs (2001, 109–110) noted that those foremen who were former workers and had climbed up in hierarchy were seen as a threat by the community of manual workers because they knew too much: sharing the same expertise and knowledge of social norms gave them an advantage in their new role as supervisors. In Elsa's narrated world, the boundary between workers and social climbers, the working class and their social superiors (the lower-middle class), was also based on the division between blue-collar and white-collar labour and education. Elsa explained how some people who had achieved a better position would act all high and mighty. At work, these people were called "sharp heads" *(terävät päät)*. In Finnish, "sharp head" can mean either a clever person or literally the sharp end or point of a pencil. Niina Lappalainen found that the workers of Tikkakoski used similar social distinctions and mocking expressions. Those workers who did not have to perform physical labour were called "pencil pushers" *(kynään nojaajat)* (2010, 252). In Kaisu Kortelainen's study of the Penttilä Sawmill community, the workers also referred to office workers as "sharper" than ordinary workers (2008, 98). In the context of class distinctions, all these expressions are pejorative. They refer to the need to emphasize the new position of the former workers and their dependence on book learning, which is a form of knowledge different from that possessed by labourers: manual work and its hierarchies are based on practice and apprenticeship, learning by doing and the gradual earning of respect.

When talking about social climbing, Elsa did not point to anyone in particular or name anybody as a social climber. Neither did she offer any narratives about social climbers. She merely let it be understood that there were some people in the community who, after becoming foremen or other supervisory or managerial staff, in some way expressed their disrespect for those workers who used to be their colleagues. Maybe this anonymity is due to a bias in her own private life: her own husband became one of the "sharp heads". Niina Lappalainen (2010, 254) has pointed out that this kind of violation of categories and feelings of *otherness* within one's own group may be difficult topics to broach, even in a humorous vein. Although Elsa treated many conflicts with humour, she never joked about social climbing. The issue was a serious one, and it came too close for comfort. In her narratives, Elsa reconstructed and showed respect for the hierarchies that organized her world and offered her a clear basis for both identification and distinction.

The Self Defined by Class

Class distinctions deeply affected the ways in which Elsa saw the world, other people and herself. For her, belonging to the working class was a source of both negative and positive experiences. This is an interesting aspect of identification and social identity, with potentially strong and controversial connotations. Elsa's experiences of social class are connected to materiality and embodiment. As a child, her class identity was formed through the concrete experience of material scarcity. Later in life, her social position became intertwined with the relations and experiences of manual labour. Elsa learned the skills and routines and coped with the harsh physical circumstances.

Material Scarcity and Social Ranking

Folklorist Eija Stark (2011), who has studied agrarian poverty, has stated that experiences of scarcity and the social hierarchy create a need to both reflect on the reasons and meaning of poverty and negotiate one's identity in relation to poverty. This was also true in Elsa's case. At the beginning of the 20th century, the social position one occupied was still highly visible from the physical appearance of the body. Bodily practices such as dressing and hygiene created outward differences between the lower and the higher classes in a way that stigmatized the extremely poor (E. Stark 2011, 150). From the time she was a very small child, Elsa knew that she belonged to a poor lower-class family. Even though her father worked and earned some extra money as a self-taught cobbler, he had twelve children to feed. Poverty was present in every aspect of their lives in concrete ways, as the following narrative illustrates:

> Wealthy Girl Wonders about Patched Clothes
>
> I had a friend who came to visit us, and she was from a well-off family. They had a Swedish name, but she wanted to be in our gang. And [my brothers] Pauli and Eero had patches on their trousers, and once she came to our house and she looked at their trousers and asked us what they were. She had never seen a patch before. And we told her that they'd been patched. The trousers had been patched. (7/12, 15, p. 20.)

This girl who visited Elsa's family was one of those whose parents or grandparents had moved to the ironworks village of Inha from other ironworks, most probably from the Swedish-speaking coast. Her family members thus belonged to the highest levels of esteemed craftsmen, the skilled workers of the Ironworks such as ironsmiths or rolling masters.[27] The girl bore other markers of her family's superior status: the name of the family was Swedish, which in Elsa's view, was a sign of a more prestigious background.[28]

In addition to patching, Elsa's family passed down clothes and shoes from the older children to the young ones. Going to school made social differences visible, and comparisons were difficult to avoid. In poor Finnish children's reminiscences of going to school lack of or low quality of shoes and clothes are symbols of impoverished circumstances (see Tuomaala 2004, 288–290; also Virkkunen 2010, 91–94). Elsa recounted how she got shoes from the municipality:

Boots with Curled Toes

> So everything that you learned had come to the shop, you'd go through hell and high water to get it. Otherwise, you wouldn't have anything to wear. We got shoes from Töysä Shoe Factory, or those who got there, got them. But when I went to school, the municipality gave one pair of shoes to schoolchildren from large families, to the family. And I remember how, when I got those shoes, they were boots, boots with curled toes. And other girls were able to order proper shoes with laces, the kind of boots they have today: half boots that lace up. But I thought, "Always me, I have to have that kind of high boots." When my feet grew, the boots went to the boys [Elsa's younger brothers]. We had to save money like that. [...] I had to wear these big boots, when other girls had their pretty small shoes. And when I didn't need them anymore and I grew out of them, then the boys were growing, and they went on wearing them. Our father repaired them himself, and they lasted well. They lasted for forever. [Laughs.] And he put tar on them. You can't imagine. (11/12, 15, p. 15.)

The recycling of clothes and books was (and still is) common, even in wealthier families. What made Elsa feel bad were the ugly-looking, unfeminine and old-fashioned boots she had to wear to school. She underlines how the boots marked her socially: the fact that they were a social benefit provided by the municipality and that she could not choose their appearance made it obvious that she came from a poor family. In her study of the mentalities related to poverty, folklorist Eija Stark has pointed out that poor relief was public, and in small communities everybody knew who received this assistance (2011, 327). Consequently, the poor were stigmatized by the benefits they received.

When the law on compulsory universal education was ratified in 1921, the benefits for children of poor families became part of the system and were channelled through the municipal school offices. The benefits included clothes, shoes and food (Tuomaala 2004, 284–86; Virkkunen 2010, 92). During the school week, Elsa and her siblings ate lunch at home (5/12, p. 1). She never mentioned hunger or a lack of food. However, she recalled how food was prized in her childhood family. They did not waste any bits: for example, her father always ate the heads of herrings and would never peel a potato, and the children ate the skins of sausages with great relish (2/12; p. 1).

Many of Elsa's positive childhood memories, too, are inextricably linked to material concerns. For example, she remembers the exceptional gifts, goods, and clothes she received from persons outside the family (see also Samuel & Thompson 1990, 10). Elsa calls these occasions "high spots". Market days, which took place once a fortnight when workers got their wages, constituted an exceptional high spot, bringing local traders and their customers to the Inha Ironworks.[29] The children of the community also gathered to watch the crowds and to marvel at the wonders. Sometimes a kindly seller was in a good mood and gave the children a treat like a lollipop or a piece of sweetbread, *pulla* (1/12, 20, p. 14; 5/12, 9, pp. 4–5). The children also knew other tricks to get some treats:

Memories of Market Days: Asking for Pulla

... I'll always remember how I was with Pirkko [name changed], she was our chum and the same age as me. She later got dementia, and she's now passed away. We were sitting there on the steps, and we knew some gentlefolk were coming – it was around midday when they came to buy meat and *pulla*. Pirkko said then that they had girls and [the girls] came to play with us. And we played together there, and I guess they spoke Swedish, those girls. Well, we ran up to them, and Pirkko told one of the girls to ask them [their parents] to buy us pies. The girl went to them and spoke Swedish to them and she brought us pies. And we almost got a belting at home. [Laughs.] Pirkko's mum asked us, "Where did you get those [pastries]?" And we told her that the little girl had brought them to us. She didn't believe us at all, that we hadn't been begging. But she let us eat the pastries when we said that [the girls' families] were rich. And Pirkko did say she'd asked the girl for the pastries. (1/12, 20, p. 14.)

It has been argued that in hierarchical factory communities, it was easier for children to cross the boundaries of social class (see for example Spoof 1997, 268–269; Ahvenisto 2008, 153). Playing outside, for example, brought together children from different backgrounds and gave them opportunities to socialize with their peers from different social groups.[30] The children of Inha were aware of the class differences and the social hierarchy, but they did not pay attention to all the codes and limitations inherent therein. Elsa mentioned, for example, that the parents of working-class families had told their children not to beg from the traders.[31] Therefore, children who wanted to get their share of the treats appealed to higher-class children from wealthier families to ask their mothers to buy them some pastries. The mother of Elsa's friend did not like this, but the girls were allowed to keep their treats.

Material scarcity continued to affect Elsa's life even after she began wage labour. When rationing came into force in Finland during the Second World War, most daily commodities and food supplies could be purchased only with ration coupons.[32] Every family was issued a fixed number of coupons based on its size, the ages of the children and its income. Farmers were supposed to keep only what their families needed and to surrender the rest of their produce to the state. Nevertheless, the black market flourished. Buying food on the black market is a common theme in Finnish oral history material relating to the Second World War (see for example Saaritsa 2002, 219–224). Social networks made it possible to purchase food and other commodities under the counter or from farmers in the surrounding countryside (ibid.). Together with other young women, Elsa too, travelled to countryside to buy flour, cereals, meat, and eggs.

One of Elsa's crystallized narratives of wartime black-market shopping describes the contrasting behaviour of a rich land-owner's wife and an old woman from a small cottage (3/12, 4, pp. 8–9; 5/12, 20, p. 10). When Elsa and her friend first visited the more prosperous farm and asked if there were any food to buy, the mistress of the house was silent but took the guests to a storage building, opened the door with a big key hanging from her belt and showed them what she had. The store house was full of long loaves of sweet bread. The mistress of the house remained silent and despite the abundance of food, the guests had to leave with nothing. When the hungry travellers came to the next house, a small grey cottage, they found an old woman there. They politely asked her for a piece of bread to eat and soon the table of the small cottage was covered with variety of delicious dishes. The old woman sold Elsa and her friend some products, even some real coffee, which was a rare luxury at the time. This narrative reflects a mentality that is common in the discourse of poverty: that abundance leads to spiritual poverty while material scarcity is a sign of spiritual nobility (see E. Stark 2011, 146–151).[33]

Journeys to the countryside and black-market trading were exciting events for the young Elsa. She described vividly how she managed to buy some nice fabrics:

Cloth under the Counter

> … and you know, we got clothes – I remember how we, a friend of mine and I, found out that they had got some fabrics in Jekunen's shop beside Inha railway station. It was eight o'clock when we went there, straight across the ice, to the railway station. We went through their home, and they sold us that cloth. I bought some, too, and I got a beautiful dress out of it when I took it to a dressmaker. There were no ready-made clothes to buy. There were good dressmakers at Inha Ironworks. I knew three of them, and they sewed dresses for me. This dress was really pretty. I still remember what it looked like. It was possible to get some nice clothes, but you had to be pushy. And I don't know, well, there were always some older people who heard about everything, they always told us where you could get something and where to go for it. (5/12, 21, p. 10.)

Young people wanted to be look good and be fashionable, even in the days of rationing.[34] Nice fabrics and rarities like nylon stockings[35] were sold under the counter, on the black market (Turunen 2005). In some cases, however, the black-market trade worked in favour of those who were better off (see also Räikkönen 1993, 184–185). Elsa told an interesting story about of this kind of situation:

Trading with a Class Bias

I: What did you get from the shop then, during the war?
E: All the coupon things. Everything was rationed.
I: Everything? Flour too?
E: Yes. Sugar, there was no coffee, only ersatz.[36] And butter, meat, everything. Also clothes were rationed.
I: Ahah..
E: But there were lots of things you could buy under the counter.
I: Yes.
E: Those who could get them.
I: You could buy them with money?
E: I remember how I once went to the consumer co-op, and it wasn't easy to get raisins in those days. And there was one man who'd come from a nearby village, I knew him, and he had a loud voice, and he didn't realize that he should have kept the raisins a secret. He asked if they had some raisins, and the shopkeeper tried to gesture somehow, I saw it, but I didn't say anything, I thought, "Let's just see what happens." And the man asked again, in a louder voice, "What about the raisins?"
I: And?
E: Yes, and the shopkeeper looked uncomfortable again, and she looked at me. And the man asked for the raisins a third time really loudly. And still nothing happened. So I told the shopkeeper to give the man the raisins, I didn't care. And he got a bag of raisins then.
I: Ah.
E: So things like that happened.
I: Yes, that was really something.
E: I didn't even know there were any raisins. But it became clear there were. Hm.
I: It's quite strange that there were such goods, but…
E: There were… But of course they were very scarce so they couldn't give them to everyone. (3/12, 1, p. 4–5; variant 7/12, 16, pp. 21–22.)

This version of the narrative is told in the context of trading and wartime (Interview 3/12). Interestingly, according to the narrative it is the shopkeeper who was confused and embarrassed in the situation, in which the unequal opportunities for accessing the black market became obvious. Finally it was Elsa who broke the tension by saying that she did not mind about the raisins. A variant of the same narrative (7/12, 16, p. 21) was followed by a long evaluation and a discussion about the nuances of social ranking. In the beginning, Elsa stated that she was not informed about the raisins because of her social status:

E: So caste was involved in this too. Even though I visited this shop every day, I wasn't offered any [raisins]. I didn't know anything about them. I would never have known if this man hadn't asked for them. A little batch had come. They were [for sale] under the counter. And the lady gave them to him. But, oh my, she blushed. [Laughs] When I said that I didn't want them.
I: You must have said that because he…?
E: Of course. There was nobody else there. When I got home from, there I told Eino, "Do you know, they have raisins there, but not everybody can get them."

[Laughs.] The man spoke so loudly. You know, I was amused when the man bawled like that. He came from the village of Kukkeenkylä. From there.
I: Yes.
E: So they knew [about the raisins] there, but I had no idea even though I lived right by the shop.
I: Interesting that such things happened.
E: Yes. That's how it was. But I don't know on what basis they selected those that got some. (7/12, 16, p. 21.)

At the beginning of this evaluative part, Elsa used the word *kasti*, a strong expression of class division, which came into the Finnish language from the Swedish word *kast* (cf. English "caste"), which in turn was used as a synonym for "estate" (in the sense of a social rank). This is a word that Elsa associated with inherited class privilege and with the dichotomy between the workers (*työläiset*) and the "gentlefolk" (*herrat*). However, she was not sure how the lines between different groups were drawn, especially in the case of outsiders to the ironworks. The man who wanted raisins was from another village (cf. the group of outsiders in the Appendix 3). I would assume that one of the confusing things about the situation was that Elsa was a frequent customer in this shop, which, according to her, was a cooperative.[37] The discussion continued with my questions:

I: You said previously that one of the significant differences was between big and small families, that the family size affected the wealth and position of the family? But was there a difference between statuses, between labourers and foremen and white-collar workers? Was it rank that mattered, or was it rather wealth?
E: Yes, there was, but they didn't show it, you know. They would talk to you and be friendly but you would know that they had better jobs…
I: I see.
E: You would realize it yourself. That I am not the same, I am in a lower position.
I: Yes.
E: But they had their own gatherings.
I: But they were friendly, or what?
E: Yes, yes. But there was one foreman there, and I'd been friends with his wife already when we were still girls/single,[38] and she taught me all sorts of things. I learned how to spin from her. And Eino was friends with this man, and they visited us … so it depended on the individual, how high they put themselves. (7/12, p. 22.)

When I asked Elsa directly about the hierarchy, she underlined the fact that people were generally friendly and talked to each other despite the class boundaries. People in a lower position did, however, realize that certain boundaries existed. She also referred to a situation in which social boundaries were blurred: a friendship between two couples whose male members belonged to different social ranks. I assume that socializing with social superiors close to one's own status was common and became all the more common when people educated themselves and moved into new social environments. If the divisions were not referred to directly and were not visible, how did the class positions become obvious? In what kind of situations did Elsa face rejection?

RELEGATED TO A LOWER CLASS: DOMINANCE AND HUMILIATION
In narrating her life, Elsa described many situations in which she was shown her place in the social hierarchy. Many of these narratives were highly emotional, evoking feelings of shame, pride, humiliation and hatred, even years after the experience. These experiences of contempt and subordination followed Elsa throughout her working life from domestic service to being a retired production-line worker.

When Elsa started to work as a maid servant in middle-class households at the age of twelve, she experienced feelings of otherness. At first, she served in the family of a teacher, Mr. Latva, who worked in the nearby Tuomarniemi Forestry Institute. There were as yet no children in the family, which consisted of Mr. Latva, his pregnant wife, her mother and an English teacher who lived in the household as a lodger. The family needed a maid to assist in cleaning the house. An educated middle-class family would not have expected a girl with a working-class background to be serving in the youth section of the Lotta Svärd Organization (a voluntary women's auxiliary corps, whose members were mostly middle-class and popularly called "Lottas").[39] But Elsa was a member of this organization, although she never mentioned this to the Latva family. One day she was assisting the local members of the auxiliary corps who were cooking food at the Inha railway station for soldiers returning from the front by train. The middle-class women were surprised to see her in a Lotta's uniform:

A Maid Servant with the Latva Family: A Gift for a Member of the Women's Auxiliary Corps

E: ... once, on one Sunday, I had a Lotta shift, a girls' unit shift, at the Lotta cabin. It was on the opposite side of Inha railway station [close to the Forestry Institute]. When soldiers came from the front, they stopped there for a rest.
I: Yes.
E: So I went there in the morning, I put on the Lotta uniform already before I went to work. And I did my tasks. And the old lady was so pleased [to see that]. So pleased that she asked whether that was Elsa was serving in the national defence. I said that I was only in the girls' unit. She gave me a package of wrapped sweets, which were rare that time; there weren't any sweets available...
I: In the wartime.
E: In the wartime. It was such a surprise.
I: Yes.
E: And, I don't know, I got the impression that I was accepted. (4/12, 8, p. 6.)

Before the war, many working-class women had been reluctant to join the Lottas (see for example Leminen 1996, 179). The youth organizations' activities, however, attracted also working class girls.[40] The Lotta's uniform showed the higher-class family that Elsa, a working-class girl from a factory community, was playing her part "in the civil defence". Furthermore, the grey uniform with white collars and cuffs symbolized purity and high morals (Olsson 1999, 82–86 and 2005; Turunen 2011, 367; Heikkinen 2012, 178–190). The girls were not expected to wear a Lotta's Uniform (Olsson 1999). Elsa never explained to me her motivation for joining the girls' section nor how she was treated there. However, it seems that this gave her social superiors, the Latva family, a reason to be satisfied with her. Despite this, however, Elsa was not happy with the way they treated her:

Elsa's Service with the Amberg Family

E: [continuing from the last sentence of the preceding story] …but when the lady of the house left to give birth to her child, I stayed at home, and then I went to the Ambergs' house. Then the mistress came back home from giving birth, and the war was still going on, but I was at the Ambergs'. She called Mrs. Amberg and asked if she could have me back. And Mrs. Amberg came to ask me if I would go back since Mrs. Latva needed me. I said I wouldn't; you see, I'd had to give them my food coupons, and I never got the same food as the gentlefolk ate. They served me after they had eaten, I went to do the dishes, and I had food waiting for me there, some potatoes and some margarine on a plate, sometimes rye porridge, and I never ate, not really. I gave my food to the dog. In the end, I had it better at home.
I: How about at the Ambergs'?
E: At the Ambergs', everybody got fed [the same food]. I ate in the kitchen, but I got the same food. They had good food. And it was so that they never looked down on me in any way; even if I was a maid, they never called me that. (4/12, 9, p. 6.)

Food was often used as a mark of the social hierarchy in large agrarian households. Farm hands and other agrarian workers were often served different food from the fare of the farmer's family. According to Eija Stark, this practice continued relatively late, in some parts of Finland right up to the 1950s (2011, 118, 123–124). In the Latva family, Elsa was not supposed to eat with the family. In addition, although they used her food rationing coupons, they never offered Elsa the same food that they themselves ate. The food given to her was, in fact, poorer than she was used to at home. The Latva family showed Elsa her place symbolically through the food they served her.

Historian Marjatta Rahikainen (2006) argues that the institution of domestic service perpetuated the strong class divisions and class boundaries of Finnish society. It is important to note that this institution was based on intersections of class and gender that affected the lives and self-image of young females in particular. The status of maid servants was not only low but also a matter of contention within both the family and the maids' own peer group: by crossing the borders of the nuclear family and their own social class, they became outsiders, others.[41] The position of a young working-class girl could change when she married or when she took up a factory job, which offered better paid work and also socialized women into the new ranks of wage-earning workers. When Elsa started working in the factory, she attained this more respectable status:

University Students

E: I remember how we [I and my friend who also worked at the factory] were coming from a dance once. We were already working at that time, and we went to Ähtäri Workers' Hall. At that time it was the Workers' Hall.
I: The sports hall?
E: Yes. And we were walking from there. We were just going up Hankola Hill, the road that starts from the railway station. It was the Ähtäri road. And there were two male university students walking there [interviewer laughs.] They caught up with us and they looked at us like this. They had their student caps on. And they looked at us like this, and finally one asks if the maid servants were having an evening off. And Siiri [name changed] pulled herself up – you see, she was a stout woman. She said, "We're no maid servants. Is that what they teach you at university?" The fellows left, they didn't hang around.
I: They didn't have the courage to stay.
E: We've laughed many times about this.
I: It was good that she said that.
E: Yes, we weren't servants.
I: No, you were…
E: We were working.
I: Workers.
E: Yes, we worked at the factory. And you know, then they thought that maids were sort of cheap.
I: Yes.
E: And they were sort of looked down on everywhere.
I: Yes. (12/12, 5, p. 3.)

What made the students think that Elsa and her friend would be maid servants? Was it their age or perhaps their appearance? I do not know, but it is obvious that in the narrated situation there was more than just class at stake: it was also a matter of morals and respectability, which were tightly interwoven with class. The realist Finnish literature of the early 20th century produced fictitious descriptions of relations between maids and university or college students, typically offering warning examples of (forbidden) love and seduction that resulted in the maid having a child out of wedlock (Halme 2006, 183–184; Hyttinen & Melkas 2009).[42] In the case related by Elsa, the male university students underestimated these young women, who were not innocent, easily seduced girls, but autonomous adult women who were in respectable and paid jobs, workers who had already adjusted to the male working environment and had learned to put up with sexual jokes and talk back to men (see Chapter 3 p. 70–74 earlier in this study).

Even if factory work gave Elsa a better status than she had enjoyed as a maid servant, it too entailed certain oppressive relations. Elsa told, for example, that she always felt bad about the way the wages were handed to the workers in the early days of her career:

Waiting for the Wages

...and at that time, the wages, for example, they brought them from the accounts office to us in front of the laboratory. The workers stood there waiting. I felt ashamed. I don't know why I felt like that, but I had the feeling that even though I'd worked hard, I was begging there. Do you understand? I always felt ashamed, but then the office manager distributed the pay packets. Nobody said anything – nobody told how much they got. (5/12, 5, p. 3; 8/12, 2, p. 3.)

In Elsa's view, waiting and queuing was humiliating, almost as if the workers were begging for their wages after hard physical labour that they had performed. In so doing, the workers took physical postures which symbolized subordination. The situation had remained in Elsa's mind and had transformed into a crystallized narrative. The image of workers queuing is indeed strong and symbolic. The silence of the situation adds to the uncomfortable feeling of the labourers. The feeling of *shame* is an interesting emotional response to the situation, in which Elsa felt *dependent* on other people. Folklorist Niina Lappalainen, too, has used the word "ashamed" to describe her informant's response to the social divisions in the factory community she studied (2008, 62). Her informants were not willing even to talk about the distinctions or tell about their experiences of class differences. It has been argued that a person feels shame when forced to recognize that s/he is in a subordinate position (Kilborne 1992; Stark 1998, 186). Thus, shame can emerge as a response to revealing one's weakness to other people such as members of higher classes. In another version of the narrative in Interview 8, Elsa told me how relieved she felt when this practice changed and the wages she had earned were paid into her bank account. In her view, this was a significant change, a sign of development and progress.

Despite positive changes in some aspects of working life, however, Elsa felt that as a worker she was still in a lower-class position. This evoked feelings of otherness, subordination and humiliation. When Elsa went to sort out her retirement and monthly pension at the office of the Social Insurance Institution (KELA), she reported that she felt belittled:

A Visit to the Social Insurance Institution

Yes, yes, we moved into the Ähtäri centre in '84. Grandpa said: "You're not going to [retire] yet, let's do it at the same time." Well, I didn't do it at the same time as the other [workers] did, and I regret that I didn't, I should've done. Well, Grandpa, he couldn't retire, he was a white-collar worker, and he had to work for two months more before he got the decision on a pension. So I worked there for two more months as I didn't take it [the chance to retire when I could] at the beginning of the year, in January, so I stayed on. And I had it hard because everybody else had already visited the Social Insurance Institution to sort out their pensions. I went there alone. And they were so nasty to me. They asked me what I had done. I said I had been a production line worker. And the woman said contemptuously that I should try to remember what I'd done. I burst into tears. I said I'd been on the production line. And then she found a paper, looked at it and said, "Yes, so you have." That was the last straw. How I still hate that woman, or I don't feel anything when I see her. I see her very often. I just pass by her without nodding to her. It was such a blow to me when she suggested I didn't know what I'd done. She said it in such a nasty way. (8/12, 4, p. 4.)

When Elsa, at the age of 57 years and with decades of work experience at the factory, wanted to arrange her future with the pensions office, the clerk did not recognize the job description that Elsa offered. The feelings evoked by the meeting with the female official are strong: humiliation and rage. Elsa tells how she was so deeply hurt by the fact that she did not get recognition for the work she had done that she did not actually "feel anything" anymore. Stating "that was the last straw," she connected this experience with previous incidents of being placed in a lower, oppressed position. Both of these emotional narratives (*Waiting for the Wages* and *A Visit to the Social Insurance Institution*) exemplify the paradox between the lower-class position of workers and their strong vocational identity, the pain of not being recognized and valued as workers. In my opinion, Elsa's experiences of being belittled conflicted with her need and experienced right to define herself and make her own life, virtues that are highly esteemed in many local[43] and national cultures, and in the modernizing Western world in general. When other people stigmatized Elsa as lower-class or denied her vocational status, her working-class identity caused her to feel shame and humiliation. However, being categorized and identified as a worker did not produce only negative experiences in Elsa's life; it also brought her pride, dignity and a sense of being able to cope in life.

Skills and Dignity: "I knew the job"

Youth has been seen as the crucial time for the assumption of social codes such as gender roles and class identities (I. Young 1990). In the early 20th century, the lives of young Finnish people were strongly marked by the class from which they came (Lähteenmäki 1995, 105). Before the Second World War, most young working-class persons finished school before the age of 15 and worked full time thereafter. School attendance was gendered as well. Many families did not see any point in educating girls, especially in rural areas, and few working-class girls had a chance to undertake further education (Lähteenmäki 1995, 162). In urban areas such as the city of Tampere, girls from the lower classes had more possibilities. They could, for example, enter the extension school (a two-year continuation of the primary school) or apply to vocational schools such as business colleges. Admittedly, most of the vocational education that catered for girls pertained to domestic science subjects. In the 1920s and 1930s, secondary school education and upper secondary school education became more common for the offspring of wealthier farmers and the urban middle and even working classes (Kaarninen 1995). The Second World War changed the working life of many young people. Immediately before the war, only five per cent of the industrial work force was under 18 years old. During the war, the proportion of underage workers increased to ten percent (Rahikainen 2003, 161).

Juha Kauppila (1996, 74–75), a historian who has studied the significance of education in Finnish people's lives, has pointed out that despite the fact that the Second World War cut short young people's formal education, it did on the other hand provide them with unique learning experiences. Many people who had struggled on the home front felt that after such tough experiences they could survive anything. Young Elsa rapidly became acquainted with physical labour, obtained skills and won appreciation at work. Her vocational skills and occupational identity contributed to her sense that she was able to cope with the demands of life, and added to her self-esteem. Through her wage labour, Elsa became a member of the community of workers, and obtained a place in the world. Elsa started her career in the factory by assisting a handyman, in her own words, being a dogsbody's dogsbody *(sällin sälli)*, carrying boxes of new horseshoes and spikes. The work was physically demanding, but the fact that she managed it well led to her promotion as a machinist:

From a Dogsbody's Dogsbody to Machinist

[…] when I turned seventeen I got to… The "laboratory" was a kind of place where the technical manager and the foremen were, it was a kind of office for them, it was next to us. So Suutala [the foreman] came out of there [the "laboratory"] and said, "Elsa has turned seventeen, so you can go to [work at] that machine. And for many years I'd watched how they operated it, so I could handle it. (5/12, 3, pp. 2–3; 12/12, 14, p. 8.)

Elsa got a position that had earlier belonged to an older male worker. This might not have been possible if it had not been wartime. Because of the war, Elsa did not have much of a choice regarding her own education and future work. However, she emphasized the fact that the factory work she was trained to do required certain skills and qualities.

It was just the skill that we learned there. We had the skills for that work. We could operate the machines and do the job. It has its own rhythm. (7/12, p. 22.)

Elsa's relationship with machines was similar to that described by ethnologist Christer Eldh (1996) in his article regarding changes in factory work from the standpoint of the bodies of workers. The 40-year-old factory worker he interviewed underlined the fact that workers had to master their machines. Occupational skills were gained by respecting and even fearing the machine. Different phases of work at the factory had to follow a certain rhythm, or otherwise the production lines would not run smoothly. According to Elsa, the machinist's work was precisely about handling the rhythm. She described this rhythm using an interesting metaphor:

With them [the machines] you had to have your own rhythm so you would be fast enough, because, you see, there was iron coming out of the furnaces all the time. [...] and in the meanwhile, the piece of iron was not supposed to cool. It needed to be like continuous waltzing. (4/12, p. 8.)

Metaphors typically refer to multiple meanings which are both shared and subjective (Laine 2007, 32). The Finnish word *valssaus* that Elsa uses has several meanings: in addition to waltzing, in Finnish technical language it also means rolling, the processing of iron, which was heavy work performed by skilled ironworkers. "Continuous waltzing" is a poetic expression describing skills and team work between the machinists and the reciprocal relationship between the workers and the machines. Such time-space routines within a particular location can be characterized as place ballets, embodying rhythms of life that create feelings of belonging within space (Creswell 2004, 34; see also Seamon 1980).

Reflecting on her own identity as a labourer, Elsa often stated how nobody would do such work today, if they had other options available:

[...] it was work, and people today wouldn't do it. There was no heating other than the furnaces, and we always stood beside the boxes of horseshoes and spikes to warm ourselves up.[44] And the doors were so that we couldn't close them, even in the winter. They were simply so frozen. We could move them a bit to get in and out. Hmm [sighs]. And we didn't even have proper clothes, you see: it was wartime, there was rationing, and if we got some cloth – there weren't any ready-made clothes. They got some overalls from somewhere at the factory, and these were distributed to us. But no proper shoes or anything. It was really rough sometimes. (5/12, pp. 2–3.)

The descriptions of difficult working conditions – heat and cold, dirt and danger – and complaints about the lack of proper equipment were based on real hardship and embodied memories. In the context of her life narrative, these descriptions emphasize Elsa's own courage and persistence. In my interpretation, Elsa does not, however, suggest that people today would lack these qualities. According to her, the main difference is that nowadays people can choose whether they want to do physical labour or educate themselves:

E: It was the kind of work that people of today wouldn't do, not at all.
I: Hm.
E: But we had to. I got to stay at home. It was better than chopping wood in the forest. I did that, too, with my father.
I: Yes.
E: Yes, I did it with my mum while our father – we took him coffee to the forest. So we had to carry the branches that he cut on our shoulders. That's why I know what it's like. We had to try our best even if we weren't really up to it. People don't do that anymore, they go to school.
I: Yes, well...
E: Not today, no.
I: Well, they have to. But I've also done that kind of work.
E: Yes, you, but it's up to the individual if they want to.
I: Yes, if you want to. You don't have to. (7/12, pp. 23–24.)

At this point I ended up challenging her ideas about today's people by introducing my own experiences of physical work as an example:

I: Well, I don't know. In a way, I think I had to.
E: Well…
I: To get money.
E: Well that is what I mean, that was my job.
I: It was my job, too. I have also cut firewood as part of my job.
E: OK.
I: As part of the work on a farm.
E: Well I suppose you have.
I: And unloaded meat deliveries…
E: You see that is already a different thing. If you worked in a grocery store, for example, you would already be on a different level. (7/12, pp. 21–22.)

This exchange is interesting: it seems as if we were talking about different things. I tried to show Elsa that I also had experience of "real (physical) work" in my summer jobs, whereas she, who was reflecting on the conditions of her own life, emphasized that, unlike me, she had no other options. Referring to her own youth and the exceptional time of the Second World War, Elsa underlined the necessity and the *obligation* to work. She had no choice, and neither did many others. She also connects the issue to social class. There was no choosing between studying and working in her world. Physical work was her only option, and that was what she managed successfully, despite being a woman and having less physical strength than men. Today, on the other hand, almost all young people can go to school and get an education. Even so, in Elsa's view, factory work was not the worst work she could have ended up doing. Cutting firewood, which was normally a male duty, was one of the tasks in which women had to participate during the Second World War and is often mentioned in Finnish women's reminiscences of working during the war (see for example Kirves & Näre 2008, 66–68; Hytönen & Koskinen-Koivisto 2009). Elsa refers to this work when contrasting the modern world with her own past experiences:

I Know All about Chopping Wood

E: Men came back from the front to work there [in the factory]. We were there, and they didn't fire us since we'd learned the job anyway. I don't like to say so, but nowadays people can't get a job at all if they haven't been to school. And not even then. I can't get my head round it. Sure, I understand that industry needs its own share, and it's never enough.
I: And people today are altogether overeducated.
E: Yes, they are. And they won't do any kind of work. Like in the old days. I've done… I was told not to go cutting wood in the forest. When I got my replacement hip and I had this last operation, and I asked what I was allowed to lift, he [the doctor] said [I could do anything] as long I didn't go logging, cutting and trimming. I felt like saying I knew what it was like. I'd had to help my father cutting timber. Cutting firewood. He felled the trees, and Aili [Elsa's sister] and I

cut the branches off and sawed them into logs. Aili was on the other end of the saw. We sawed while he [our father] took measurements. I have also debarked the trunks. There you go. What else could you do? That's what the body needed. All hustle and go. Dragging things. (10/12, 21, p. 16.)

In the beginning, Elsa wonders about the paradoxical situation of today: people study but there is not enough work for everybody in contemporary Finnish society. For her, it is difficult to understand this. Her positive experiences of factory work, attaining the skills involved in it, getting a better and independent position, and coping with the circumstances in which she had to work made Elsa celebrate physical work: the waltz she used to dance when she was young and strong, when machines required enormous amounts of labour, working bodies – men and women.

Worker Identity and "a greasy skin"

Many of the narratives I have thus far analyzed contained experiences and emotions related to Elsa's sense of self and dignity. Elsa lived her life in a small, tightly-knit factory community, where one's identity was tied to one's social positions. Being a worker made for a contradictory identity. As an active member of the working-class youth, Elsa was part of a loyal network of peers. Through factory work she obtained independence in the outside world, acquired skills and a position in the factory environment, and experienced pride and joy. However, the same position brought class discrimination and sometimes humiliating treatment from other people who were higher in the social hierarchy.

Patricia Sawin (2004) notes that her informant Bessie Eldreth, who had worked hard through her life, served other people and suffered from her husband's tyranny and neglect, emphasized her innate willingness to be of service, her constant diligence and obedience, by using other people's voices and reported speech. Eldreth did not praise herself directly but used the voices of authoritarian figures such as doctors, priests and preachers to construct for herself the figure of a hardworking, respectable woman. Sawin has reflected on Eldreth's need to present herself in this manner. In her view, Eldreth's stories reflect and reconstruct a cultural framework of reference in which certain features count and make uneducated and relatively poor elderly working-class women worthy (2004, 51).

Elsa seldom used other people's voices in the form of reported speech to represent herself. Instead, she herself evaluated other people's attitudes towards her and placed value on her mental and physical strength as well as skills and life experience. It has been argued that in the Finnish context, in which there has been a powerful moral and ethical impetus to define oneself through work, hard work and struggling to cope have constituted the marks of a good man or a good woman (Kortteinen 1992, 50; Taira 2006, 92). This ethos which is rooted in Protestant ethics and nationalism is based on the connection between work and piety and the rational endeavour aimed at achieving economic gain (Weber 1985). Religious studies scholar Teemu

Taira (2006), who has studied the changing values of work-related culture in the autobiographical writings of unemployed persons, points out that in the Finnish context, the strong work ethos has not emphasized economic success and the maximizing of profit but is rather a cultural image that has been evoked in difficult circumstances (2006, 92). Taira reminds us that in the Nordic countries, capitalism has taken a collective form and the ethos of work does not emphasize individual success as a way to economic prosperity (Taira 2006, 92).

In her research on the school experiences of Finnish children in the 1920s and the 1930s, historian Saara Tuomaala (2004) analyzes the processes of subject formation of school children. During her research process, Tuomaala interviewed several elderly narrators who told about their childhood, youth and early adulthood. She draws attention to children's learning of both school knowledge and working skills. Learning happened through the body, especially the hands and fingers. According to her (2004, 53–54; 2009a, 81), the experiences of different life stages can be approached from the perspective of *bodily layering (la sédimentation)*. Following Tuomaala's thoughts, I argue that the narratives about embodied experiences presented by Elsa in this study construct Elsa's working-class and worker identity. In Elsa's childhood, the weak economic situation of the family correlated with a lower social status. Children of large families whose fathers worked in the Ironworks did not enjoy of much in the way of material commodities and were used to having to wear patched clothes, for example. When growing up, working-class children like Elsa learned to perform physical labour, enduring the dirty conditions and hard work, adjusting their bodies to the rhythm of the machines. Thus, for Elsa, being a worker was a result of the material conditions of her life and her practical skills, in other words her physical being in the world (cf. Merleau-Ponty 1962; Tuomaala 2004, 53).

Elsa never got the opportunity to receive any more than a basic education. She told surprisingly few narratives about her time at school. The one of the few narratives of her school years described how the children of a large family had only one school book that they had to share (see the other case of recycled shoes earlier in this chapter p. 97). Elsa's time for studying was late at night, and she still wonders how she managed to complete her school education (5/12, 1, pp.1–2). Referring to her siblings, Elsa pointed out that "nobody else studied at that time". Interestingly enough, there was a precedent for (self-)education in Elsa's mother's family. Elsa's maternal uncle Hermanni was a man who held a number of respectable jobs in the village: for instance, he had been a dairyman and a bank clerk. He had taught himself to write and do arithmetic, and therefore he handled financial matters for his fellow villagers.[45] Hermanni was in many ways an active, modern and exceptional person. He studied and wrote poems and humorous articles for local newspapers.

Elsa did not have any vocational training: she learned the factory work by doing it. In Elsa's life, her feelings of otherness relate to the situation in which she found herself after her husband had educated himself, obtained a higher position and became one of the "sharp heads" in the office. She felt different from her husband as well as from the other workers, who now saw her as the wife of a manager, not simply as another labourer. Her identity as a manual labourer continued to define her narrated self. The following comment occurred when Elsa and I were discussing Elsa's daughter's studies:

Let the Others Study

E: At the same time it happed that Grandpa was studying…
I: To be a technician.
E: Yes. Through a correspondence course. Hm. I was working hard. I tell you, I'm a greasy-skinned work*man*. [Laughing] Let the others study. But I've done OK.
I: Yes. (10/12, 9, p. 8.)

In the above Elsa refers to the key narrative "Back to work", which I analysed earlier in this study (Chapter 3, p. 66ff): I reacted by confirming that I understood it. The reference to a longer narrative makes this micro-narrative an example of a small 'narrative-in-the-making', which is not fully articulated and is connected to the process of constructing identities in interaction (see Bamberg & Georgekapoulou 2008). The micro-narrative summarizes the fully-fledged narrative and is an interesting identity performance, especially when it comes to the chosen expressions. Sociologist Paul Willis, who has studied working-class culture and identity, has pointed out that experiences of heavy manual labour are often expressed through metaphors that emphasize physical strength and masculinity (1977, 53, 104). The Finnish language is often gender-neutral, but in the case of some professional titles, the forms are either gendered or only a male version exists. In this case, Elsa used a masculine term *työmies*, (literally a work*man*) which, in my view, emphasizes the physical quality of the work she performed.

Having a "greasy skin" meant being tough and capable. In my interpretation, this metaphor had a positive connotation for Elsa: well-oiled leather is waterproof and strong. Folklorist Jyrki Pöysä, who has analyzed the culture of lumberjacks, notes that "greasy skin" was mentioned in the list of different expressions used for lumberjacks by one of the respondents to an inquiry about the lumberjack tradition (1997, 125). The informant had added the words "genuine" and "sleek" to explain the meaning of the phrase "greasy-skinned lumberjack".[46] According to Pöysä, the expression had a respectful tone. Persons who could be characterized as greasy-skinned were authentic, diehard lumberjacks with long years of service and lots of experience (ibid. 130). By employing this strong physical metaphor, Elsa placed herself among those who did bodily work.

Elsa used the expression "greasy-skinned workman" twice in the interview (8/12; 1. p. 2; 10/12, 9, p. 8. Earlier in interview 8/12 Elsa had recounted how this period in her life was very difficult for her, how she felt like an outsider in her own family and how she eventually decided to go back to work against her husband's wishes. Here, Elsa once again contrasts her life with the lives of other members of the family, explicitly with her husband's and her daughter's lives, and implicitly with mine as well. Niina Lappalainen

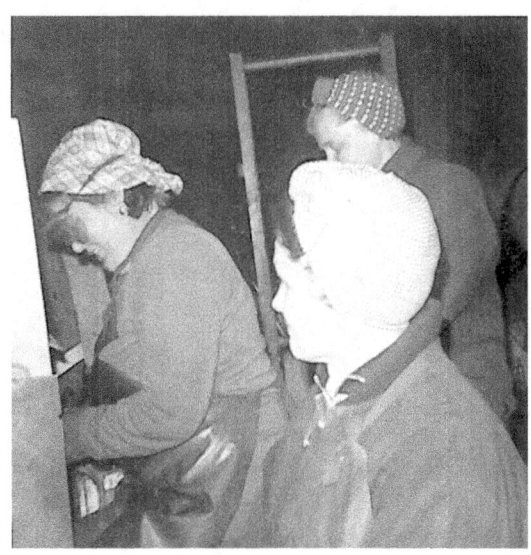

Elsa and her fellow workers in the production line. Elsa is in the front. Elsa Koskinen's family album.

reports how her interviewees from the Tikkakoski worker community never lamented their lack of education (2010, 254). She assumed that they were talking to her as a fellow worker, not as a researcher with an academic background (cf. Kortteinen 1992; Sawin 2004). I would argue that my education and the fact that Elsa knows that these interviews are related to my studies provoked her need to reflect on her working life and the possibilities for education that were unavailable to her.

Psychologist Katri Komulainen (1998) has studied the narratives of Finnish women with regard to education during the late 1980s and early 1990s. She argues that in order to become modern autonomous individuals, women needed to break the mould of the subservient figure who had been denied sufficient education. These new social actors came into being in the narratives the women told Komulainen about their later choices. She approaches these narratives as dialogues not only between the self and the past, but also between the self and the future. Komulainen analyzed the conversational partners who participated in the discussion in the women's narratives. These partners included not only other persons and other narratives, but also the various voices of the different selves, often the past selves that these women had been and the future ones they wanted to become. But education is not the only means of becoming an empowered subject and to narrate oneself as such.

In the excerpt above, Elsa describes herself, her situation and her life by employing a series of short but powerful first-person sentences that constitute her own voice: "I was working. I tell you, I'm…" By telling me that she resigned herself to what she eventually became, Elsa shows that she, too, had made a choice, even though there were fewer options available to her. She chose not to stay at home and therefore, not to be defined according to her family's new status but to choose her own. The result was a positive conclusion: "I've done OK." These expressions, in my opinion, describe how

Elsa became who she is, and how she, somewhat paradoxically, became an empowered subject, at least in the narrated situation. However, her laughter could suggest that she has, at some point, experienced bitterness over her situation. In earlier interviews, she told me that other workers, especially her female colleagues at the factory, no longer saw her as a worker or member of the working class anymore even though Elsa herself considered herself as such, and still does. Instead of defining herself according to her husband, she chose to represent herself as loyal to the class of manual labourers and as proud of it.

5. Change and Continuity in a Life Narrative

> "Mennyt ei näyttäydy [...] nykyisyyden peilikuvana tai negaationa, vaan erilaisuutena, joka osoittaa nykyisyyden mahdollisuudet." (Hyvärinen, Peltonen & Vilkko 1998, 22)
>
> "The past does not appear [...] as a mirror image or as a negation of the present but as something different which reveals the potential of the present."[1]

The first two research questions I posed at the beginning of this study were: 1) How have gender, class and work shaped the narrator's subjectivity? 2) How does Elsa position herself in relation to shifting cultural ideals, and what kinds of narrative means and strategies does she employ? Both questions concern the creation of the continuity and the sources of the self in relation to social change. The focus of my analysis in this chapter is on Elsa's experience of both concrete and material change within the work environment and the physical environment of the factory village. I also consider the different narrative strategies she used to evaluate social change and her past selves. I therefore analyse how she positions herself in biographical time and space in terms of what kinds of experience function as sources of the self and establish the continuity of the self in a life narrative, and how it is possible to narrate the transformation and development of the self as well as the passage of time.

Embodied Change: Experiences of Advance and Loss

Studies of oral traditions and oral history have shown how material culture and the physical landscape, objects and sites, can epitomize the personal and shared meanings attached to a person's past life.[2] The realm of concrete material reality offers symbols of abstract processes of change as well as the expression of experiences and emotions related to transformation and loss. Folklorist Ray Cashman (2006) argues that in the villages of Northern Ireland, material culture such as old amateur museum collections of individual villagers, commemorative traditions related to certain sites, and the display of agricultural machines and tools enunciates critical nostalgia. According to him, the outsider's first indications of a nostalgic mood are more visual than verbal (ibid. 142). But what if there are no physical traces left that could be ascribed symbolic value? What happens when social transformations take people away from landscapes familiar to them? The old factory community of Inha has not left many physical objects in the lives of former workers. They could not claim ownership to machines or tools, not to mention land or dwellings. Technological advances necessarily change the industrial landscape. However, the factory community and its physical environment continue to live in the memories and narratives of elderly persons as well as in photos of family albums. In the following section, I analyse how Elsa narrates the transformation of factory work and its social and physical environment and connects her personal experience to complex processes of change.

Modernizing Factory Work: Embodied Experience and the Worker Identity

Rationalization and mechanization are part of the logic of industrialism and capitalism: both work to enhance production and profit.[3] These two processes also transform the work itself, the relationship between people and machines as well as the social dynamics among people involved in factory work. It is often argued that production line work together with economic rationalization subordinates workers to time-space relations dictated by *machines* (see for example Arvastson 1987, 27–28; Shilling 2005, 80). Ethnologist Christer Eldh (1996) has studied changing circumstances in production lines, technical advances and rationalization from the point of view of skilled manual workers, and the oral historians Judith Modell & John Hinshaw (1996) have analyzed masculine identity of former steel workers. These studies draw attention to the subjective and embodied experiences of male factory workers and interpret technological change and the globalization of industry as threats to the worker's subjectivity and identity. I would argue, by contrast, that the relationship between worker and machine can also be productive. Furthermore, the rationalization affected not only the relationship between the workers and technology but also the prevailing social structures and dynamics at work.

According to historian Pauli Kettunen, who has studied the history of industrial safety, the history of labour protection is linked to the development of rationalization and working conditions. In addition to creating means by which working conditions were controlled, such as industrial safety legislation and networks of inspectors, labour protection movements encouraged workers to take more responsibility for their work.[4] Altogether, the development of industrial safety helped to transform working bodies into more knowing subjects. The process thus included both subjectivity and discipline (Kettunen 1994, 12–23, 26, 232–239; Foucault 2005[1975]).

Industrial safety is an issue encountered by Elsa when she started working on a machine during the war at the age of seventeen. Elsa told, for example, how one old machine on the horseshoe line tended to break down, often almost smashing the workers' fingers:

> [This machine] had a board and in the centre there were two round wheels. And when you stamped [on the pedal], the machine would cut the horseshoes apart from each other, and I had to take the pieces and throw them to the next machine. It was dangerous because sometimes the plate that had those two wheels came off on its own and you would always have to hold the tongs so that your fingers didn't get caught in-between. It happened often. It gave you an awful scare because it happened so suddenly. It shouldn't have done that. Then it was always repaired, but the tongs were smashed. (5/12, p. 3.)

Elsa calmly described how the plate with two wheels on the machine often came off and smashed a pair of long tongs she had in her hands. She does not describe the incident as a personal experience but rather gives a neutral report of the matter. In the interview situation she did, however, demonstrate the movements and her frightened reaction by means of gestures.[5] In my view, her narrative strategy, the seemingly calm reporting style, emphasizes her skill and experience. Earlier I quote Elsa's rather poetic description of the skills required by a machinist and production line worker: she described the rhythm of the job as "continuous waltzing" in which verbal expression intermingles with bodily movement. I also analyze how she, as a young worker was proud of performing jobs on the machines that she had learned by watching others while assisting them as a handyman's assistant. Elsa often emphasized the strenuous nature of the working conditions, the dirt and the sweat, but also the poor working conditions and lack of industrial safety.[6] I have argued that many of Elsa's experiences of production line work, including coping with the dangers of physical labour at Inha Ironworks, became resources through which she negotiated her subjectivity and assumed a positive worker identity. In Elsa's eyes, the development of industrial safety was indeed a positive thing. From the point of view of her presentation of self, however, the lack of industrial safety was a challenge overcome by the narrated self.

At the individual level, narratives of coping can be a means of dealing with the effects of social change and ageing. Social psychologist and gerontologist Marja Saarenheimo (1997), who has studied the reminiscences and life story narration of elderly Finns, has pointed out that the relational self, whose coherence lies in the way other people perceive her/him and in the continuity of memory, must compose a story of survival and successfully overcoming vulnerability in order to frame her/his subjectivity and agency within her/his current life situation. Saarenheimo introduced the term superwoman discourse *(teräsnaisdiskurssi)* to describe the process through which older women were able to remember and narrate the often contradictory experiences of their corporeal beings and physical resources, of being vulnerable and encountering the limits of survival (1997, 182–184). Survival did not depend on conscious choices or actions but on coping with physically and mentally harsh circumstances that could not be easily altered. This narrative process, the superwoman discourse, and the notion of getting by or adapting *(sopeutuminen)* were gender-specific. According to Saarenheimo, male narrators did not talk about their lives in a constant flow like this but rather described specific incidents and heroic deeds such as being wounded in the war (ibid. 184).

The reminiscences of the male steelworkers in Pennsylvania studied by John Modell and Judith Hinshaw (1966) emphasized the physical demands and dangerous nature of their labour, which had left permanent marks on their bodies (cf. Salmi-Niklander 2004, 304–305). The scars and illnesses can be seen as the combat badges of workers, as in the case of the fishermen of Lake Erie interviewed by the folklorists Patrick B. Mullen and Timothy Lloyd. The fishermen were proud of the marks on their skin left by their exposure to constant sun and wind (Lloyd and Mullen 1990; Mullen 1992, 136–138).[7] Elsa does not mention visible marks such as permanent scars, but she says that work has left her with aches and pains. She told me how she and her female colleagues developed similar kinds of illnesses: arthritis and cancer, which she referred to as "legacies of the factory" (5/12, 4, p. 3).

Although Elsa welcomed all the improvements in industrial safety and working conditions such as new warm factory halls, some changes bothered her. In her life narrative, Elsa also touched upon her encounters with new cycles of factory work and new specialists: the rationalization resulting from the work of time-and-motion analysts. Elsa saw this as a new way of controlling the workers. She felt restricted and controlled, even subordinated:

Time-and-Motion Analysts

But it began to change then. I certainly remember that we were not allowed to do the work freely. The timekeepers came. Then we were no longer able to have too long breaks from work. […] And then each person's work [began to be timed,] mine, too, since I was the dogsbody's dogsbody. I fetched the coal from a faraway shed, and they began to follow me. That was the first change, which a workman couldn't understand – that they timed the work with a watch, how long we spent on each job. Now I understand it. […] But not then. And the timekeeper walked behind me and looked at his watch, all the time writing down all the different tasks I did. […] And when I was last working there, we weren't allowed to have a coffee break (7/12, p.18.)

Elsa reports feeling sad about the lost possibilities for breaks and free socialization she had earlier described to me so vividly. In the narratives describing the industrial work she did as a young girl, the working day did not consist of continuous toil but rather of cycles of work and various breaks, and momentary pauses which were often caused by the breakdown of some machine. In Chapter 3 (p. 83–84), I mentioned the significance of breaks and small moments of freedom in which the young workers carved out some time and space for themselves, hid from their supervisors in order to have some fun, sang or smoked cigarettes. Elsa told me that if workers detected problems in the machines they would not let anyone know, but instead let the machines break down in order to get some time off for themselves. I would suggest that the workers themselves did not consider the machines to be the source of any oppression. Rather, the vulnerability of the machines enabled different tactics to be employed within the factory system (de Certeau 1984, xix). Furthermore, I argue that changes in the work process were what created a new kind of control and subordination: these included time-and-motion analysts and their measurements which aimed at increasing efficiency, achieving production targets, and using the factory to its full capacity.

New innovations that changed the cycle of work and reduced breaks were not welcomed by the workers. Neither were the new social dynamics. When Elsa first went to work, the factory processed mainly iron and produced horseshoes and spikes. Later, iron processing gave way to the more complex manufacturing of steel and aluminium products. In 1974, Fiskars Corporation transferred the production of hinges and aluminium boats from another factory to Inha. New technologies gave rise to new infrastructures and different kinds of skills. Elsa reported that one thing that baffled the workers was the new professionals and their status:

> And then there came so awfully many of those engineers. And we wondered at it. There were so many office workers. And we didn't know what they all actually did (7/12, p. 18.)

These new professionals were mostly engineers, educated people who, unlike the foremen, sat apart in their offices.[8] Women like Elsa, who had no secondary education and who had learned to respect their social superiors understood that these people were distinct from the workers but did not know why they were there or exactly what they did. As previously mentioned, these new white-collar workers were called "sharp heads". When a former labourer like Elsa's husband suddenly became a member of office staff, the situation must have been confusing. It was possible that this confusion and conflict that caused Elsa to cling to her status and identity as a worker, to narrate herself as a *greasy-skinned* worker and to celebrate manual labour and a worker identity that was based on skills, the rhythm of work and the collectivity.

An Easier Life Equals a Better Life?

In western world, the grand narrative of the *modern* presents technological advance as straightforward evolutionary progress, a step forwards towards something better, rather than a loss or disappearance.[9] However, this is not necessarily how people themselves experience the complexity of the social transformation that it involves. A factory worker interviewed by Christer Eldh was sceptical as to whether the new technologies of industrial life had made the life of the workers any easier (1996, 135). Eldh points out how new technologies changed the social structures of worker communities, for example by reducing the respectful distance maintained between the older and younger workers (1996, 130). Mullen and Lloyd (1990) noted in their study of Lake Erie Fisherman that occupational changes caused the older men to indulge in nostalgic reminiscing and the narration of heroic deeds (Lloyd & Mullen 1990; Mullen 1992, 138–139). The discourse of these fishermen emphasized how the work back in the old days was harder and the men better. They defined themselves in opposition to other groups related to fishing such as sport anglers. For the elderly fishermen, antagonism and nostalgic storytelling were two means of reinforcing a positive identity. Mullen and Lloyd reflect on this nostalgic tendency, referring to Santinos' thoughts about workers who in every industry seem to have a conception of a golden age, a time before the present when things were different or somehow better (Lloyd & Mullen 1990, 165–166; Santino 1978, 204). The need to construct a positive identity emerges in the face of changes such as technological advances that transform whole branches of industry, rendering some modes of production skills obsolete and inefficient, closing down factories, leaving skilled workers unemployed and thereby affecting not only the lives of individual people but also of whole societies and communities.

In the metal industry, both the forms of control and the actual composition of the work together with the value of labour changed along with the development of mechanization and automation. This is how Elsa sees the development:

> The work changed there. There were an awful lot more office workers than before, and the plant expanded in every way, but at the same time as it became mechanized, some workers always lost their jobs. So that there weren't any workers left, and when we retired, when I retired, we all left, and there were dozens of us, and we all agreed to leave with the idea that we were sort of giving jobs to the younger folks. (8/12, p. 4.)

In the end, Elsa did not want to continue working, saying that there were so many without work. When speaking of the past, she often observes that when she was young there was too much work but today there is not enough for everyone. She does not blame technology or other innovations, but emphasizes the changes that have taken place: there are no more jobs for working bodies capable only of performing raw physical labour.

It was not only on the job that easier work and new machines were encountered: Elsa and other women of her time also became familiar with new technologies at home.[10] Her memories of learning to use and accept new devices in everyday life inspired many stories like the following:

Dryer

> Then the machines [for drying laundry] came. I remember the first time when I was with Sylvi Saarela [name changed] in the laundry room, and there was the dryer. You see, it dried the laundry. And there was also a room where you could spread it out so that [the machine] spun it dry. And it did. [Laughs.] The woman who was in charge of it was horrified when she saw both of us lying on top of the spin-dryer. Because we thought that it was going to take off in flight, because it wouldn't stop. And we lay on top of it, shouting, "Now it's going to break." And after that somebody came to show us all how it worked. [Laughs.] Well, Sylvi and I were there listening, and first we didn't say anything, but then when they showed us the spin-dryer, well [laughs], we burst out laughing. And

everybody was staring at us: "You didn't have any problems with it, did you?" [Laughs.] (5/12, 28, p. 15.)

This narrative is a humorous and self-ironic description of Elsa's first encounter with a dryer.[11] Before washing machines and dryers, doing the laundry was extremely physical and arduous work. Obviously, Elsa did not know how to use the machine or how it was supposed to work or the kind of noises it should make. She presented this experience as a funny event that was not at all humiliating, although one could easily imagine that it might have been. In my interpretation, self-irony was one possible attitude which helped Elsa to remain an active agent in the face of change. Another way of reaction to modern novelties was nostalgic reminiscence and celebration of the good old days. In narrating her life, Elsa adopted both these attitudes. Her narration shifts between sharp critical comments which reflect an understanding of larger-scale societal developments and an emotional nostalgia for the good old days. The following is an example of a nostalgic attitude to the taken toward the development of laundry facilities and a potentially easier life:

> We had a sauna on the river bank, and we went there. The gentry had their own sauna, and the laundry hut was right next to it where we could do the laundry in the old-style way. You didn't need ... you used a washboard. The river was right there, it was easy to rinse the laundry in it. I enjoyed that life. Today, everything's too mechanized (8/12, p. 5.)

In the narration of Patricia Sawin's informant, Bessie Eldreth, the washboard functioned as a symbol of backbreaking labour (if also a reminder of her youthful energy and industriousness) (2004, 61). In Elsa's mind, it played

Elsa's mother, Hilda, Elsa and Elsa's daughter Raija doing laundry on the lake shore in the 1950s. Elsa Koskinen's family album.

a different, nostalgic role: non-mechanized labour as a simple pleasure of everyday life.

Nostalgia is a common narrative tendency in reminiscences about childhood and youth. For example, researchers studying family narratives have noted that when talking to younger persons, elderly narrators often describe a golden age of family traditions, thereby reproducing a powerful myth according to which the family was held together by love and harmony (Samuel & Thompson 1990, 10; Finnegan 2006, 180; Korkiakangas 1996, 37–38). Sociologist Fred Davis (1979) divides nostalgia into three different orders: First-order or *simple* nostalgia is a sentimental feeling, a longing for bygone days. Golden memories of childhood serve as an example – a longing for bygone days when life was pleasanter, simple and controllable (Davis 1979, 17–25; Korkiakangas 2002, 198).[12] Second-order or *reflexive* nostalgia juxtaposes the past and the present, and includes reflection on the course of change. Thereby it helps one to consider the nature of change and its complex significance. Finally, Davis refers to third-order *interpretive* nostalgia as reflection on being nostalgic, or an awareness of nostalgic thinking. (Davis 1979, 17–25.) All three orders are present in Elsa's narration, but give no explanation of the reasons for the nostalgic feelings.

Folklorist Ray Cashman has studied storytelling in Northern Ireland in an area that has undergone "a staggering amount of change over the past century" (2006, 137). He has pointed out that material culture can provide resources from which people revise their memory of the past and their identities in the present. Cashman's elderly informants had started again to build old-style rustic houses and to use old rural artefacts and vehicles on their home farms. They explained that they wanted to keep something from the old world and teach the younger generation how different life was back in the old days. Cashman conceptualized this practice as *critical nostalgia,* as a way of coping with the surrounding changes and striving for a better future.[13]

Life narratives often include moral contrasts between the past and the present that work as vehicles for social criticism and a condemnation of the present difficulties of life (Skultans 1998, 86). Anthropologist Marianne Gullestad has analyzed the rhetorical use of community and family values in the life story of an elderly Norwegian man (1994). According to her, the cherishing of collective responsibility and family solidarity may be a response to the crises of the welfare state, increasing individualism and the loss of family values in today's society. A sense of community and sharing are values that Elsa cherishes and misses. She often contrasts her childhood with what she thinks is the cold and individualistic world of today:

> We always had [company], and we always pulled together. But children today, they are only one or two, and in my opinion, they are like orphans. I often [think about this] when I'm out for a walk and I hear, I see first-graders coming. They have heavy satchels hanging on their backs, and there's no one at home. I almost cry when I look at them. That's what life's like [now]. That's what it has become. (11/12, 6, p. 2.)

Seeing the past as a golden time and the present as foreign and colder, longing for coherence and a sense of togetherness in today's fragmented world, and for lost freedom and authenticity, are central dimensions of nostalgia (Turner 1987; Knuuttila 1994, 11–13).

The reflexive or critical nostalgia in the context of her life narrative reflects Elsa's present life and the narrated situation. At the time of narration, Elsa was a widow, living alone in her flat in the municipal centre of Ähtäri. All her siblings had moved away a long time ago. Her grandchildren (I and my brother), who had long been present in her daily life, had grown up and moved elsewhere to study. In telling about her past, Elsa cherished memories of these aspects of life that have made her who she is: communal bonds, togetherness, physical strength and the activity of her *youthful* working body.

SITES (DIS)CONNECTING PEOPLE

I have noticed that Elsa does not primarily organize her memories chronologically but, instead, navigates her past life via material and spatial attachments. Interestingly enough, Elsa cannot point out *when* any of the events she narrates happened. Often, the time of the event does not matter to her. As a researcher, I am more interested in the chronology than she is (see also Passerini 1988, 8). Elsa, by contrast, remembers things according to the place and the house where her family lived at the time:

> I: When did the washing machine arrive? When did you wash by hand? Approximately?
> E: Well we lived at that time in the "Engineer's manor" [a huge log house comprising three flats].
> I: OK.
> E Until the time that...
> I: It was either the 1960s or the 70s?
> E: Well, you see, Asko [the interviewer's father] was already an adult when we lived in the "Engineer's manor".
> I: It must have been in the 70s then. (5/12, p. 16.)

There are only a few major events in her life that she can date: the time she entered working life (when the Second World War broke out and everybody over 15 years old had to do productive work), the times when her children were born and left home, and the time she retired from factory labour (she retired at the same time as her husband in 1984). Other events and narratives, and her reminiscences in general, are attached to certain places and spaces, some of which seem to act as more than just a backdrop. In my view, they become sites that orient the storytelling and define Elsa's life and identity; in other words, for her, place is a way of understanding the world (see Cresswell 2004, 11; check Massey 2005).

The condition, size, and location of a family's dwelling expressed its status in the hierarchy of the factory community (Spoof 1997, 278–279; Koivuniemi 2000, 84; Kortelainen 2008, 113). During the early years of their marriage and family life, Elsa and Eino moved frequently to bigger and better flats. They did not, however, build a house of their own, which for Finns, as for many others, is a symbol of the good life (Saarikangas 1993; Apo 1995, 222–223; see also Assmuth 1997, 141; Stark 2011, 293–302). Elsa does not seem to attach strong symbolic significance to the houses or flats of her married life as physical and material sites for recollection or to regard them as symbols of home. This is interesting because I know that the last place in which Elsa and Eino lived before retiring and leaving the factory village was a detached house, an old log building in which the Amberg family (the family of the former general manager and his son, the technical manager) had lived earlier. The house was naturally no longer new, nor was it owned by Elsa and Eino themselves. Nevertheless, the house was located in a very beautiful spot beside the River Inha right next to the factory. For me, this is a symbolic location, the place that I associate with my childhood memories of the factory village. I was a very small child when I visited the house, but I clearly remember the floor plan, the view overlooking the river and the garden. Once I began reminiscing about the house with Elsa. Together, we produced a joint reminiscence about the house:

Sliding on the floor

E: […] We lived there on the river beside the Ironworks, right next to the rapids. It was a detached house.
I: Yes, I remember.
E: It was very nice, but it was so terribly old, it sort of lurched towards the river.
I: It was a bit tilted.
E: Do you remember how you used to slide along the floor?
I: Yes, I do, it was slippery. Especially in the kitchen.
E: Yes, well, you see, the dining room where the stairs led upstairs, it was obvious that you'd slide there.
I: Was it too then owned by the factory?
E: Yes, it was an old house, it was valuable. It was built, would it be in the 19th century or even earlier, and that's why they weren't going to demolish it. But when it started to … they had to
I: To lean over
E: It leaned. Nobody dared to go there anymore. But it was nice.
I: There were inky cap mushrooms in the yard?
E: Yes, an awful lot.
I: And berry bushes.
E: And then there were lilies of the wally.
I: Yes, especially right on the river bank.
E: It was a beautiful place. The lawn was so good, especially when the grass was cut short short. And you could go swimming from there. Just put on a swim suit and wrap [a towel] and when you could go swimming in the rapids. It was nice like that. But those days are gone.
(8/12, 5, p. 5.)

This occasion was one of the few times on which Elsa told about the physical space and interior of her home, other than that of the house in which she had lived as a child.

What seems to be of major significance for Elsa, rather than the houses and the flats themselves, is the communal space and landscape of the factory community, the factory village of Inha. The yards in front of the dwellings, the porches and steps of large houses that contained flats for numerous families, and some buildings of the old factory community of Inha were places for social gatherings. Not all of them, however, were open to everyone; some were reserved for particular groups such as higher-class people or factory workers, men or women. In Elsa's stories, there are traces of the symbolic borders that marked the spaces, sites and routes connecting people of different groups. The shared mental boundaries were often not visible but manifested themselves in social practices, especially when they were crossed for some reason or another. For example, Elsa has narrated several childhood memories in which she and the other children were secretly playing in the yard of the factory owner's manor house, which Elsa calls *Pytinki*:

A Big Snake

You weren't supposed to go to the grounds of *Pytinki*. But we went anyway. There was a housekeeper there. It was a kind of straight driveway about half a kilometre long to the yard, which was well tended. Nowadays they don't look after the yard like that. And it was always decoratively raked, and the woods were well kept. We went there to the end of the drive. There was a big crowd of us girls, as usual, because the families were big in those days. And there were the neighbours' girls too. The housekeeper always shouted out – she had a loud voice – she shouted, "Children, don't come here! There are snakes here. There's a really big one here!" She didn't know what to say. (1/12, 7, p. 5, *variant* 2/12, 4, p. 8.)

One version of the story (2/12, 4, p. 8) continues: "Some of us shouted back that you are the big snake yourself!" This story could be interpreted as an expression of working-class children's own culture. However, it also demonstrates the existence of conceptual boundaries and prohibited areas where working-class children were not welcomed. Interestingly enough, the children were not explicitly told that they were unwelcome, but the implicit message was clear. Symbolic boundaries are often somewhat flexible and change over the course of time (see also Leminen 1996, 167–186; Tuomaala 2004, 316). I point out earlier that the factory owner's manor house serves as a scene for different stories; for example it is the location of several popular ghost stories that local people still narrate today. In fact, the manor house is one of the few places left as a reminder of the old factory village of the days of the *Patruuna*. By the time Elsa was a child, nobody was living in the house any more. Nevertheless, it was still a very special place with limited access even for the villagers themselves.

Elsa's narratives about crossing boundaries as a child tell a great deal about the social rules and norms of her community and about different groups and their identities. Interestingly, the factory and its yard were open to anybody, even to outside visitors (see also Salmi-Niklander 2004, 300).

5. Change and Continuity in a Life Narrative

In Elsa's view, there used to be much more spatial freedom than there is nowadays:

> [Talking about the factory yard:] You can't go there [now]. [...] at that time the riverbank was free. You could go along it beside the factory, and people went fishing there. But you have no business going there anymore. When the bridge [Hamarisilta] was there, there was a road leading from it, and people went to work and school over the bridge just next to the smelting furnace. Nobody stopped you ... (8/12, p. 9.)

Today, the factory area is closed to outsiders who are prevented by a fence from entering. It is clear that Elsa feels sad about the fact that she is not able to visit these places anymore. She has lost contact with the mental landscape of her past in a concrete way:

> E: The river isn't the same anymore. It's overgrown with all kinds of weeds. You can't see it at all anymore.
> I: Yes, it's still there. You can see a bit of it.
> E: And the mill bridge was there, it was a romantic place, the old mill. And the power station, that white and yellow building, where the electricity came from...
> I: Was it right next to the factory?
> E: No, the mill bridge was there. [...] You don't know that. It's been demolished. It was really a sad day for the old workers when they had to tear it down. They didn't need to demolish it. It could have been kept as a pedestrian bridge since people didn't dare to go over it in their cars anymore, although they used to. Somehow it was a nice bridge and the oak tree that still stands there. We spent a lot of time there, walking and hanging around. (8/12, 6, pp. 5–6.)

The changes occurring in the factory village have also transformed the physical location and its nature: the river that used to be clear of vegetation is now filled with it. These changes cause not only nostalgic longing and melancholy but also a deep sadness and ache. When I asked Elsa to describe the big changes that occurred in the factory community during her lifetime, she first mentioned that many of the places where people used to meet each other such as shops, the bank and the post office, had been closed down. She misses the sense of community that existed in these concrete spaces: the open factory yard, which was always crowded and served as a market place, and the old bridges, where people had gathered, were all demolished one by one:

> It went a little bit too far. All those places started to disappear. Places that were basic conditions of life for the old factory workers. The bridges went, and in the end all the dwellings disappeared. The houses, our homes, they've been pulled down. There are only a few left there: Hurutlinna, where we lived for a while, and Lumppulinna, and some private houses, two of them up on there in Kallio. And the Workers' Hall is left, they renovated it, it's the village community hall [now], and I have heard it looks nice. But I don't fancy going there anymore; there's nothing left there. Bushes grow on the roads and in all the ruins of the old buildings. They're gone. I only feel sad if I go there. (8/12, p. 9.)

In this excerpt, Elsa describes both subjective and collective reactions to the transformation of the factory community by referring to "the old factory workers" and narrating how she herself felt about the situation. It is not clear whether Elsa counted herself among the old factory workers, but anyway she shared their views and emotions: the disappearance of the sites that were essential elements of communal life and connections between community members meant the loss of "basic conditions of life".

Disappearing Landscapes – The Amputated Sites of the Factory Community

Everyday life consists of streams of changing events and developments such as the closing of entire factories or the opening of new ones, the building of new houses and the demolishing of old ones. On the other hand, people preserve traditions and mentalities both consciously and unconsciously. The longevity of cultural values and practices can be seen in social phenomena such as Finnish ideals regarding self-sufficiency and gender roles. Based on ethnographic field work among different communities in Turkey, Ireland and Bangladesh, folklorist Henry Glassie (1998) suggests that what matters most to communities and individuals is the continuity, stability and integrity.[14] Stability seems to be important to Elsa, especially when it comes to the physical environment and the social world connected to it. She misses the physical landscape of the factory community that was dominated by the mill and the big smokestack, which seems for her to represent a symbol of the old industrial community and of the change that has occurred in the industrial and social worlds and their dynamics:

> The Demolished Smokestack
>
> E: And all these things disappeared. You feel it, you know. And then the smokestack. It was the last thing they demolished. They say that the old men cried that day [in a touched voice]. It was so hard to bear. Who would it have hurt if they'd left it standing?
> I: When did they demolish it?
> E: I was still working then. It was the time of technological progress. The old men like Gunnar were still there. It was a sad time for those old men who had seen the smokestack everyday of their lives. It was hard for me too. It felt like death was visiting the village. The smokestack had a lightning rod so we didn't have to be scared when there was thunder and lightning. And it never struck anything, it always went to the side. And everybody felt at home there ... even if you were worse-off, poorer, it didn't matter, it didn't feel bad at all because everybody was in the same boat. (8/12, 13, p. 9.)

Elsa connects the "landmark" of the demolished smokestack to a larger issue: to a sense of security and belonging, to being part of a whole. New technology brought about other changes than just lighter work at new computer-driven production lines. The social hierarchy of the community changed when ironworkers were no longer needed and in their place the factory hired engineers and other educated professionals. The younger generation

5. Change and Continuity in a Life Narrative

The Smokestack of the Inha ironworks falled down in 1962. Courtesy of the Archives of Fiskars Inhantehtaat Ltd.

started to study and move out of the village, and concomitantly its social life died. Furthermore, Elsa, who went to school for only four years and started working at an early age, now feels incompetent in today's world of higher education and information technology; she feels that there is no place for her or other old people in this new social order. Societal change, the blurring of boundaries and the opening-up of possibilities can also be a threat to a person's identity constructed in an earlier era, however contradictory this may seem at first from today's individualist point of view. According to Elsa, the old workers cried when they saw the smokestack demolished. Even though she was younger, she had also grown up in its presence. She becomes nostalgic when thinking about the village and the lost sense of belonging.

Elsa would have wanted to preserve the physical landscape and particular material sites because for her they characterize the stability of the older factory community. Structures such as the smokestack not only marked a place but also constituted a material and physical connection with the past. The industrial progress that closed down the old charcoal-fired steam engines did not stop there: the factory still exists today, but it struggles with the challenges of industrial globalization and the market economy. Elsa is well aware of current developments and often states that times have truly changed. According to her, back in the old days, there was a lot of work available, while today there are unemployed people who do not have anything to do. However, she also doubts whether the people of today would do such work anymore.

Geographer Doreen Massey sees places as processes that are not frozen in one time (2005). In her view, places do not have single identities but multiple ones, nor are they in any sense enclosures, with a clear inside and outside. Places are social processes and meeting points, where history accumulates. Following Massey's ideas, anthropologist Anneli Meriläinen-Hyvärinen (2010) has examined the experiences of the changing of change in the Talvivaara mining area in Finland. She has interviewed people who used to live there but who were forced to sell their houses and their land to the mining company. She states that the mining area is indeed a space-time conjunction, where local history, personal experiences of the place (topobiography) and the challenges of globalizing industrial business meet. This could be said of other industrial spaces, many of which grew and flourished, deindustrialized and in the process were transformed in various ways (cf. Kortelainen 2006 and 2008; Ahvenisto 2008).

Meriläinen-Hyvärinen has emphasized the reciprocal relationship between place and the human subject (2010, 75). Not only do people make places, but transformations of space also affect people. Some places offer people a sense of *stability* that correlates with the continuity of the self (see Tuan 2006, 16–19, 29). One of Meriläinen-Hyvärinen's informants, her elderly father, experienced deep sorrow for the lost place, the family summer house on a lake in an area which was expropriated, and Meriläinen-Hyvärinen compared his feelings to a premature death (Meriläinen-Hyvärinen 2010, 68). Elsa compares the demolition of the smokestack to death as well, not to a personal death but to the death of the community and the communal spirit. Apart from this single dramatic event, the transformation of the factory village and changes in the social dynamics of Inha Ironworks generally took place over a longer period of time. However, the disappearing sites are concrete examples of institutional change.

Ever since I began to study Elsa, I have wondered why she cherishes these memories of the hierarchical factory community and hard physical labour. Is it not a good thing that the world has changed and that we are more equal and do not have to work under such circumstances anymore (see Koskinen-Koivisto 2009)? Nostalgic thinking has previously been dismissed as a naïve rejection of change (see for example Lowenthal 1985). However, nostalgia can also be seen as a more complex phenomenon, a form of critical thinking.

In her study of the experiences of Finnish children and young people in the state educational system of the 1930s, Historian Saara Tuomaala (2004) was interested in the way Finnish boys and girls were educated to become proper citizens in the years when Finland was still a young nation state. Tuomaala found that many of the practices, such as hygiene instruction, discipline and moral education, have become collective embodied memories. She argues that experiences leave behind symbolic and linguistic traces which are intertwined with the cultural construction of narratives. Accordingly, narratives of personal experiences concerning feelings, emotions, moves and acts preserve sites of memory that create a past-directed *metaphorical space* in which various meanings are articulated (Tuomaala 2004, 58).

The metaphorical space created by Elsa in her narratives is full of sites that connect her to the old factory community. Both hierarchical and communal, this space offers her a sense of security, a feeling of knowing her place in the world. Sites such as the river, old bridges, the factory owner's manor house and the smokestack connect her to other people and embody both the change and the stability of the patriarchal factory community, which, while it never have been a static environment, was for her at least clearer, more familiar and more manageable. Material and physical sites constitute sources for the narration of life stories and for the sense of self even if they no longer exist. Creating the space over and over again does not mean that the narrator is living in the past, but rather that s/he is using the past to cope in the present.

For Elsa, the old factory community with its narrated sites afforded a metaphorical space of community, a safe social order and an opportunity for an uneducated, hard-working labourer to support a family. Her storytelling and the metaphorical space narrated by her transport the positive aspects of the past into the future, to another person, in this case to me – a grandchild and academic scholar who has never seen the actual landscape, experienced the everyday life of the factory village or met the people of the old community. The life there was unknown and foreign to me until I listened to Elsa's emotional personal narratives, most of which she told to me only once. Just as Bakhtinian chronotopes introduce specific time-places for readers, narrators of their own lives create metaphorical spaces from the sites of their memories.[15]

Place is created in and through social practices (Mahlamäki 2005, 46; Massey 2005). Storytelling creates a metaphorical space in which sites are connected with a sense of self and meaning in life. In Elsa's storytelling practices, the disappearing sites of the old factory community symbolize the loss of communality and stability and the clear social hierarchy of the factory and the work done there. The factory, the workers and members of the higher classes, the dwellings and the other buildings, the river, the bridges and the smokestack were once a part of a lively community that became a disappearing landscape, the social body that Elsa Koskinen was part of. The feelings of loss are deep and concrete. Thus, this change is materialized and embodied in places, *amputated phantom sites* that continue to exist and give meaning to her life through storytelling. In Elsa's case, by employing powerful metaphors and nostalgic images, her personal narratives not only communicate experiences of loss but also serve as resources for moving forward in life by strengthening her sense of self and positioning her in the constantly changing globalizing world. Thus her nostalgia for the disappearing landscapes of the old factory community also embodies the positive power of continuity.

Travelling Selves – Narrative Strategies and Biographical Time

> "There is no unified, essential identity, only a continual negotiation using terms that are themselves changed by that negotiation, a recursive but changeable enactment, a performance undertaken in the mode of belief." (Sawin 2004, 4)

Travelling, in the form of a journey, is commonly used as a metaphor for life. It has also been used as an analytic and metaphorical tool in life narrative studies to demonstrate the passage of time in a life narrative (see for example Vilkko 1993 and 1997, 46–47).[16] Moreover, travelling outside the common everyday environment can also take on other meanings. It can be seen as a breakaway, a kind of liminality (see Selänniemi 1996; Salmi-Niklander 2004). Historically, travelling was possible and undertaken predominantly by men (Hapuli 2003, 16–17).

In Bakhtin's chronotopes, travelling works as a time-space. Some examples of the chronotopes introduced by Bakhtin, the "road" and the "threshold", emphasize the individual trajectory and development of the self (1979). Bakhtin has also analysed time-spaces of romantic adventure novels in Greek literature, which include mythical journeys and metamorphoses of the protagonists, who are often male heroes (ibid. 271–271). Bakhtin notes that the time-spaces of adventure literature moves between exceptional, unusual moments and the logic of coincidences and higher forces (ibid. 276–277, 282). In these exceptional moments, the qualities and actions of the protagonists, their responsibilities and attitudes towards everyday life become crucial (ibid.).

In her life narrative, Elsa tells not only about work and everyday life at home, but also about leisure and travelling. Elsa's travel narratives describe small journeys in the immediate surroundings covering short geographical distances. I noticed that they comprised not only a movement in biographical time – a return to past selves, past experiences and past life – but also the negotiation of the development of the self. In this retrospective evaluation of her past selves, Elsa relates life experiences of her childhood, youth and adulthood to the voice of the narrating self, the elderly Elsa.

BEGINNINGS: THE SOLIDARITY OF THE FAMILY AND THE COMMUNITY
In her childhood and youth, Elsa was part both of a large family and of larger groups of neighbours and villagers. Many of Elsa's personal narratives of those times are presented in the collective *we* form instead of the singular *I*. The *we* of her childhood and youth can refer to two larger groups: we, the children of the same family, or we the children/girls/young people of the

worker community (see the Appendix 3).[17] Elsa's childhood in particular was characterized by unity and the presence of siblings, and she describes it as being "carefree, even though we were poor". The older siblings took care of the younger ones. Taking care of the younger siblings was a common responsibility of the older children in big agrarian families. The responsibility typically moved from the shoulders of the eldest sisters and brothers to the next senior ones (see Korkiakangas 1996, 96, 155). According to Elsa, it was Aino's responsibility to take care of her. Later, Elsa herself was made responsible for one of the younger ones, her little brother Pauli. The close relationship between her and her brother has lasted until the present day. She still worries over him and offers him her support especially in times of hardship (11/12, 5, p. 2, see also Korkiakangas 1996, 240). Elsa demonstrates how important the close relations were to the siblings: they all cried when any of them left home to work somewhere else or after marrying (9/12, 12, p. 6).

In narrating her childhood experiences, Elsa mentions Christmas time as a "high point" that offered many memories of togetherness and good will. One of the best gifts she remembers having ever received was a small coffee pot made of chocolate from her eldest sister Aura, who was already earning her own living as a maid (1/12, 34, pp. 22–23). The holiday goodwill also extended beyond the family circle. During the Christmas period, the factory organized a communal celebration for all the workers and their families (1/12, 37 pp.23). Sometimes, big families that were experiencing financial troubles or other hardships were given special surprise treats:

Real Santas

E: Then there was one Christmas Day that I remember so vividly, you know, because every Christmas our father got drunk, and it always spoiled things. Two Santas came to visit us. It was a great surprise. They came with fur coats on and they had masks. Two big Santas, they knocked on the door, and we wondered who was coming because our Father had already gone off somewhere, and Mom said we should welcome the visitors. So we shouted "Come in!" – that was what we said in those days, "Come in", and these two Santas came in. And it was wonderful, they were so lifelike, real Santas.
I: Did they bring gifts?
E: They did. Kilo bags of sweets and all sorts of things they brought.
I: Who were they?
E: They were from the factory. They were gentlefolk. They knew what it was like for us. They were office staff.
I: My goodness!
E: It was like – I'll never forget that, never. It was such a wonderful surprise. And we sang for them.
I: All kinds of carols?
E: Yes, all kinds of carols. It was a real Christmas for us. (1/12, 36, p. 23.)

The narrative presents the visit of the Santas as a miraculous event: in the midst of fear and disappointment they suddenly appear to the door. Elsa's family appreciated the surprise charity that they were given. In the narrative, the donors were left anonymous although Elsa had recognized the men and identified them as middle-class office workers. Elsa emphasizes their good will and understanding of the situation of poor families. Overall, Elsa's view of the factory community's social relations and closeness is positive. She never lamented the fact that everybody knew about each other's lives. In her view, people generally minded their own business but offered to help when others needed it.[18]

According to Elsa, the sense of community present in the ironworks also included closeness among of people of different ages. Her narratives often involved anonymous groups and older people who intervened in the lives of working-class children and young people, offering them small treats, a place to meet or advice about how to get access to the facilities they needed in their free time activities. These memories were part of the nostalgically narrated ironworks community which Elsa constructed in order to reflect upon the transformations that happened over the course of her life. A sense of community also played an important role in the ways in which Elsa saw her past selves and the development of her character from childhood to old age.

The Young and Wild Elsa

As a child and young woman (from the age of 12 to 20), Elsa attended various free-time activities organized by the local workers' and women's organizations, and in doing so she travelled to surrounding areas by train, on her bicycle, on the back of a truck or simply on foot (or in the winter, on skis). She was a member of the local workers' sports club *Taimi*, which offered athletic activities for both boys and girls. The girls of Inha practised synchronized calisthenics, and they trained with the help of a physical education instructor. With a small group that travelled to surrounding villages, they performed in community halls in events that included dancing, acting, reciting, and singing. Together with the boys of the Ironworks, the girls' section, including Elsa, took part in the national gala of the Finnish Workers' Sports Federation in Helsinki in 1946.

In Finland in the 1930s, sports activities were organized in a way that reinforced the prevailing gendered conception of citizenship. Youth organizations and Sport clubs organized different sports for boys and girls. For young males, sport offered an arena in which they could show off their prowess and compete, whereas for girls sport was a *healthy* pastime, a way of elevating their minds and souls (Salmi-Niklander 2004, 272–274). Sporting activities were also class-specific. After the Civil War of 1918, working-class sports clubs formed a separate central association, the Finnish Workers' Sports Federation *(Työväen urheiluliitto, TUL)*, in 1919. In Finland in the 1910s and the 1920s, sport and ideology went hand in hand. Socialistic discourse encouraged working-class boys to train and be strong and healthy in order to fight oppression (Salmi-Niklander 2004, 272). Sport and patriotism, on the other hand, were centrally bound up in the pursuits of the nationalistic Civil Guard, as well as being part of the principal ideology of the Finnish school system (see Vasara 1997, 30–31; Tuomaala 2004, 240–241; 244–247;

The girls of Taimi sports club in the annual gathering of the Finnish Workers' Sports Federation in 1946 in Helsinki. Elsa is second from the left (front row). Photo from Elsa Koskinen's home album.

Leino-Kaukiainen & Heikkinen 2011b, 20). In the 1930s, however, the previous class distinctions began to blur.

In most of the stories of her childhood and youth, Elsa presents herself as an active and outgoing child and young woman. Before the war, Elsa attended the summer camps of the Lotta Svärd Organization. These camps were one of the popular activities organized by the girls' section. In many areas, schoolteachers, who were also leaders of bourgeois youth associations, urged working-class girls to participate in activities to which many working-class parents were opposed. The agendas of the nationalistic White youth organizations created conflicts within families with a working-class background (Vasara 1997, 660; Tuomaala 2004).[19] In the 1930s, many working-class parents still had bitter memories of the Civil War of 1918 and its aftermath. But especially in the countryside, the former Whites and Reds lived side by side in social worlds that were simultaneously both separate and shared (Tuomaala 2004, 316). In the 1930s and during the Second World War, working-class children, too, were urged to join the activities of youth associations and sports clubs that were associated the former White section of the population.[20] In the following narrative, Elsa describes her father's reactions to her independent decision to join the Lottas and to her impulsive behaviour, depicting herself as "the wild one" of her family:

Shoes Too Fine to Wear

And then I remember when you couldn't get shoes. And I had to. I was like that – none of the other girls in our family were – but I was always going off somewhere to do different activities. For example I did [synchronized] gymnastics. I was always practising gymnastics at the Taimi sports club, and I was in all their programmes. And before that, when I was at school – the war hadn't broken out yet – at that time I belonged to a girls' unit [of the Lotta Svärd Organization]. And one summer, we went to a camp that was held at Peränne School. We travelled on the back of an open lorry. There weren't any other vehicles. And I had to get new shoes for the camp. And Dad said that I could go and buy a new pair of plimsolls, they cost 25 marks. The local SOK co-op had them ordered for me, and I went to get them. The girls there said that only a pair of leather shoes had come. And they cost 75 marks. I wasn't supposed to take them. But I wanted them. They were just such a beautiful brown colour. They urged me on and said that it wasn't so much and that my father wouldn't mind. But I said that my father told me that they shouldn't cost more than that [25 marks]. But I took them, and when I went home I almost got beating. He said I'd taken them without asking. I said they hadn't any other shoes there. And you know what, I checked them every night. He said that there mustn't be any scratches on those shoes. I needed them, you see, because I was going to that camp. And it was hard for me, you know, and I always checked them before he did. They had to be well taken care of. I still clean my shoes [laughing] because that fear has stayed with me, because it wasn't easy to get shoes, you see. Yes, and I had a good time there at the camp (5/12, 11, p. 5.)

Elsa's presents her father as an absolute authoritarian who condemns the independent decision of his daughter. In my view, this narrative expresses Elsa's agency at multiple levels. Even if the class dynamics and divisions associated with the youth organization were not mentioned directly, it becomes clear that it was not a simple choice for a working-class girl from a poor family to attend the activities of bourgeois organizations especially when her shoes and clothes would reveal her social background.[21] In her narrative, Elsa underlines her own decision to participate in the activities of an association that was associated with the Whites. In addition to facing her father's anger, Elsa also had to deal with some negative feedback from her siblings on this matter. When she told about this event to me, Elsa defended her actions by explaining that she had no other option but to take the only shoes that were available because she needed shoes for the camp. Buying expensive shoes made her stand out from the other children of the family, who did not have fine shoes. However, Elsa continued to serve in the girls' unit of the Lottas.

Despite the ambiguities created by her class background, Elsa seemed to look back on her participation in the activities of the youth associations with some pleasure. Regardless of the material scarcity and restrictions on organizing leisure activities such as dancing, wartime circumstances offered Elsa many opportunities to prove herself a competent individual despite her youth. She told, for example, how she was selected to go black-market shopping in the surrounding countryside:

And the black market thing. It's been left out – the wartime. You see, it was me who had to go. I hadn't even been to confirmation classes yet, and it was always me who had to go, you see. When an adult, some older person, set off to go black-market shopping, my father told me to go with them. (5/12, 18, p. 9.)

In describing black-market shopping, Elsa emphasized how other people gave up easily and showed their weakness when they encountered difficulties, for example by crying, while she managed to stay calm:

The Rocky Road

E: I remember how I was [doing black-market shopping] with a girl of my own age. She has already passed away a long time ago, she's dead and buried, but she and I, we went together to Sulkavankylä [a village in a neighbouring municipality]. […] Well, we were just kids; we were still small, young girls, so people sold us things. We got everything: cereals and flour and butter, we took everything we got, and we didn't even think about how we were going to carry it. Well, my friend had a woman's bike, and I had a man's bike, and when I got on the saddle, I couldn't stop, I had to keep pedalling, otherwise I'd fall. And my friend followed and started crying and called after me: "Don't leave me, don't leave me." So I had to stop and wait for her every so often and try not to fall into a ditch. […] The railway workers at the station, they were already waiting for us, they knew we were coming because we'd gone in the morning with our bikes. From a long way off they called out to us to hurry, that the train was already in the station. And, like, from the carriage, we saw there were some soldiers getting on the train, the train patrols, they checked the trains and the passengers. So one of the railroad workers took our bikes and put tags on them, and …
I: Hm.
E: My friend, she burst into tears when she saw how full the train was; the carriages were so full that there was only room for us in the corridor. And she cursed. There were some girls we knew there, and she said, "Just take something, for Christ's sake. The eggs, you take the eggs!" Yes and they [the train patrol guards] didn't do anything to us. Of course they knew what we were up to, but they pretended not to see us, they just went nicely past without so much as a glance at us. And we were so relieved. And we thought that when we got to Inha station we still had five kilometres left to go – to get home. Well, the Ironworks lorry was there, which had been delivering some stuff there. And we thought, "OK, now we'll get a lift. On the lorry." And we did. But guess where they went?
I: Well?
E: They didn't go straight to the factory. They went to Peränne gravel pit to fetch a load of gravel. We cried then.
I: Did you have to cycle from there?
E: Not, they took us. They didn't say anything. We'd already have been home ages before.
I: Yes.
E: Yes, and my friend cried so bitterly; she had a date that evening, and [laughing] we were too late. And she was on top of a load of gravel! (3/12, 2 p. 6; *variant* 5/12, 18, p. 10.)

Elsa vividly described her physical struggle with a man's bicycle and her friend's desperate pleas. In this situation, Elsa manages to handle the man's bike, her own nerves, and at the end, the entire situation.[22] Elsa also told that by the time the two girls got home, she was totally exhausted and could not speak anymore when her father asked if they had got anything. When he saw all the products, he wondered how the girls had succeeded in carrying them all and how they had managed to get to the station and back. Telling about her friend's despair and using her father's authoritarian voice are rhetorical devices which Elsa used to present herself as worthy and courageous. This narrative depicted black-market shopping as a kind of adventure, and the girls, especially Elsa, as heroines: she and the other girl struggled through difficult situations along the road and completed their quest (cf. Bakhtin's (1979) adventurous chronotope).

The girls of the Ironworks also travelled in their leisure time to go to exciting and entertaining events. In the writings of the young working-class activists of the 1920s analysed by Salmi-Niklander, travelling to a neighbouring village or even a nearby railway station was always presented as more dangerous for young women than for young men (2004, 437). Railway stations were regarded as sites of morally suspicious behaviour (ibid. 2004, 268, 320, 349). In most of Elsa's narratives of her youth, by contrast travelling by train and visits to the railway station were safe and fun. According to Elsa, they had little money for travelling, but they knew the tricks of dodging train fare:

Fare Dodging on the Train 1: A Stye in My Eye

That was the kind of journeys we made, and often we didn't have any money, you see. Sometimes we had enough that we divided it up so that everybody had enough to pay, if we wanted to. But we didn't always want to. So one time I had a big stye in my eye. And we were standing in the connecting section, where you go up the steps, and we stayed there. And the conductor came, and he looked at my eye, and he said: "Oh dear, what's the matter with your eye? You need to go to the doctor. Your pretty eye will be ruined." He talked to me like that, and he forgot to ask for the tickets. So he went away, and we travelled free that time. Hmm. (5/12, 24 p. 11; 8/12, 21, p. 13.)

Fare Dodging 2: Swedish Magazines

And sometimes we went to, what was it, a second-class carriage – there weren't any first class ones, so we sat in a second-class carriage and one friend of ours, she had a Swedish surname. One of the girls, she was a pretty girl, she was tall and slim and she had always a wonderful hairstyle, piled up high like this. In those days they used rollers. And she always had some Swedish magazines with her. So we sat there and read Swedish magazines. The conductor didn't stop. He probably knew that we weren't really Swedish, but he didn't bother. They knew who were getting on at each station. If it happened that there were a lot of people like at Haapamäki station, then they sometimes didn't notice that we got on at Kolho; it was right next to Haapamäki (5/12, 25, p. 11.)

In Elsa's narratives, working-class girls are not only allowed to travel and perform in entertainments but even encouraged and helped in their endeavours. On their way, other people seemed to be acting in ways that helped the girls. Elsa suspects that the conductors knew that they were trying to get away without paying but let them travel free anyway out of kindness or solidarity. In Chapter 4, I described the chivalrous behaviour of the railway workers in waiting for and helping the girls (see pp. 102–103). The good will of other working-class people is a characteristic feature of most of Elsa's childhood narratives.

The adventures Elsa narrated also had something in common with the travel narratives in the handwritten magazines written by the young worker activists of the Högfors Ironworks in Karkkila in the 1910s and 1920s (Salmi-Niklander 2004, 327–340). Salmi-Niklander notes that in the 1920s, travel narratives became primarily a male genre in which women are described as objects. Salmi-Niklander observes that female writers found reasons to avoid journeys during which young males got into fights with boys from other villages. In addition, girls travelling alone were vulnerable to harassment and open to moral condemnation (ibid. 320). The men's journeys were constructed as fantastical "odysseys" of the Ironworks boys in which different perspectives and positions overlap. The narratives were built around thematic binaries such as desire-disappointment or attainment-refusal and actions such as conquest and competition (ibid. 331). Often, the motive for travelling seemed to be to meet members of the opposite sex, the quest for romance. Some of the narratives were boastful and emphasized the masculinity of the travellers in the form of sexual conquests and disputes with other men. In Salmi-Niklander's view, travelling signified a mental break for the young male workers: a change from the chores of everyday life, from the ties and bonds of hierarchical communities and an escape from the expectations of the community that the boys would marry locally and start a family (ibid., 346). Salmi-Niklander points out that these stories of escapism are merely momentary: a more permanent distancing would have been a frightening scenario, even for young males, because it would have meant abandoning the solidarity and safety of the worker community and expose one's masculinity to the outside challenges of larger-scale power dynamics and domination (ibid. 346–347). The odysseys were, therefore, narratives of journeys within the limits of confident masculinity and communality (ibid. 347).

Elsa's narratives of travelling working-class girls contain romantic and adventurous elements. It is interesting to see how in Elsa's stories, the travelling young girls manage different situations and navigate through difficulties in unknown spaces, including encounters with men. Travelling and performing in entertainment events meant opportunities to meet men independently, without the protecting presence of the boys of the Ironworks.

Interestingly enough, the written narratives of young men's journeys outside their everyday environment of the worker community which were analyzed by Salmi-Niklander never had proper endings or homecomings (2004, 348). Elsa's travel narratives have endings, which in most cases are happy and fulfilling: the girls manage get home against all odds; they might be tired, but they are happy. Indeed, they even receive admiring comments from their families. These endings could be seen as a return to the safe situation that constituted the ideal place for young women: the home. The completion of their quests could, however, also be interpreted as a sign of collective agency.

In the narrative *Shoes Too Fine to Wear* Elsa seemed to want to distance herself from her working-class background. Despite the obstacles in her path, Elsa managed to buy good shoes and face her father's anger. In recounting *The Rocky Road* regarding black-market shopping, Elsa expressed her resilience in a situation in which the conditions of the outside world were hostile. The *Fare Dodging* narratives show how the girls dodged the conductors and rode the train free of charge on their fun-seeking travels. These elements of wildness, resilience and resourcefulness which characterized the young girls in these narratives are qualities that can also be found in the protagonists of fictitious genres such as fairy tales and in certain forms of popular culture such as children's literature.

It is worth noting, however, that "the young and wild Elsa" is an identity constructed in a retrospective evaluation of her past life and in a dialogue with a researcher of a different generation. In summarizing and reviewing her life in Interview 5, Elsa ends her stories about wartime by describing her personality as follows:

> If I think about it, I wonder how I was able to do it. I wasn't big, I was small and skinny. But somehow I had so much grit that I'd have gone through a brick wall. (5/12, p. 10)

The distance from the narrated events and from past selves often produces feelings of empathy for the younger narrated self (see also Saarenheimo 1997). In talking about how the girls of the Ironworks travelled and how carefree they were, Elsa not only displays empathy and understanding for her past behaviour but also celebrates her actions in a way that emphasizes her own courage.

Luisa Passerini (1989) has studied oral life stories of working-class women in Italy and has analyzed the paradoxes of self-emergence in women's life stories. The women she interviewed told about being wild and rebellious children, tomboys, and later capricious young women. At the same time, they also saw themselves as good, respectable workers and self-sacrificing, caring mothers. However, the ideal of motherhood was not the cornerstone of the *narrated* subjectivity that the women wanted to present about themselves in the interviews. In her analysis, Passerini suggests that presenting the self as rebellious and capricious at some point might be a *symbolic* act, a way of coping with the emancipating changes in women's role and the new demands placed on modern independent women (Passerini 1989, 189–194; see also Kinnunen 1993, 203). In the light of Passerini's thoughts, it could be argued that Elsa's narrative is a reflection on what it was like to be a woman in a different era. However, I think it is not in the least surprising that Elsa should tell me, her female grandchild and a researcher, about the challenging experiences in her life and what she had accomplished. Her narratives about choosing one's way and not giving up (having pluck) could be seen as both offering me good advice and giving me a basis on which to compare my position as a young and active travelling woman. I also believe that in talking about her different selves she wanted to show me that human life consisted of contradictory experiences, hardship and growth. During the interview process, Elsa also introduced me to a different side of herself, one that was shy and worrying, less open to the world. She depicted her adult self as being timid – the opposite of her courageous and carefree youthful self. We have to ask what happened to the wild, active young woman. Why did this change occur?

The Shy and Worrying Elsa

Elsa's narratives of her youth and early adulthood tell of an active and brave girl who manages in the world outside her own community, and on the road. However, the narrated Elsa does not take on any active individual role *outside* her family circle or her peer group. When travelling *alone*, for example, to spend a week at her uncle's house in the summertime, Elsa reports that she desperately missed home and the company of her siblings and friends. After the war, Elsa married Eino Koskinen, a worker from the same village, from the same group of local working-class friends with whom she used to travel. Other young couples, including all of Elsa's eleven siblings, moved away from the Ironworks village. Unlike her wild younger self that travelled in a group, the narrated grown-up Elsa is very careful and worries about the dangers of travelling alone and leaving behind the safety of the small community. For instance, Elsa told of a negative experience of travelling alone when she was still a young single woman and was visiting her sister Liisa in Helsinki after the war was over:

Frightened on the Train 1: Shady-Looking Men

Yes, Liisa went to Helsinki then when the war was over, and her husband was decommissioned. So she moved to Helsinki. And I remember when I went to visit her then. It was the time when it was hard to get food, and of course I'd gone to the black market. So I took food there, and the trains were so full that I hardly got a seat. But there were some shady-looking men in front of me on the opposite seat. They had been fighting, they had black eyes, and they were covered in blood. There were three men there, and I was terribly afraid. There was also another young girl there who I thought was also from some small village. So she was afraid too, and we kind of tried to stick together, and when we got to the railway station in Helsinki, I took my suitcase from the luggage rack, and one of the men grabbed it and asked if he could help. I said, "No thank you. I can carry it myself." I was rude. Luckily, on the other side of the cabin there was a nice-looking young man who was watching what was going on and might have helped me if I [...] Since then I've been afraid of travelling by train. There's no way I would go. You never know what's there. (5/12: 31, pp. 17–18.)

Frightened in Helsinki

And then it happened that Liisa was there to meet me at the station and we set off. They lived in [a place called] the Photographer's Villa. It wasn't quite in Helsinki. We went there by bus, and they would have put me up in one of the rooms. I said, "I won't go there. I want to be where you are". And that night, if I had slept there in that room, that night someone got in from the balcony, through that very same room. They stole Erkki's new suit, and they ate all the food and drank the juice. It was a burglar. And I was so afraid that I thought that if I ever got out of there I would never go to Helsinki again.[Laughs.] Things like that always happen to me. (5/12, 32, p. 18.)

The world outside the familiar realm of the small safe community of Inha Ironworks and its nearby villages is presented in Elsa's narratives as dangerous and full of unpleasant incidents. This outside world lay beyond the closest railway stations, whose staff knew the girls of the Ironworks and who, according to Elsa, were always ready to help them. The narrated world of danger extended as far away as Helsinki.

The shy and fearful Elsa who is afraid of travelling alone seems inconsistent with "the young and wild Elsa". This narrated self of a later age, that of adulthood and motherhood, is also linked to her position as a mother and grandmother:

A Worried Mother

E: That's why I am afraid for you too. I've said so. It was a joke in our household when Raija [Elsa's oldest child] went to Helsinki [laughing], so when she was getting dressed I would always go up and tell her not to show her money to anybody, not to talk with strangers, to be sure about the [train] connections. I rattled off the instructions. Then I noticed how Simo [her younger son], he still was a child, when Raija was leaving again, and I hadn't yet said a word, he said, "You shouldn't show anybody your money, when you change trains, be careful which one you get on, and you shouldn't talk to anybody." That's how he went on. So I thought that my lecture had got across. [Laughs.] But I had that fear always, that's what I was most afraid of. I know there's no need to worry, there are conductors and so on, but anyway. When a person is afraid, she's afraid. And it was so safe at the Ironworks. Yes. We had it good there, nobody gave anybody any trouble there. Everybody knew each other, and that's why I don't like to be in big places like that.
I: Yes, when you are used to these…
E: Hm. I'm used to these, these surroundings. The only [other] places when I was young, the only places were Ähtäri railway station or Inha railway station and the centre [of Ähtäri], you see, the chemist's was beside it. Otherwise we didn't go there much, only to the chemist's
I: Hm.
E: Hm, there wasn't anything else here in Ähtäri like now. (5/12, 35, p. 18.)

In the beginning Elsa, too, refers to our real life relationship and social roles outside the narrative realm. She also seems to be aware of the contradiction between her earlier narratives, which portrayed a brave and decisive self, and the later the ones, which a showed shy and worried self. Elsa needed to explain her fear, which existed when she left the familiar environment of the closely-knit Ironworks community. Later, this contradiction became a source of humorous narratives which seem to occupy a central place in Elsa's self-presentation, especially in her old age.

The Funny Elsa

When all of Elsa's sisters, brothers and her friends moved away from Inha, they had to travel to see each other. In Interview 8, Elsa recounted these travel experiences, but not until I had asked about them. I have called them a series of "road trip narratives" of the funny Elsa, a "travelling housewife". These narratives seemed to have something in common with the earlier stories that recount the adventures of the young and wild Elsa. In four of these narratives, Elsa was the protagonist of more or less intentional comic incidents, as in the following example:

Road Trip Narrative 2/5: At the Vaasa Market Square

When we travelled, we always had my sister and her husband with us, and then they only had that one child. And we had the boys and Raija, and we had so much fun together. I always blundered somehow. [Laughs.] It was awful. Once we were in Vaasa, and we went to the market place there. And I had a beige-coloured jacket suit and beige-coloured toe shoes. And the market place had somehow been repaired or something had been done to it. There was some fresh tar there, they put some on the pavement and between the paving stones, and I, of course, stepped on a ball of sticky tar. It made a squeaking sound when I walked. I tried to scrape it off and the others were walking on a long way ahead from one stall to another, and I saw a man with the same kind of clothes as Grandpa, my husband, and he was as short as him, and I put my arm around him and I scraped and scraped my shoe on the ground and I howled, "They make a bloody mess everywhere…" He didn't say anything, and I looked at him. And I said, "I'm sorry, you're the wrong man." [Laughs.] The others were walking there, and they were enjoying it. They saw what had happened, but they were always playing tricks on me. Later, Eino comforted me, saying, "You never know, he mightn't have understood you if he was a Swedish-speaker."[23] Well, that calmed me down quite a bit. (8/12, 17, pp. 11–12.)

Elsa explained her funny behaviour by using the very same term that she had attached to her childhood and youthful self: that of being a free soul (what the Finns would call "a child of nature" (*luonnonlapsi*):

Road Trip Narrative 5/5: Making Faces in the Back of the Car

[…] the car was the kind that had a luggage compartment in the back. The kids started to say they didn't always want to [sit] there, they wanted to sit on the back seat. I said, "OK, I can go in the back." [Laughs.] And I was there, and there were some young lads in a car behind us, and they saw me there in front of them. And I did this, I played all kinds of tricks, all kinds, and in the end, Ville said, "Stop it, for heaven's sake. They'll check my number plate, and they are going to recognize the car wherever I go." After we'd been going for a while, I had to get out. They wouldn't let me to be there anymore. [Laughs.] I was like that, wild. Sointu [Elsa's sister] just laughed at this. […] but the lads had fun in the other car. Oh my lord. And now I'm timid. I don't dare go anywhere out of the house. [Laughs.] (8/12, 20, p. 12.)

In telling about her crazy behaviour, Elsa shifts between the wild and the humorous Elsa and ends with to current narrating Elsa, whom she describes as shy. Distinguishing between one's past and present selves often inspires the use of irony (Portelli 2006, 38). Mikhail Bakhtin (1984) considered that talking about different aspect of the self makes people use language in the same way as authors do when handling the voices and thoughts of their characters. Both kinds of narrators need to use *double voicing*: the present voice (the narrating self) juxtaposed with the voices of other past selves (narrated selves). Irony helps the narrating self to gain distance from itself, and interpret and evaluate its previous experiences, behaviour and emotions. The presented (narrated) self is thus (re)presented as having learned a lesson and being wiser than before (Bakhtin 1984; Löyttyniemi 2004, 76). Elsa's narrative contained hints indicating the presence of different selves, temporal comparisons such as "once, you see" and "now", as well as ironic laughter. The voice of the narrator is that of a wise and ironic elderly lady, a humourist reminiscent of the older female colleagues from the Ironworks discussed earlier in connection with female workers' crazy jokes (Chapter 3 p. 75ff). Kirsti Salmi-Niklander's material also contained an ironic retrospective travel narrative, a causerie describing a journey by car in which the individual first person "I" and the collective first person "we" interchanged and in which the narrator occasionally takes the role of an outside commentator (2004, 357). In Salmi-Niklander's view, the narrative, which lacks a coherent plot and involves two different episodes where young single men and married men go on a journey by car to find women, was about the limits of proper behaviour. In my view, Elsa, too, parodies the roles of the responsible housewife, homemaker and mother, roles that require correct behaviour, the boundaries of which she cannot transgress in her everyday life.

Humour and irony have many functions in the life narrative. One is to comment on the norms and ideals of life as it is lived. Often, irony functions as a means of distancing oneself psychologically from the experienced event. A humorous tone may also indicate that the narrator has experienced difficult situations and times, when laughing at oneself was not possible (Kinnunen 1993, 208). Irony and humour also embodies elements of continuity. One of Patrick Mullen's elderly informants built his self-image around humour. He made it a practice of joking and fooling the interviewer, demonstrating his verbal superiority (Mullen 1992, 226). In Mullen's view, the purpose of this was to indicate that a joker personality was an essential part of his self-image and his attitude to the world, even in old age (ibid). Elsa's case is similar in that the humourist appears in later life and at the end of the interview process, in her narratives about the amusing, travelling housewife, and in her encounters with severe illness:

Some Excitement in Life

We joke, otherwise we couldn't take it. There must be some humour there. You see, when I was in the hospital, the nurses laughed at me when they came, you see, when I had some fluid here, and I had to go back there, although I'd already got out of hospital, to have the fluid removed from my armpit, here. And the nurses went to work and put me in bed, and they always stayed there for a while to listen to me [and I said], "Now I've got a bit of excitement in my life; it's really been pretty dull. [Laughs.] You see, every day the same." They thought it was so funny. They told me that I'd got it right (9/12, 15, p. 8.)

Illness as a High Spot

E: Yes. And later, I got this, the so-called "modern disease". In the past, nobody talked about cancer. It wasn't even known. But when it hit me, it was in a way a high spot in my life. You know, you always have to have something that makes life meaningful.
I: Yes.
E: Otherwise, it gets boring. As you've seen, I didn't mind having cancer. [Laughs.]
I: No, on the contrary, it was something you had to get over.
E: Yes, it was a fight. And a human being needs that, every moment. When they said to me in the hospital that they didn't mind if I cried, I said that I didn't feel like crying. I fancied saying to them, "Get on with it. This is much easier than any of the jobs that I've done in my life." (10/12, 10, p. 9.)

Elsa, too, seems to believe in the power of humour. In the above examples, she turned the situation of having a severe illness upside down and claimed to be having a good time, enjoying "a high spot" and "and getting some excitement in her life" her life. Interestingly enough, Elsa uses the same expression "high spot" when talking about her childhood memories (discussed earlier in this chapter) and when referring to her illness, breast cancer. In Elsa's words, "there must be some humour" especially when times are hard. In reflecting on the self-representation of his elderly informant's, Mullen noted that humour was one of this man's favourite ways of dealing with threatening, authoritative figures, if not in the actual situation then afterwards when he narrated the event. In Mullen's words, "The life review can add humour to situations that may not have been humorous as they were experienced, another means of giving a sense of control after the fact" (Mullen 1992, 224). In Elsa's case, illness which is a physical condition and a serious threat can – at least retrospectively – be tamed by means of humour. This is interesting from the point of view of embodied experience. Elsa, who in other contexts presented her illnesses as a result of hard physical labour and as part of her worker identity, does not recount physical or mental suffering but emphasizes instead her will to fight and her capability to see these challenges in a positive light.

When Elsa got breast cancer, she was an elderly widow and was living alone in the municipal centre of Ähtäri. Having told about her earlier life, her active childhood and youth and her working and family life, she presents illness as part of a natural continuum, and by employing humour to do so, she demonstrates that she is aware of the ironic side of the situation. Elsa's narratives of her attitude towards the illness diminish the power that the medical staff have over her sick body, and thereby also over her mental health. In telling me how she refused to cry and grieve, but chose rather to face the situation defiantly through the use of humour and her experience of life, Elsa introduces yet another self, and thereby continues to control her life narrative in which selves of different ages meet. In my view, the power of her humour lay not only in the feelings of control and inclusion it aroused, but also in the distancing and different perspective it provided.

Completion: the Humorous Storyteller

After studying Elsa's retrospective travel narratives and the experience of her different selves, two questions arose in my mind. The first was: How can the appearance of the different Elsas who developed in the course of her narrated life story be explained? "The young and wild Elsa" was a brave young woman who, despite doing monotonous production-line work, filled her life with all kinds of free time activities and challenging tasks, which she managed well. "The shy Elsa" was scared of travelling alone, which she explains referring to some negative experiences she encountered and the fact that she had not explored the world outside the Ironworks. She was the only one in her family and close group of female friends who stayed in the small village, who did not leave Inha Ironworks to go out and discover the world. In "the funny Elsa", a wild, free soul and a prankster, appeared again on family road trips and ended up in comic situations. A humorous, self-irony seems to be part of her current self, commenting on her previous somewhat contradictory life experiences and on her present life.

I believe that by portraying herself as a *humorous storyteller*, Elsa is following role models taken from the working-class community. In her narratives, Elsa provides examples of the humorous attitudes of the older women who worked at Inha Ironworks. Two female workers, one significantly older than Elsa and the other nearly the same age, were constantly joking and making self-deprecating comments about their lives and their difficult circumstances (their narratives are analyzed in more detail in Chapter 4). Elsa enjoyed their humour and attitude toward life, and later she shows that she, too, is versed in the art of absurd humour. According to folklorist Niina Lappalainen (2008, 61) who studies the Tikkakoski factory community, humour and especially a self-ironic attitude brought the members of the workers' community closer together.[24] Lappalainen's informants explained that a humorous attitude was an essential feature of everyday life in the close-knit working-class community (ibid. 70–71).

Folklorist Eeva-Liisa Kinnunen, who studied humorous features in women's life narratives, points out that different genres and plots are not mutually exclusive in the life narrative (Kinnunen 1993, 205). On the other hand, totally opposing narrative features rarely fit in the same story. Although 'wild' and 'shy' may seem like opposing qualities, it is important to note that in the narratives of the "young and wild" adventurous Elsa, she was travelling in the safe company of a larger group. This may be why she refers to her present self as "shy", since she no longer has a large group to travel with. Alone, she would not have dared to violate the boundaries of proper behaviour by fare dodging on a train or making herself the centre of the events.

I have wondered whether the narratives of "the shy and worrying Elsa" also express a sense of getting older and weaker and of becoming distanced from the world of contemporary young people. In her narratives of her travelling selves, Elsa expresses her feelings of the loss of communal bonds, both by telling about the pleasure of the immediate presence of family members, peers and the people of the local community who all knew each other, and by describing her fear of being alone without any contact with her own people. Elsa's seemingly different selves can thus be viewed as expressing emotions and reactions to changes in society and to social life.

Another question that bothered me is whether Elsa was trying to tell me something with all these different presentations of herself. Is it that she knows that I, a representative of a different generation and time, in fact left my childhood community to explore the world? Is it that this mental travelling in biographical time and transformations of her self are her ways of assuring herself that her life worked out well even though she stayed at the Ironworks? And is it that she wants to show me that she is aware of the changes that have taken place in the world, such as increased individualism and the different expectations placed on the young people of today? All these are intelligible ways of explaining Elsa's self-representation and narrative attitude. I doubt, however, that her message was fully intentional. In my view, the different characters she attributes to herself serve as a way not only to explore her past and present selves and to examine the conditions of her subjectivity but also to address possible futures. The role of the humorous storyteller could, thus, serve to demonstrate to herself and the listener that it all depends on one's attitude to life – a guiding principle offered to a listener of another generation.

6. Conclusions

Life narrative operates in three temporal divisions: past, present and future. Even if the source of the life story telling is the lived past, the life story is a future project, an outline for potential change (Hyvärinen et al. 1998, 13). Studying a life narrative and scrutinizing the context in which the narrator lived her/his life reveal less about a past social reality than about the strategies and attitudes the informant has chosen to represent the life s/he has lived. Life narratives and the narrated self can thus be seen as interpretative models offered to the listener.

Almost any life story is potentially suited to the analysis of experiences of gender, social class and work. What makes Elsa's narrative special was that her narratives and reflections shed light on the power dynamics and the constant negotiation of social status that takes place in everyday life. Elsa's retrospective view and our dialogic relationship encouraged her to not only narrate personal experiences about incidents which evoked positive, negative or contradictory feelings and had shaped her self-image, but to comment on

Elsa and I at the opening of a photo exhibition on Inha Ironworks in Ähtäri, 2004. Photo: Tarja Riihimäki.

6. Conclusions

complex issues such as the transformation of social categories and gender roles, industrial working culture and a sense of community.

In this research, I have studied Elsa's narratives related to changes in the role of women, ambivalence regarding social hierarchy and class position, transformation in working life and the industrial community. I have analyzed Elsa's narrated experiences within their socio-cultural as well as material contexts and have pointed out the different narrative strategies employed by Elsa to create continuity in her life narrative and to overcome the challenges brought by social change. I found that different identities and social positions enable the narrator's agency and autonomy while others constrain it. The focus on one individual's life narrative provides the opportunity for a deeper and more nuanced analysis of personal experiences and the social forces shaping the narrator's subjectivity.

Narrating Subjectivity: Continuity and Renegotiation

Elsa negotiated her identity by positioning herself in certain ways in relation to gender, class and work through different stages of her life. Throughout the interviews she explicitly reflected on what it meant to be working-class. She knew from her childhood that she belonged to the working class. For her, belonging to the working class and being a worker were primary cornerstones of her identity. Growing up in the factory community, Elsa had learned and internalized the identity of a worker. Having been socialized into the world of the old hierarchical factory community, Elsa saw the social hierarchy as something inherent and natural. The higher classes had the right to higher social positions and to better material wellbeing. Nevertheless, although she accepted the social order as given, Elsa felt offended in situations in which other people somehow tried to demonstrate their superiority.

Gender roles were clear, and gendered differences were often taken for granted in Elsa's narratives. Femininity and sexuality became somewhat problematic when she entered working life and later when she made the decision to continue working instead of staying at home. In narrating her life as a female labourer, Elsa emphasized both collective sharing and individual agency. The women of her narratives were able to cope in situations that they themselves had not chosen. In this sense, many of Elsa's narratives that emphasize women's agency maintained and reify the grand narrative of the strong Finnish woman. The strength of the women she depicted did not, however, lie in emancipatory actions but in perseverance and coping against the odds. The working-class women of Elsa's mother's generation lived in a situation in which gender, class and sexuality together created a relatively oppressed position – or at least circumstances that challenged their wellbeing: constant pregnancies and endless household work. Nevertheless, Elsa represents her mother as heroic, as a kind of superwoman who coped with the repeated pregnancies and cared for her family, never complained and accepted the conditions of her life.

On the other hand, women who worked outside the home in addition to taking care of their families and households had to cope not only with physically demanding tasks both at work and at home but also with the conflicting ideals attached to homemakers and rough factory workers. The humour these women shared was dark, based on ironic notions of their own situation and the demands made upon them by other people. Young girls were socialized into the factory workers' culture through this humour and through the men's sexual banter. Young factory women also created a culture of their own, one that tested the boundaries of proper behaviour and displayed agency, for example in the form of joking and playing defiant games like hiding from the factory foremen.

When Elsa recounts her life, she does not tell much about her activities as a homemaker and mother or about domestic work in the private sphere. Most of Elsa's narratives about her childhood and youth depict young girls – girls who took up factory work at an early age – in environments other than the home: working at the factory or travelling outside the home environment. In Elsa's narratives, the young working-class girls travel, are active and brave and have fun. They stick together to avoid their morality being called into question.

It has been maintained that in the 1930s, both middle-class and working-class girls were expected to become homemakers. This expectation governed the gendered ideals of education (Kaarninen 1995; Tuomaala 2004). However, in her life narrative Elsa hardly mentioned her school education, which in her case was brief short but instead narrated experiences of her service as a maid servant in middle-class families, a task which, according to the lady of the house would equip her with the skills needed for a better life as a homemaker.

However, it was not, after all, her role as a housewife with which Elsa wanted to identify. From the beginning of my research process, my attention has been drawn to the narrative I have titled *Back to Work*, which summarizes the narrative strategy of Elsa's life story with regard to her gender and class position: she chose to be the agent of her own life. I have reflected on Elsa's choice to abandon the role of housewife. Did she really not want to become a member of the middle-class? Had she not earlier, when narrating about her experiences as a maid servant in a higher-class family, referred to what she had learned there as "the keys to a better life"? What exactly did a "better life" mean to her? Better material conditions?

Elsa did not talk much about money or wealth, not even in relation to her husband's new status. She welcomed the changes that made everyday life easier and more manageable. Communality seems to have been more important for her than a higher social status. It is interesting to note that she could have attained a higher rank in society as the wife of an office worker but chose to continue to identify with the role she had occupied when she felt secure, part of the group of the workers, even if that group had changed or disappeared. In my interpretation, Elsa resists the interpretation of working class identity as a social constraint. This does not mean that she would not narrate any negative experiences of class-bound hierarchies, but she embraces the working class solidarity and communality which characterized her childhood, youth and early adulthood, and stresses an identity founded on mastery of manual tasks.

In my interpretation, her longing for the good old days of the clear social order does not mean that she did not welcome development, but rather it expresses the pain she felt at losing her place in the communal order. The significance of community, groups bonds, loyalty and help or care from both her peers and other members of the workers' community of different ages, is manifested in nostalgic and metaphorical narratives such as The *Demolished Smokestack*. Philosopher Maurice Merleau-Ponty (1962) used the metaphor of a *phantom limb* to describe bodily layered memory (see Tuomaala 2009a, 80). Places that have disappeared and only exist in collective or eventually in individual memory could be described as the phantom limbs of culture's body. Narratives about sites that used to exist verbalize the feeling of loss and embody the process of change. Thus narrated sites of memory are the amputated limbs of a disappearing landscape.

In patriarchal factory communities, the clear social order offered a sense of security. Whether the master narrative of social advancement is connected to individual success or social welfare, the achievement of better living standards and a higher social status can also be an ambivalent issue, attended by mixed feelings of hope and pride, shame and betrayal. Elsa's worker identity became threatened in her later life when her husband educated himself and climbed the social ladder. Elsa felt that after this, she was no longer treated as one of the workers. Her own self-identification was strong, and she represented herself as being a greasy-skinned worker, a genuine labourer.

For Elsa, the factory was the place where the body submitted to hard work in difficult circumstances, but also a place where she became a skilled labourer. Elsa vividly describes the material world of manual labour in a metal factory, its demanding rhythm and difficult working conditions, cold, heat and danger which shaped her physical being and self-identity as a hard worker and skilled labourer. In the letter Elsa wrote me in 2003, commenting on my Master's thesis presentation, she mentions the smells and noise of the factory, "the sound of work", stating that "nothing today can compare to it". Learning the rhythm of work meant that young girls like Elsa had access to a professional identity and could become full members of the working community, which had its own culture, humour and rules. The work, which Elsa performed well, left permanent marks, both positive and negative, on her body and her identity. Elsa summarizes her career, social position and sense of self by contrasting her experiences of having "a greasy skin" with those of other people who had a chance to study. By claiming that she has *always* been a greasy-skinned worker, she establishes continuity between the young female factory worker and the later self, the wife of a technician.

The central value of work in Finnish culture is also tied to gendered ideals. In agrarian Finland, women performed many physically demanding tasks and household work (carried water, milked the cows, washed laundry by hand, etc.). One of most important characteristic of a good wife was to be a hard worker (Markkola 1990, 26–27; Stark-Arola 1998, 90). The Second World War intensified the value of Finnish women's work and sacrifice. Men sacrificed themselves at the front, while women worked in various jobs on the home front.[1] Women at all levels of society had to do men's work. In Elsa's case, the significance of her wartime work efforts for her life and identity as well as to the society in general were considerable. The key dialogues of her life narrative aim to emphasize the continuity of her worker identity and agency and her ability to cope with rough factory work and a masculine working environment. Elsa's narrative titled *Back to Work* demonstrates that while she was fully aware of the emancipating changes that had occurred with regard to women's roles during her lifetime, she experienced these changes in an ambivalent fashion. Despite this ambivalence, she nonetheless chose to portray herself primarily as a manual labourer.

Reflections on Narrative Means, Strategies and Agency

Narration establishes new connections between past experiences. Narrative positioning anchors actors and events to time and space, producing a variety of narrative strategies and narrative agencies (see also Palmenfelt 2006b, 2007). In my study, I have studied micro-narratives of Elsa's life story and scrutinized their relationship to an individual's life history and to cultural ideals and model narratives. I have argued that the analysis of micro-narratives, their actors and content, and their relation to the entire life narrative as a whole, can provide the researcher with a methodological tool for examining the myriad ways in which narrators strategize to build a multi-vocal life story by contrasting different experiences and adapting conflicting and even contradictory attitudes.

Elsa's social position as a young girl – a maid servant or dogsbody's dogsbody – tied her to different expectations than when she became a homemaker. Her narrative orientations were linked to the different selves associated with different periods in her life. In narrating her life, Elsa portrayed four different kinds of narrated selves and narrated agencies: first, she depicted herself as calm and courageous in narratives of coping which emphasized Elsa's personal qualities, embodied experiences and challenging situations; second, she described herself as nostalgic in reminiscent narratives in which past events were juxtaposed with the world of today. Third, the elderly Elsa described herself using self-irony and absurd humour, portraying herself as a humorous storyteller with life experience; and finally, in a few micro-narratives we see a confused voice through which Elsa depicted herself as shy and worried or scared. How did these narrative strategies and narrated situations differ?

In my analysis, I paid attention to the relations between different actors. In narratives which emphasize coping and agency, Elsa is the centre of events. Her calm attitude and perseverance contrasts with other people's emotional reactions to difficulties and demanding situations. Her peers, young friends and fellow workers cry or give up whereas Elsa keeps fighting and manages against all odds. The courageous Elsa stands up to physical hardship but also to the 'Others', the gentry and officials. Her current self tells about past situations in a calm reporting style. Elsa stresses her courage and perseverance when talking about social situations that did not threaten communal values or communal identity, togetherness, but simply created discomfort (mental or physical) for individuals. By narrating about coping, survival and coming to terms with challenging life events, the narrator can provide the listener(s) with models that have helped her in difficult situations (see also Frank 1995; Skultans 1998). Elsa's narratives of coping could be seen as models offered to me and my generation regarding the right kind of attitude towards difficulties. Some are moral lessons of socially shared cultural values such as the importance of a strong work ethic, but others can be seen as local and personal narratives of resistance.

Nostalgia, which is a common feature of intergenerational dialogue, often irritates the representatives of younger generations. Melancholic longing may seem purposeless and naïve. Nevertheless, nostalgic representations, reminiscences tied to places, and metaphoric expressions can include different perspectives, not only emotional but also critical, pointing towards the values the narrator wishes to cherish (Cashman 2006). For Elsa, remembering the old factory community is a daily practice which does not always involve narrating or a need for an audience. In her letter commenting on my Master's thesis essay, Elsa writes how, while reading my essay, she relived the ironworks again. The factory village exists in her mind and she "visits" there regularly. Elsa not only misses the familiar landscape but especially the sense of community created by the daily shared work. Thus, the nostalgia in her narratives is not always about missing the everyday toil of the past but rather underlines what is missing from her current life: a sense of togetherness and feeling of purpose. These were perceived to be lost in the course of the industry's development and the structural changes which took place at the Inha ironworks village as well as within Finnish society as a whole.

I have argued that nostalgia functions as a narrative strategy to highlight the importance of values such as social responsibility and togetherness. In addition, nostalgic narratives can also be seen as reclamation of agency, an attempt to control change. When situations arose which threatened Elsa's values such as solidarity and a sense of community, Elsa reacted with nostalgia. In general, Elsa's narratives of her past are full of strong emotions. She expressed sadness over the loss of the community and identified with the group of manual workers through verbal expressions and metaphors. Although these narrative strategies highlighted Elsa's agency, some narratives also introduced her vulnerability and confusion under changing circumstances. In depicting herself as shy and worried, even scared and frightened, Elsa reflected upon the challenges of facing an external world different from the environment in which she grew up. The settings for her narratives, some of which were large cities, were portrayed as dangerous and unpredictable. In my interpretation, through representing herself as shy and worried, Elsa underlines the difference between her world and my world, demonstrating the scale of change that has occurred within her lifetime.

Positioning herself within a spatial dimension and anchoring of her experiences to physical sites helps both of us to appreciate the transformations.

In addition to narrative strategies that emphasized coping or employed nostalgia, a humorous attitude to life seem to have been of great importance to Elsa. She learned the art of situational banter and the use of a self-ironic voice from her female colleagues at Inha Ironworks, who transformed their fatigue, their lack of time for themselves, and the expectations placed on them into absurd jokes. In her later life, Elsa talked about aging and illness in a similarly absurd and humorous way. In the working community, humour arose when the social dignity of female workers was at stake. Later, Elsa joked about her uneventful life when it was threatened by severe illness.

It is noteworthy that even individual micro-narratives can contain different attitudes adopted by the narrator, offering possibilities for varying interpretations. Elsa's narrative *Back to Work* which explains her choice to return to factory work when her husbands' new social identity placed the family in a higher social position was an open dialogue in which she reflected on her own feelings and needs, other people's choices and the ways things had been previously. This narrative, which touched upon the central themes of Elsa's life and narrated subjectivity, gender, class and work, was an example of how the narrator constructed and negotiated her agency against the backdrop of a changing world. From the beginning, it was the core dialogue upon which I based my study and analysis because it implied many potential directions in which the research could lead: a discussion of women's roles at work and in the family, class expectations, working-class pride, limits of self-determination, and the yearning for a prior 'habitus'.

Unlike many others, the key narrative *Back to work* was not repeated in full in any other interviews: it was only referred to and summarized on one occasion. Although the narrative did not have an established form, an expression it contained, greasy-skinned worker (or work*man*), embodied cultural ideas of what it means to be a labourer and working-class. This expression truly underlined Elsa's narrative positioning.

The Potential of Micro-level Analysis and a Dialogic Approach in Life Narrative Research

As I have demonstrated, research into the narrative construction of self entails difficult but at the same time crucial questions of multivocality as well as controversy over individual versus societal authorship of stories. We narrate our experiences from multiple points of view and use other people's narratives and various narrative means to represent ourselves. We are categorized in multiple ways which may differ from the identities we ascribe ourselves or which may contradict cultural ideals. How do we narrate ourselves as autonomous individuals and members of our own cultures and communities? Which experiences of our life path do we emphasize and why?

6. Conclusions

In this study I have examined how Elsa used narratives and narrated experiences to represent herself. Scrutinizing the micro-narratives within one life narrative draws attention to the complex process of narrative positioning. Dialogues with the self, with other persons and with other narratives are actualized in these numerous micro-narratives, which set the scene for the analysis of social dynamics among various actors and events. The analysis of micro-narratives allowed me to examine the ideals related to intersecting social categories and to bring to the fore the complexity of hierarchies and social dynamics which shaped one individual life in a small factory community. The position of a female labourer depended on various historical, cultural and even situational factors and conditions. Similar micro-level scrutiny of lives of representatives of different generations, other social groups or other genders could open up new insights into varying forms and spheres of agency as well as illuminate the range of subject positions which individuals live and to which they aspire.

The key narratives or dialogues I interpreted to be cornerstones of Elsa's narrative identity all concerned her experiences as a female labourer. This, I came to realize during the research process, was attributable not only to her choice to represent herself this way but also to my eagerness to hear about her experiences related to gender and class in particular. Portraying herself as a skilled worker who could handle her job, but also recalling the painful and contradictory sides of her experiences related to social class, she could show her life and experiences in a positive light. She could also offer me a role model in terms of managing and getting by, despite the harsh conditions, with the help of humour and a sense of togetherness. I could have further exploited the potential of dialogic analysis in shedding light on the dynamics of our mutual interaction and reflecting on how my interpretations evolved during and after the interview process. However, it should be noted here that the qualitative research process is always directed by subjective choices and can never be explained thoroughly (see also Ojanen 2008).

One of the aims of this study was to analyze the ways in which an individual situates her/his narrative in relation to cultural ideals and model narratives. It was a challenging, but intriguing, task from the beginning. Many of Elsa's narratives appeared to involve elements that resisted dominant interpretations of modernizing changes, interpretations I was eager to deconstruct. However, the concept of a cultural model narrative appeared to defy precise definitions. I have found that Elsa converses with a range of culturally and historically specific ideals regarding femininity, motherhood and respectability, core values of the Finnish society such as the ethos of work and education, as well as narratives of modernizing developments such as women's emancipation through paid labour or the success story of technological progress. Many of these cultural narratives exist parallel to each other in shaping our understanding of life in the 20th century. Some compete with each other or are challenged by individual narrators.

Elsa's life narrative reflected many contradictory events and developments in modernizing Finland. She was born into a society that was relatively poor and in many ways unequal. Most girls of worker families did not receive any more than a basic education. In Elsa's case, war ended her school career exceptionally early, but it also gave her the chance to gain experience of men's work at the factory. Her post-war life followed the ideal. She married another worker and had her first child during the post-war baby boom, and stayed at home throughout the 1950s rearing her three children. However, although married women in the 1940s and 1950s were expected to become homemakers, ideals regarding motherhood and womanhood in general were already changing. This development reflected the other major changes in Finnish society that accelerated in the 1960s. Elsa, who went back to work even though she could have become a middle-class housewife, told me how she acted according to the new ideal of the modern independent woman, which she found somewhat contradictory. Many of the developmental stages of life she found painful were already easier for members of her children's generation, who were free to proceed to vocational or even higher education, for example. I was the first of her children or grandchildren to receive an academic education, however. This must have affected her narratives and the dialogue between us: our lives and opportunities were, indeed, very different.

The awareness of different perspectives and potential interpretations forces the narrator to reflect upon her life trajectory, the situations in which she ends up, and the choices she makes. References to cultural ideals can be found in these reflections, some of which form key narratives and dialogues with the individual's life narrative. Simple explanations and interpretations seldom exist because the narrator's perception of her past is affected by cultural ideals existing at different times. The listener who is simultaneously interpreting also influences the act of narration and the emphasis placed on each perspective or narrative. Despite the complexity of the concept, an analysis of the relationship between an individual's micro-narrative and cultural ideals can offer new perspectives on transformations in cultural values and mentalities. The method might be most fruitful in the analysis of the life narratives of multiple persons, where the researcher could point out shared interpretations and narrative patterns as well as differences between individual experiences and representations.

In sum, individual life narratives offer unique perspectives onto the dynamic relations between narrative and experience, culture and individual. Micro-level scrutiny of personal experiences and biographical materials is thus at the core of ethnological research which is interested in the everyday lives of ordinary people, their relationship to social change and their home environment. I am curious to see how my generation in Finland will narrate the material world of the 21st century which is characterized by affluence, interconnectedness, and information technology. How do these factors shape our subjectivities? And how will new forms of work, communication, and cultural ideals transform the practice of life narration?

Notes

1. Introduction: Understanding Her Life

1   I choose to call the narrator *Elsa* – and not my grandmother – to allow room for her subjectivity and personality and not limit them to a single dimension or role. The use of her first name also enables distancing and analytic thinking, both of which are needed in writing an ethnography and especially when the study is of one's own a relative. In a casual everyday life setting, I call her *Mummu* (Grandma) or *Elsa-mummu* (Grandma Elsa). I myself appear in the interview excerpts in the first person as "I". I chose this to indicate my position as both the interviewer and the interpreter.
2   The sociologist Eeva Peltonen (1997, 103), who has interviewed her own mother about her experiences and interpretations of the Second World War, uses the term *perusluottamus* (basic trust) to describe the rapport that exists between relatives (on the establishment of rapport between interviewer and interviewees of different generations, see also Strandén 2009 and 2010).
3   Some folklorists and oral historians who have studied their relatives have also applied a dialogic approach to their analysis. Katherine Borland (1991), for example, who studied her own grandmother, negotiated with her about the interpretations she had made. During this process, Borland learned a great deal about feminist epistemology and feminist research practices.
4   The word *ruukki* comes from the Swedish word *bruk*, which means a "mill". In Finland, the word referred primarily to ironworks (Spoof 1997, 275). The word has a more old-fashioned connation than the word *fabrik* (factory), which was first used in urban industrial settings (see Häggman 2006, 189).
5   The historian Kari Teräs, who has studied the social and organizational relations of the modernizing metal industry in Finland in the late 19th and early 20th centuries, points out that the process of modernizing industrial working life was not a straightforward unidirectional development but rather a fluctuating trajectory, a mixture of different sets of options and agents that all influenced and determined the content and pace of developments (2001, 34).
6   The Swedish folklorist C.W. von Sydow (1878–1952) called storytellers "tradition bearers" and made a distinction between active and passive tradition bearers (1948). Finnish folklore studies have tended to focus on active tradition bearers, the expert storytellers of certain communities such as Juho Oksanen (a storyteller studied by Annikki Kaivola-Bregenhøj's [1988, English translation 1996]), a village eccentric called Heikan Jussi (the subject of a study by Tuija Saarinen [2003]), the Pastor of Kalkkimaa (studied by Pälvi Rantala [2009]), a self-educated folklore collector Heikki Meriläinen (Kurki 2002), or Marina Takalo from Viena Karelia, whose repertoire and worldview Juha Pentikäinen studied 1971 (English translation 1987). Other related subjects studied in Finnish research have included the opposition between educated and non-educated persons and the marginal positions of healers, jokers and storytellers.

7   Folklorists have themselves criticized the concept of "the good storyteller". Studies of expert storytellers and their oral performances can lead to overemphasizing the artistic nature of folklore and ignoring its role in everyday communication (Lehtipuro 1980; Peltonen 1996, 98).
8   Ehn & Löfgren 1982; Bringéus 1990; Frykman & Gilje 2003, 15; Snellman 2012. 'Everyday life' became a central concept when the focus of ethnology turned towards contemporary culture and when definitions of 'folk' and 'folk life' became problematic (Knuuttila 1989, Sääskilahti 1999, 151).
9   As in ethnology, early folklore scholarship also represented folk culture and folk, the (agrarian) common people, as uncomplicated and apolitical, ignoring their involvement in political activism and failing to address the existence of possible conflicts between the social classes (Abrahams 1993; Salmi-Niklander 2004, 36).
10 In Sweden, Nordiska Museet began to collect workers' written biographies in the 1940s and 1950s. Ethnologist Ilmar Talve who had Estonian origin but worked in Sweden and Finland began documenting life and work in different industrial communities in Finland, especially in fields of industry that were about to vanish in the face of technological advances. In the 1970s, "the hidden history" (den dolda historia) of workers' lives became a popular subject of research among Swedish ethnologists and historians (Arvidsson 1998, 9–10) and in the 1980s, Swedish ethnologists conducted several studies on workers and the working class (see Ehn 1981; Skarin Frykman 1987 and 1990; Arvastson 1987; Ambjörsson 1988.) Since the end of the 1980s, several interesting ethnological studies have been carried out on various groups of workers and industrial communities in 20th-century Finland (see Nurmi 1989; Snellman 1996; Spoof 1997; Sappinen 2000). A list of earlier studies is given in Ilmar Talve's book Finnish Folk Culture (1997, 384–385).
11 See for example Pentikäinen 1971; Siikala 1984; Knuuttila 1984; Kaivola-Bregenhøj 1988.
12 See for example Nenola 1986; Nenola & Timonen 1990; Apo 1995, Stark-Arola 1998, Apo, Nenola & Stark-Arola 1998.
13 By contrast, in the United States, studies of the workers' oral culture, which are often called "occupational folklore" or "labourlore" (the folklore of the labour movement), had already started to emerge in the 1960s and 1970s (McCarl 1997).
14 In her study on the oral histories of women of her own family, sociologist Mary Patrice Erdmans (2004, 3) argues that the voices of white working-class females are not heard in contemporary gender studies. According to her, researchers are more likely to acknowledge race than social class. White working-class women's experiences are considered when researchers are interested in their position in the labour market, in wage-earning or in labour activism. The private lives and domestic circles of such women continue to receive little attention. Erdmans argues that ordinary lives are seldom studied because the category of "normal" does not generally attract the attention of researchers.
15 According to ethnologist Ilmar Talve, industrial workers comprised nine per cent of the total population in 1890, rising to 14 per cent in 1914 (Talve 1997, 318). The numbers grew significantly (more than doubled) in the 1920s and 1930s. However, farming still employed more people than industry in 1940. The proportion of industrial workers of the total population was 20 per cent in 1940, 29 per cent in 1950 and 30 per cent in 1960, whereas the corresponding figures among people making their living from agriculture and forestry were 59, 41 and 32 per cent. (Alapuro 1985, 61, 78, 81, 87–88; Talve 1997, 326.)
16 In addition, new opportunities also arose in logging and timber floating, and on urban building sites, the railways and canals (Talve 1997, 321).
17 Chief justice Erik Gustav Roschier was given the right to start an Ironworks in 1841. However, he never did, but sold his rights to Gustav Adolf Wasastjerna who owned a mill in Seinäjoki and wanted to expand. However, Wasastjerna died

before he could do so, and it was not until 1851 that his son Gustav August, who was studying mining engineering in Sweden, founded the ironworks in Inha. The "Gustafsfors Bruk" was completed in 1954. (Rautainen tarina, 6–7.) Later, the river Inha gave its name to the ironworks. The name also appears in the names of two villages in the municipality of Ähtäri. The village that formed around Inha Ironworks is officially called "Inhantehtaat" on the map. The other village, which sprung up around the railway station of Inha, is located five kilometres away at the other end of Lake Hankavesi and carries the name "Inha". The locals often call this other location "Inhan asema" (*Inha station*).

18 The first Finnish ironworks were established in the 17th and 18th centuries. Inha Ironworks was founded during the second wave of the Finnish iron industry when small ironworks were established in the lake areas of central and eastern Finland (Salokorpi 1999).

19 The Finnish word *patruuna* has no exact equivalent in English: it is used to refer to the typical 19th-century patriarchal and often paternalistic factory-owner.

20 In 1895, Keirkner ceased producing iron from lake ore and built a new Siemens-Martin steam furnace. In addition, he started nail and stack production lines (Hahne 1994, 51; *Rautainen tarina*, 24–27). A new horseshoe line was started in 1901. In 1915, Inha Ironworks signed a contract to produce horseshoes for the Finnish Army. Finnish Railways ordered spikes from Inha factory starting from the beginning of 1920s (*Rautainen tarina*, 24; Hahne 1994, 76–77, 79).

21 The history of the Inha Ironworks community *Rautainen tarina* [The story of iron] (1991), is a brief history of the facility published to celebrate the 150th anniversary of its founding. It was produced by a company called Kynämies Kyriiri Ky, and the author's name is not mentioned. Historical writings by local amateur historians include a history *Inhan ruukkiyhdyskunta 1833–1964* [Inha Ironworks community 1833–1964] by Reino Hahne (1994) and the memoirs of Matti Ranta *Aikamatka ruukinelämään* [A journey in time into the life of the Ironworks] (2006). Both Hahne and Ranta were former employees of the Ironworks. Another text that concerns Inha Ironworks is the history of the local branch of the metalworkers' trade union *Inhan metallityöväen ammattiosasto 51 100 vuotta* [The Inha Metalworkers' Union, Branch no. 51, 100 years] (2009), which I will henceforth refer to as "IMA".

22 In 1910, Ähtäri had 5991 residents of which 9,9 % were industrial workers. During the years 1911–1915, Inha ironworks employed approximately 120–160 people (Viertola 1991, 18–19, 28).

23 The divisions varied locally. In rural Osthrobotnia, for example, many crofters who wished to become independent farmers supported the Whites (see Norrena 1993).

24 Työväenyhdistys 25 vuotta. Text by Juho Kask. The Finnish Labour Archives / Inha worker's association *(Inhan Työväenyhdistys)* / folder 2. Despite this, 23 Reds were executed in Ähtäri (Viertola 1991, 45).

25 The minutes of the meeting of *Inhan Taimi* 1923–1930 (Sport Archives / Inhan Taimi / folder 1).

26 The number of the Inha industrial council was 24. In 1930, the council was abolished, and a new Inha Metalworkers' Union branch was formed, the number of which was 51 (IMA 2009, 13).

27 In 1925, the average residential density in Inha was four persons to a room (IMA 2009, 12).

28 The factories also depended on a skilled work force, so the relations between workers and factories could best be described as mutual interdependence (Koskinen 1993, 18; Kortelainen 2008, 162).

29 There is a picture of Kaarlo Kiikkala and accompanying caption in Hahne 1994, 60.

30 Vihtori was a member of the board of the Workers' Association for 35 years (1914–49), as secretary to the board in 1919–21 and 1929, and as president in

1922, 1930–32, 1936–40, and 1949. *Kertomus Inhan TY:n toiminnasta 50 vuoden ajalta.* TyArk: Inhan TY: kansio 2.

31 For more on the process and experience of deindustrialization, see for example Koskinen 1987; Ahvenisto 2008; Kortelainen 2008.

32 Experience is a person's subjective relation to the surrounding reality and to the world in which (s)he lives (Laine 2007, 29). Experiences consist of perceptions which human beings structure through their consciousness.

33 Scott 1991; Gergen & Gergen 1991; Koivunen & Liljeström 1996, 276; Vilkko 1997; Shuman 2005; Saresma 2007, 89.

34 Like any constructionist in this field, I do not see narratives as directly mirroring the reality, or as plain (imaginary) constructions: they lie somewhere between life and storytelling (e.g., Taira 2006, 40).

35 Written autobiography is a fixed mode of representation, which means that researchers do not have access to the process of creating (writing) the life story. The authors can choose the limits and style of their representation. The oral life narrative, on the other hand, is interactive and open to negotiation. Typically, life narrative interviews are mixtures of chronological and descriptive sequences, narratives, free associations, question-and-answer chains and interviewer's comments (Oring 1987). Both the interviewee and the interviewer can return to earlier topics, ask for more detailed information and clarifications, and add to what has been said and offer new interpretations of it (Arvidsson 1998, 7; Pöysä 2006, 229).

36 In addition to this division, many other differences in emphasis exist. According to the anthropologists James L. Peacock and Dorothy C. Holland, the term "life history" connotes that the narrative is true (1993, 368). In her study of Holocaust survivors, the folklorist Ilana Rosen (2008) preferred the term "life history" over "life narrative" because, in her view, "it keeps alive the ties between history and story" and offers a "balance between the individual and the masses that he or she is part of and inevitably represents".

37 Performance-oriented methodologies of folklore studies which were developed in the 1970s produced an interest to study (new) non-traditional genres such as personal narratives (see for example Stahl 1977; Virtanen 1982). At first, genre-oriented folklore studies struggled with the definition of personal experience narratives. Sandra Dolby Stahl (1977) was one of the first scholars to define personal narratives, which she called narratives of personal experience: dramatic, truth-based and presented in the first-person. Other scholars were not as strict about the first-person form but rather underlined the personal significance of the narratives for the narrator (see for example Dégh 1995, 73–78, 131–132; Virtanen 1982; Kaivola-Bregenhøj 1989, 11–113; Aro 1996, 50).

38 In similar vein, folklorist Lena Marander-Eklund (2011) uses to the term micronarrative (originally *mikro-narrativ* in Swedish) to refer to personal narratives and anecdotes of written autobiographical material because the term embodies the idea that they are produced within a larger framework of life narratives and in the context of life narrative interviews.

39 Dialogic relation between the experience and its expression see for example Bruner 1986, 5; Bauman 1986, 10. Experiences can be analyzed at multiple levels such as action, discourse, emotion, morals/values. These levels are not separate but rather intertwined (Saresma 2010, 63).

40 It is noteworthy that in English, "subjectivity" can have two rather different meanings: 1) the state of being a subject and 2) the quality of being subjective (versus objective). I use the word in both senses. In this introductory chapter and in my analysis, I refer to subjectivity in the former sense. However, I use it in the latter sense in Chapter 2 to describe the nature of my research material and process. The Finnish language distinguishes between these two meanings with two different terms: *subjektiviteetti* refers to the former meaning and *subjektiivisuus* to the latter.

41 In this research, the term agency signifies two dimensions: positioning in relation to social structures and becoming a unique person/self. Agency is thus understood as an ongoing dialogue between relatedness and autonomy. In the context of this research, agency is primarily *narrated agency,* produced through language and narration (see also Saresma 2007, 192).

42 Identity and self come very close to the concept of subjectivity. Identity emphasizes the public aspect of self-representation and belonging, whereas self refers to subject's own conception of his/her qualities. In my view, the process of negotiating subjectivity entails both dimensions. But unlike self or identity, subjectivity does not imply unity or sameness but rather highlights the multivocality and situatedness of the narrating subject.

43 Dialogism, as developed by the Russian literary theoretician Mikhail Bakhtin, is widely used in literary studies and also in anthropology. According to Bakhtin (1981, 1984), no individual voice can exist in isolation. Every person is influenced by others and by different voices embedded in their inner dialogue. In a life story, for example, the narrator both speaks to and listens to her-/himself, asks and answers at the same time. Thus even one person creates a dialogue. In a life narrative study, both the inner dialogue and communication with other people are crucial.

44 Olney 1980, 247; Komulainen 1998; Skultans 1998, 33; Tuomaala 2004, 313, 339; Saresma 2007, 105–106.

45 Ricoeur 1991, 195; Widdershoven 1993; Aro 1996, 51; Löyttyniemi 2004, 17–18, 62–64; Sääskilahti 2012, 55.

46 I am aware of the weight and the complexity of the term "class". It is infused with political connotations and can be analyzed at different levels, for example, in terms of structures, identities, consciousness and action (Skeggs 1997, 6). Historically, the term is connected with the birth of wage labour societies and the worker movement. In the 18th and 19th centuries, industrialization and capitalism transformed the economic and social structures of Western societies; the working class emerged and formerly agrarian societies developed into wage-labour societies. In the late 19th century, the term "class" began to replace hereditary classifications such as "estates" as a means of organizing society into hierarchical divisions (Heikkinen 1997, 72–73). This corresponded to a general decrease in the significance ascribed to hereditary factors and increased the significance of wealth and income as indicators of position in the social hierarchy. Marxist theories emphasize the role of capitalism in shaping class relations. According to them, the capitalist stage of production consists of two main antagonistic classes: the bourgeoisie, the capitalists who own the means of production, and the proletariat or 'working class' who sell their own labour power to the capitalists.

47 Sociologist Alejandro Portes (1995, 12) has defined social capital as 'the capacity of individuals to command scarce resources by virtue of their membership in networks or broader social structures'. According to him, the resources themselves are not social capital: the concept refers instead to the individual's ability to mobilize them on demand.

48 The concept of intersectionality was first introduced into feminist studies in 1989 by Kimberlé Crenshaw, a scholar of critical race theory. Some scholars have used the concept only in dealing with women of colour (and other attributes that can be assigned to them), whereas other have used it as a general term applicable to any group of people (Yuval-Davies 2006, 201).

49 See for example Scott 1986 and 1988; Moore 1993; Jordanova 2002, 121; Boydston 2008, 558; Laine & Markkola 1989; Markkola 1994; Lähteenmäki 1995, 11.

50 In addition to issues of gender, class and work, this study also deals with *age* and different life stages which are significant dimensions of both social life and life narrative practice.

2. The Dialogic Research Process and Analysis

1 Narrative ethnography, which has developed within the so-called narrative inquiry of the social sciences, examines the contextual organization and situational character of narrative interaction rather than the internal logic and structure of narratives (see Gubrium & Holstein 2008). Studies based on narrative ethnography focus on particular narrative environments and brief stories in everyday communication (see, for example, Georgakopoulou 2007; Bamberg & Georgakopoulou 2008; Gubrium & Holstein 2011).

2 Folklore scholars have long studied how narratives and narrative devices are used in different ways in everyday communication, in passing on oral traditions and beliefs by applying both textual and contextual oriented methodologies (Klein 2006; Palmenfelt 2006a and 2007; Ukkonen & Koski 2007). Folklorist Ulf Palmenfelt (2006 and 2007) has written about "the ethnography of narrative" by which he means an approach that pays attention to both the act of *narrating* with all its cultural, social, communicative and emotional power and to the *narratives* themselves: their form, contents, meaning, function and aesthetics. His approach is a combination of detailed textual analysis and the analysis of narrative interaction. Folklorist Jyrki Pöysä (2012), on the other hand, refers to his research on the workplace culture of office workers as "narrative ethnography", which in this context means an emphasis on social interaction and oral performance, as well as the use of methods resembling the ethnography of speech.

3 This is also what distinguishes oral life narratives from the written autobiographies solicited in contests organized to collect written essays and other textual materials, a method commonly used in Finnish folklore studies and ethnology for eliciting life stories. From the 19th century on, Finnish archives have organized competitions to solicit materials which document oral traditions and knowledge of popular customs and beliefs. Since the 1960s and 1970s, Finnish archives have concentrated more on the collection of oral history materials. In the 1980s and 1990s, archives and researchers became more interested in the autobiographies of ordinary Finnish people (Peltonen 1996; Salmi-Niklander 2004, 38–39; Latvala 2005, 24–33).

4 For example, heroic survival stories often collapse in the course of longer interview processes (see Rosenthal 1991; Peltonen 1997, 107). Oral historian Alistair Thomson (2010) has reflected on the confusing and conflicting versions of some elderly people's life stories. In the case of an Australian WWI veteran whom Thomson interviewed, the first versions of the narrated life experiences were distinctively patriotic. At the beginning of the interview process, this interviewee recounted a narrative about an experience that crucially affected his life, the story of how he was enlisted. This narrative was clearly directed at younger generations of Australians, to which that the interviewer belonged. However, direct questions and later discussion with the researcher produced different voices challenging the patriotic tone of the first version, which represented a kind of "comfortable story of the war". Folklorist Anna Hynninen's (2004, 2011) research on the written and oral self-representation of an elderly woman who has written about her life for several Finnish archives sheds light on the impact of different contexts on life story telling and illuminates the similarities and particularities of written and oral accounts by the same person.

5 The ethnologist Hilkka Helsti (2000) has studied conflicts between maternity education and actual experiences of motherhood, analyzing, among other things, women's written reminiscences of childbirth. She has pointed out that, when they get the chance to do so, people are often willing to share intimate experiences, as this both helps them to organize their own experiences and allows them to give valuable information to today's people about the conditions of life in the past (ibid.

163

28–32). According to Helsti, the writers in her study were inspired by the chance to participate in producing *popular, unofficial history* (see also Peltonen 1996, 282; Ukkonen 2000, 35–38).

6 On open questions in life narrative interviews see Atkinson 1998.
7 A story is usually repeated if it receives an appropriate response from the audience (Mullen 1992, 5). These *variants* can, however, be used in different ways on different storytelling occasions.
8 This is a mark of a skilled performer (see Mullen 1992, 166).
9 For example, together with Saima Kilponen, Elsa discussed her childhood experiences and life during the Second World War. From the beginning, Elsa led the discussion. At this point, she was an experienced interviewee and encouraged Saima, too, to share her experiences with us. At first Saima hesitated, but soon these two ended up reminiscing about the period of the Second World War, and in the end they even produced joint narratives.
10 For examples of studying one's own cultural environment and background, see Myerhoff 1978; Lawless 1988; Zerubavel 1995; and Ruotsala 2002; On studies of family members, family history and family narratives, see Suojanen 1978; Steedman 1994 [1986]; Stahl 1989; Wilson 1991; Borland 1991; Thomas 1997; Eskola 1997; E. Peltonen 1997; Jaago 2002; Finnegan 2006; Haanpää 2008; Rosen 2011.
11 Reflexive positions should cover the whole research process. In addition to self-reflection, positioning involves reflection on the researcher's epistemological and methodological commitments, questions concerning the cultural context of the research and research ethics (Aro 1996, 28–30; Fingerroos 2003; Fingerroos & Haanpää 2006, 40–41).
12 This piece of factual information prompted Steedman to study her mother's life and her own memories. It seemed to function as a clue to larger social issues in a similar manner than in microhistorical research, which studies so-called *normal exceptions*: people with obscure, strange, and even dangerous qualities which are kept hidden from the outside world (see M. Peltonen 2006; Haanpää 2008, 42–43; Magnússon 2011).
13 For an insider perspective, see for example Suojanen 1978, 22–25; Ruotsala 2002; Vuorinen 2002; Haanpää 2008; on the insider-outsider dichotomy, see Reinharz 2011.
14 The references to the interview excerpts give the number of the interview and the page of the transcript (e.g., 1/12, p.1).
15 For example, people who have gone through hardships often tell about their lives in order to share their stories, to comfort co-sufferers and to facilitate the process of adjustment of both themselves and their listeners (see for example Frank 1997).
16 Several folklorists have reminded us that we should not see elderly people only as the memory of the nation; they are still active experiencing subjects in the present (Kirshenblatt-Gimblett 1989b; Mullen 1992, 2–3; Vakimo 2001, 24; Heikkinen 2007, 34). This is important to remember since the work of folklore scholars and ethnologists is influenced by what is still generally regarded as its goal: the preservation of disappearing traditions, although these traditions often continue without us and our work (see Glassie 1982; Abrahams 1993). Traditions and stories are dynamic and constantly changing.
17 Psychiatrist Robert Butler (1964) introduced the concept of *life review* to gerontology in the 1960s. In his view, advanced age is characterized by a naturally occurring, universal mental process of return to past experiences and particularly to unresolved conflicts. Even if there has been a lot of criticism of the age-specific nature of reminiscence, it is important to note that Butler's ideas, namely, his positive attitude towards reminiscence, has significantly changed views on elderly people's reminiscing, which was earlier seen – at least in the American context – as a sign of degeneration (Saarenheimo 1997, 33–34).

18 The Finnish sociologist Eeva Peltonen has analyzed the differences between two generations of Finns in their interpretations of their experiences related to the Second World War (1997). She has noticed that she writes her research for two different audiences: the patriotic generation of older Finnish people who lived through the war years and an academic audience, who, in Peltonen's view, represent a counter-voice composed of people who were young in the 1960s and in 1970s and who wanted to distance themselves from their parents' legacy. Peltonen herself belongs to this radical generation. After interviewing people of her mother's generation and reflecting on her own reactions, Peltonen understands better the attitudes of both generations. According to her, a dialogic relationship is possible only if the parties can acknowledge the possibility that the other party might be "right", and if both parties can communicate the reasons behind their thinking (ibid. 98–99). Peltonen believes that later generations may succeed in analsing the war experiences of her mother's generation more deeply and from a more dialogic perspective (1997, 132–134).

19 On talking to a future archive researcher, see Palmenfelt 2006a, 113; for more on the presence of other audiences, see Yow 2006, 66.

20 The names of many of the villagers – including my relatives – appear in Elsa's stories. In cases where a person might take offence, I have chosen to replace their names with pseudonyms. I have indicated this in the quotes of the interview material. In other cases, such as the case of factory owners and managers, I have used the names Elsa mentioned. In the context of a small community, individuals are in any case easily recognized from their position, style of speech and other contextual information.

21 The oral historian Joanne Bornat criticizes studies in her own field for valorizing the narrators' voices while often leaving them out of the interpretive process (2006, 465–466). Examples of practices that allow the dialogue to continue after the actual interview situations have been introduced in the context of, for example, community projects (on the notion of *shared authority*, see Frisch 1990) and feminist oral history (see Borland 1991). Following these examples, Bornat considers that the outcome of the research process should be a "partnership which both includes and controls academic powers" (ibid. 466). Bornat's ideas are very close to the principles of reciprocal ethnography.

22 Folklorist Dell Hymes (1975) coined the term "breakthrough into performance" to describe such moments.

23 I designate the micro-narratives with the number of the interview, the number of the narrative in the listing and the page of the transcript (e.g. 1/12, 1, p.1). If the quoted example has been defined and listed as a micro-narrative, it also carries a title. The parts of the interview dialogues that are excerpts from a conversation that did not entail micro-narratives are only marked with the number of the interview and the page of the transcription.

24 In psychology and sociology, significant others are those persons who are of sufficient importance in an individual's life to affect her/his emotions, behaviour and sense of self. Significant others play an important role in the development and maintenance of identity.

25 The grand meta-narratives of science include for example Enlightenment ideas such as rationalist thinking and human control of nature. According to philosopher Jean-François Lyotard, these meta-narratives have collapsed in the late 20th century. Lyotard proposes that metanarratives should give way to *petits récits*, "localized" narratives, which bring into focus a singular event (1984).

3. A Working Woman: The Negotiation of Gendered Ideals

1 It is important to note that in the 1920s and 1930s, all areas of industry grew and an estimated 100 000 new workers were hired. Many of these were women (Hjerppe et al. 1976, 43–44).
2 Sulkunen 1989b; Kaarninen 1995; Helén 1997; Nätkin 1997; Tuomaala 2004; Vehkalahti 2000.
3 At the end of the 19th century, the concept of modern citizenship for Finnish women was oriented towards "societal motherhood" (*yhteiskunnallinen äitiys*), meaning that the ideal role of middle- and upper-class women was to take part in social movements and to participate in public life and political decision making in areas that came within their sphere of responsibility, namely education and social policy. Thus women came to be active in the temperance movement, religious organizations and in women's and youth associations (Sulkunen 1986; Ollila 1993, Markkola 1994).
4 In the process of creating a civic society and the Finnish nation, the "home" was made into a centre of both middle-class and working-class ideals (see Saarikangas 1993; Markkola 1994, 230; Rojola 1999). Similar developments also took place in other Western countries such as Sweden (e.g. Åström 1985; also Löfgren 1987, 79).
5 Many researchers have drawn attention to parental figures in life narratives and autobiographical writings; see for example Passerini 1988, 23; Määttänen 1998; Vilkko 1997; Roos & Rotkirch 1997; Komulainen 2001; Latvala 2005; Rosen 2008.
6 The authoritarian conception of parenthood of the first half of the 20th century based on distance and inequality: children were supposed to respect their parents, know their place, behave well, be silent and, above all, obey the rules. They were expected to stay out of the way while the parents took care of their daily duties (Ruoppila 1954; Korkiakangas 1996, 42; Tuomaala 2004, 84; Latvala 2005, 206). The strict rules often had to do with practical issues such as security (Korkiakangas 1996, 256; Tuomaala 2004, 84). Children showed their respect for their parents by using the formal form of "you" (the equivalent of the French *vous* or German *Sie*) when addressing them. In Elsa's family, the only exception was made for the youngest child Sointu, Elsa's little sister, who according to Elsa was pampered in other ways as well.
7 Elsa's father was 33 years old and her mother 24 when they married.
8 The reason the other workers could see Elsa's mother going to the outhouse was that her home was right next to the factory yard, and anytime anybody went to the outhouse, they had to cross the factory yard.
9 For more on the notion of respectability in analyses of social class, see Skeggs 1997.
10 Elsa's narrative Soldier at the Window (6/12, 1, p. 1).
11 Reinhold Amberg was the general manager between the years1917 and 1938. The next general manager was his son-in-law Birger Illman (Rautainen Tarina 1991, 42).
12 Until the 1910s, the most common occupation for females working outside the home was that of maid servant (see Vattula 1989). This was true even of women from farming families. Working-class girls often served in middle-class households. Elsa's eldest sister Aura, for example, worked as a maid servant for the stationmaster of the nearby Ähtäri railway station. In 20th-century Finland, agrarian maids were young. If they were really young, that is under the age of fifteen, they were not necessarily even paid for their work, but were only offered food and board. In the 1920s and 1930s, there was a lack of servants especially in the cities, and during the whole interwar period most of the maids in the cities were relatively young. In official documents from the year 1928, young servants in the cities were called either maid servants (*kotiapulainen/apulainen*) or nannies *(lastenhoitaja)*, whereas more experienced maids were household assistants *(talous-*

apulainen), housekeepers *(taloudenhoitaja)*, matrons *(emännöitsijä)*, or cooks *(keittäjä)*. After the Second World War, domestic work was more common among adolescent women than among adults, and the shortage of maids continued to grow. (Rahikainen 2006, 228–229.)
13 E.g. Sulkunen 1989a, 37–44; Ollila 1993, 47; Markkola 2002b, 221–227.
14 Another factor in determining the transition from childhood to adolescence was basic education. When primary school was made obligatory in 1921 and extended to age 16 instead of age 14 as before, the boundary between childhood and youth shifted. (Tuomaala 2004, 99–155; Tuomaala 2009b, 61.)
15 The obligation to work had already been enacted for adults in 1939. In 1942, the law was extended to include young people above the age of fifteen (Kirves & Näre 2008, 66–68). A similar kind of legislation determined the wartime lives of women in Britain. In particular, this affected young unmarried women, whom the state saw as free agents and a mobile work force (Summerfield 1998, 45).
16 Approximately 70 000 women served the war industry in Finland during the Second World War. These women were not trained or used to this kind of work, which sometimes led to accidents (Lähteenmäki 2000, 159)
17 Satka 1993, 1994; Lähteenmäki 1994; Hytönen & Koskinen-Koivisto 2009.
18 The wartime period increased the value placed on motherhood and maternal sacrifice. Mothers were crucial for the reproduction of new citizens and for safeguarding patriarchal values on the home front (see Satka 1994; Kemppainen 2006b; Hytönen 2011). Motherhood was also a uniting factor for women of different social backgrounds (see Olsson 2005, 58–59).
19 The idea of the husband as the primary breadwinner has its roots in bourgeoisie ideals and wage labour society (Häggman 1994, 89; E. Stark 2011, 194–199). In the agrarian society, the work force of both men and women was needed and the physically demanding work was divided between men's jobs and women's jobs (Stark-Arola 1998, 87). When capitalism and industrialism brought about the wage labour economy, rural Finnish men – also landless and lower-class men – could earn money for themselves and their families. This development, along with industrial wage labour and modern mechanized agriculture, created a gendered division of labour in which men became breadwinners for their families.
20 For other examples of situations in which men who had become foremen did not want their wives to work outside the home, see Lappalainen 2008, 71; Steel 2011, 115.
21 See Ollila 1993, 46–65; Häggman 1994, 223–224; Helén 1997, 317–324.
22 Löfgren's study is part of a larger research project that studied culture and class in 19th- and 20th-century Sweden. Instead of examining separate groups such as workers or the middle-class as such, it focused on relations between such groups.
23 Middle-class girls, too, gained more freedom and independence through education and white-collar jobs (see for example Pohls 2001). The morals of female teachers, post officers and shop assistants were, however, controlled by employers (see for example Hentilä 2001, 171).
24 Kinnunen 1988; Kaivola-Bregenhøj 1998; Bergholm & Teräs 1999, 114; Teräs 2001, 47; Lappalainen 2008.
25 Testing newcomers with language games and jargon was often part of factory workers' informal initiation (cf. Rossi 1988; Teräs 2001, 45). Knowing the working culture and its humour ensured group membership and increased a worker's social competence.
26 For more on agrarian communities see for example Stark 1998; for more on lumberjack culture see Pöysä 1997.
27 On women's reputation and the use of the word *huora* (whore), see Saarikoski 2001; Olsson 2007.

28 Both women are long deceased. I chose to let these two women remain anonymous. In some of the interviews, Elsa does so, too, but on some occasions, she mentions them, especially the friend of her own age, by name. In these cases I have used a pseudonym.
29 On incongruity theory, see for example Oring 2003, 1–12.
30 Folklorist Eeva-Liisa Kinnunen (1998), who studied expressive genres of humour in a community of laboratory workers, identified the different genres by their content and the storytelling situation. The other genres were teasing, put-downs, self-mockery, ridicule, pranks (or practical jokes), jokes and witticisms (ibid, 412–413).
31 The original Finnish version of this exclamation adds an extra feature of humour: Fuck you (*Haistakaa vittu*) was addressed to the main engineer using the formal form of address (equivalent to the French *vous* form).
32 According to Lüdtke, *Eigensinn* should not be regarded as a dichotomy between us and them, but as the individual agency of workers who balance between the contrastingdemands of their foremen, fellow workers and their own need for space. Finnish researchers (Teräs 2001; Suodenjoki 2010) have used *Eigensinn* to represent a collective form of contestation (Torninoja-Latola 2011, 65).
33 The second part of the word, -*väli*, means a break. The first part *hitsi*- is a word that can mean "weld" but also "damn" or "hell".
34 I have not found any detailed description of the work rhythm at Inha Ironworks. Nor have I read about similar systematic breaks in any other factories.
35 Philosopher Michel de Certeau (1984) created the terms strategy and tactics to describe the routines and practices which shape our everyday lives within power relationships. Strategies are practices located in a place or institution whereas tactics practiced by the weak do not assume a place but are situational and momentary, events turned into opportunities (ibid xix-xx).
36 In the 19th century, smoking was a common and respectable activity among male metal workers. The idea of a woman smoking, on the other hand, was considered totally inappropriate (Teräs 2001, 95). Smoking women were despised and suspected of having low sexual morals. Literature and magazines in the 1920s warned young girls against ruining their reputation by smoking and drinking alcohol. The disapproval maintained a clear distinction between a respectable and a fallen woman (Vehkalahti 2000, 142, 146; also Häkkinen 1995, 29–33). In the countryside, on the other hand, some women smoked pipes and roll-your-owns from home grown tobacco. Agrarian children were not allowed to smoke until they could earn their own money and thus afford to buy tobacco. Therefore, smoking was also a symbol of adulthood (Korkiakangas 1996, 61–63).
37 For ideal concepts regarding the behaviour and education of girls in first half of the 20th century, see for example Vehkalahti 2000; Korkiakangas 1996, 257; Olsson 2007, 219, 221, 222. The ideal of a good woman as humble and obedient is common to the Finnish fairy tale tradition (Apo 1990, 255). The ideals have persisted through the centuries, and some of them are still extant in the education of Finnish girls today (see for example Ojanen 2011, 189).
38 See for example Arvastson 1987, 111; Löfgren 1987, 83; Kortteinen 1992; Modell & Hinshaw 1996; Lappalainen 2008 and 2010.
39 The word "master" (in Finnish *mestari*), which relates to craftsmanship, could refer to the top manager of the working unit or to the closest foreman. The roles of foremen tended to vary according to the specific location (Teräs 2001, 109–110).
40 In her study of discussions of women's trouser-wearing in women's magazines 1889–1945, ethnologist Arja Turunen (2009; 2011) argues that trouser-wearing was seen as a symbol of the new independent, active woman. In Finland in the 1930s, trousers were still not an everyday garment for women but were recommended mainly for those women who performed physical activities such as skiing. During the Second World War, Finnish women were encouraged to wear trousers

at work, but leisure time clothing was nevertheless always a skirt or dress (ibid. 345–353).

4. Social Class: Identification and Distinction

1 Translated by E.K-K.
2 The dichotomy between the common people who performed physical labour to survive and those who belonged to one of the three higher estates (nobles, clergy, and burghers) was deeply rooted in the agrarian world view of the times of *ancien régime*. This dichotomy continued in the class society which was divided into to the owners, the bourgeoisie, and common people (Soikkanen 1981, 438). These dichotomies characterized the mentality of the Finnish people at the turn of the 19th and 20th centuries. The division was situational and fluctuating but nevertheless clear: it divided people into "us" and "them" (Haapala 1995, 99). For studies of the social hierarchies and group identities of skilled workers in industrial communities, see for example Nurmi 1989; Spoof 1997; Koivuniemi 2001; Ahvenisto 2008; Kortelainen 2008.
3 For more on antagonisms among different groups and professions see for example Pöysä 1997, 241ff; Paaskoski 2008, 226–228; E. Stark 2011, 140ff.)
4 Historian Pertti Haapala, who studied the industrial workers of Tampere, the largest industrial city in Finland, states that before the organized workers' movements, workers did not constitute a single coherent group but rather many different groups. The only thing that unified them was their lack of power (1986, 100). Haapala calls this powerless class the "estate of work" (*työn sääty*) (ibid.).
5 Haapala 1986, 62; Häggman 1994, 134–136; and 2006, 189; Vilkuna 1996, 10, 84–94; Karonen 2002, 13 and 2004, 140.
6 The Finnish word *patruuna* is used to refer to the typical 19th-century patriarchal and often paternalistic factory-owner. Keirkner was the most influential *patruuna* of Inha Ironworks, and was mostly called by the name *Patruuna*, perhaps because his Swedish last name was difficult to pronounce. His wife was correspondingly known as the *Patronessa*. Elsa sometimes abbreviates this to *Nessa*.
7 The industrial action impasse was resolved when, after government arbitration, the workers signed an agreement that included a rise in their wages (Koivisto 1959).
8 This description corresponded to the qualities mentioned in local histories (see for example *Rautainen tarina*, 15–17; Hahne 1994, 42).
9 The translation given here does not reflect the fact that Elsa mimics the poor Finnish of the *Patruuna*'s outburst: some words were mispronounced, and the sentence was grammatically incorrect.
10 According to sociologist Erik Allard (1964), the division between Finnish-speakers and Swedish-speakers was one of the basic group oppositions that persisted in Finland until the 1960s. Other basic oppositions that caused tensions in society included the divisions between rural and urban inhabitants, workers and bourgeoisie, and communists and members of the other political parties (see also Stark 2005, 25).
11 In Finland, one presidential term lasts six years. Kekkonen was re-elected three times, and his third term was extended by four years.
12 In Finland, Kekkonen was regarded as a kind of national hero. He was extremely popular in Finland for three decades and was portrayed in the media as a model citizen: extremely hardworking, sporty and civilized. However, his authoritarian acts as well as extended presidential term were also widely criticized.
13 Elsa uses two forms of the man's name in the interview: "Vasilev" (a surname) and "Vasili" (a first name). It has not been possible to establish the man's name from any documents or popular histories.
14 I have not included all the belief narratives of Elsa's repertoire in this study. They appear especially in the interviews 1, 6 and 9 and are numerous. In interview 9,

Elsa has also reflected on questions of faith and religion, acknowledging a personal faith in god and Christian beliefs. She is religious and a member of the Lutheran church, but like the majority of Finns does not frequently attend church. Her belief narratives offer material for further study and analysis.

15 The official name of the house is the Marble Palace, not the Glass Palace. The house, which is located in Kaivopuisto in Helsinki, was built by the Keirkners for their later life and served as the residence of the Patronessa until her death.

16 Serving good food and eating together with the residents of her former home village can be seen as a symbolic way of strengthening relations between the higher and lower classes, the *Patronessa* and the men of the Ironworks (cf. Stark E. 2011, 168–169).

17 The slang verb *duunata* which means "to do", "to carry out a task", appeared in the dialect of the longshoremen of the Sörnäinen district in Helsinki in the early 20th century (Paunonen 2005, 158–159). The actor noun *duunari*, which is derived from this word, was first used in the Helsinki area, but later, presumably in the 1960s and 1970s, it became widespread throughout the country.

18 Despite the symbolic and central role of alcohol in working-class culture, it is important to note that socio-historical research has shown that workers and the working classes generally did not drink any more than other groups (Sulkunen 1986; Haapala 1986, 166–167; Apo 2001, 202–205). The workers' movement was progressive in promoting the ideal of the active and self-educated modern citizen and in nurturing the values of the temperance movement (Haapala 1986, 177; see also Salmi-Niklander 2004, 259–260). However, in the eyes of the upper classes of the late 20th century, the stereotypical picture of the worker was of a malnourished and uncivilized creature, a way of thinking that is connected to the ideology of race (Sulkunen 1986, 31; Apo 2001, 205).

19 These dances included popular versions of ballroom dances such as the foxtrot, the waltz and the tango as well as folk dances such as the *jenkka* (a traditional Finnish dance similar to the polka). The Finnish tradition of partner dancing evolved from ritual folk dances and young people's village dances of the 18th and 19th centuries, which were primarily group dances (Laine 2005). In the early 20th century, partner dances displaced the group dances (Hoppu 2003, 37–38). In the late 19th century, new social institutions, such as the temperance movement and youth organizations, started to criticize the dancing activities of young people. Dancing, especially partner dancing, was thought to be immoral and to lead young people into irresponsible pre-marital sexual relationships (Nieminen 1995, 59–60; Siltala 1999, 525; Salmi-Niklander 2004, 254).

20 Most parents accepted that their confirmation-aged children participated in social evenings and dances, but girls' journeys and behavior were more strictly curtailed than boys'even after confirmation (Salmi-Niklander 2002; Tuomaala 2009b).

21 The Tuomarniemi students were mostly from middle classes and were studying to become foresters, forest engineers and technicians (the supervisory ranks of the logging sites). Foresters, especially, have been seen as a part of gentlefolk (Paaskoski 2008, 226–228). In the Civil War of 1918, the school served as a training ground and military base for the Civil Guard, the military unit of the nationalist Whites.

22 The views presented by Elsa in this narrative come close to what the anthropologist James C. Scott (1985, 322–323) calls "internalized inequality", a view of the world that is characterized by a harsh economic reality and that is not even meant to be equitable. Scott found that such an attitude prevailed among the poor peasant classes of Malaysia. Similar views concerning the natural order were also found in the life narrative material and proverbs of agrarian Finns studied by folklorist Eija Stark (2011, 159). The social order and divisions of traditional agrarian communities continued to shape the worldviews of the people who moved from the

countryside to industrial and urban environments in the 19th and 20th centuries (ibid. 159–160.)

23 In the 19th century and early 20th centuries, projects of social reform and enlightenment did not aim at removing social distinctions but rather at offering the best possible life for each individual within their own social circle. The common folk and especially workers were to be civilized in order to guarantee a stable social order, not to encourage them to climb the social ladder. In the 1920s and 1930s however, new ideas of citizenship and individual potential gained ground. Individuals were encouraged to rise from poor backgrounds with through perseverance and nobility of mind. (Koski 2011, 169–174.)

24 Service as a maid was often only a temporary occupation (see for example Rahikainen 2001, 18).

25 Like the Finnish word *hän* (she/he), *se* is grammatically neuter in gender, and is commonly used in colloquial language to refer to persons.

26 Social climbers who did not know how to behave in higher social circles were popular characters in Finnish films and literature throughout the 20th century (see, for example, Rojola 2011, 209). The question of language also relates to this phenomenon; social climbers from Finnish-speaking families did not know Swedish, which was commonly used among management.

27 As in the other ironworks (see Vilkuna 1996, 28–29), some foreign labour from Sweden and Germany had been recruited to work at Inha. In addition, some workers had moved to Inha from Swedish-speaking areas of Finland. These persons were mainly skilled workers such as smiths and master craftsmen (foremen), who were higher in rank than the ordinary workmen. Most Finnish-speaking workers did not understand Swedish at all. To their ears, it was the language of social privilege (Rautainen tarina 1991, 31).

28 A Swedish name did not always correlate with a wealthier background. Swedish names were common among farmers and fisherfolk in Ostrobothnia and other west-coast areas of Finland, as well as among the working class of Southern Finland and the Helsinki region.

29 In the 1930s, several Finnish factory communities held market days according to the salary cycle (Spoof 1997, 278). At Inha Ironworks, workers were paid their wages every two weeks. This was the day when families could purchase food and other necessities for their families, but it was also a day when the men drank and played cards. The life of workers in other industrial communities such as Penttilä Sawmill in Joensuu (Kortelainen 2008, 105) were marked by similar market days and the same wage-payment period.

30 Cultural historian Inkeri Ahvenisto, who studied the Verla Sawmill community in Southwestern Finland from the late 19th century to the 1960s, points out that the feelings related to the crossing of the class boundaries were very personal and situation-dependent (Ahvenisto 2008). Some children of workers' families did not experience any discrimination, whereas others felt very uncomfortable in the company of higher-class children and their families (ibid. 155–156).

31 In agrarian Finland, begging, even when it was absolutely necessary, was regarded as a source of shame and humiliation (see for example Pentikäinen 1971, 97–99, E. Stark 2011, 242). Coping with scarcity and resigning oneself to the prevailing circumstances, one's given lot, were cultural ideals that were intimately bound up with self-respect (E. Stark 2011, 330, 334, 349ff). Since 1883, vagrancy had been prohibited by law. Times of crisis such as the Great Depression of the 1930s forced people to go on the road to look for work, to use their social networks and to rely on other people's good will (see for example Häkkinen 2002; Virkkunen 2002). In most cases, however, people did not beg but looked for work in exchange for food.

32 The rationing began in 1939. The rationing of sugar and coffee went on until 1954 (Räikkönen 1993).

33 The noble poor are also common characters in Finnish fairytales written by the 19th century cultural elite (Apo 1995, 146–147).
34 In Finland, the rationing of textiles and shoes began in October 1940 (Aikasalo 2000, 205).
35 Nylon stockings came on the market in the 1940s and became very popular in the USA. In wartime Europe, it was difficult to acquire these novelties. American soldiers who served in Europe during the Second World War traded nylon stockings on the black market (Kopisto 1997).
36 During the Second World War, chicory or roasted grain were used for making ersatz coffee.
37 The co-operative movement came to Finland at the turn of the 19th and 20th centuries. The first cooperatives in Finland were workers' consumer cooperatives. In 1904, the SOK Corporation (Suomen Osuuskauppojen Keskuskunta) was founded in order to coordinate joint purchases, advice and guidance. In 1916, cooperatives owned by the working classes formed their own Corporation Osuuskauppojen Keskusliitto (KK). The disintegration of the cooperatives reflected the strong political dichotomy of the Finnish society at the time. The store mentioned in the narrative belonged to the SOK chain.
38 The Finnish expression *"tyttönä ollessa"* used could mean either "when we were young" or "when we were single".
39 During the Second World War, Finnish women participated in the civil defence effort through the Lotta Svärd organization. The Lottas worked in hospitals, manned air-raid warning posts and carried out other auxiliary tasks in conjunction with the armed forces. The Lottas were mainly unarmed. The Lotta Svärd organization had been founded in 1920. The girls' section was started in 1931 in order to offer Finnish girls healthy, useful and patriotic leisure-time activities such as camps, games and sports as well as training (Nevala 2003, 247–248; Pohls & Latva-Äijö 2009, 120–125). In the 1920s and 1930s, the Lotta Svärd organization was associated with the Finnish Civil Guard, a nationalistic right-wing movement. During and after the Civil War of 1918, and in the political tensions of the early 1930s, Finland was divided between the right-wing Whites and the left-wing (mainly working-class) Reds. The Reds' workers' movements also had youth sections and organizations such as *Työväen Urheiluliitto* (the Workers' Sports Association). The division between the White and the Red organizations began to blur in the mid-1930s. During the Second World War, in 1940, *Sosialidemokraattiset naiset* (Social Democratic Women), the most powerful leftist women's organization concluded a cooperative agreement with the Lotta Svärd Organization in organizing women's work service (Lähteenmäki 2000, 152–153; Pohls & Latva-Äijö 2009, 213–215).
40 Either the Lotta Svärd organization did not collect information about the social background of its members, or the documents were later destroyed when the organization was prohibited according to the demands of the peace agreement with the Soviet Union in 1944. The majority of them were from the agrarian middle class. It has been argued that joining Lottas seldom had a political motivation, but was rather motivated by patriotic values. Furthermore, in many smaller countryside villages there were only few organizations and free time activities, and Lotta Svärd offered agrarian girls an opportunity to engage in activities other than school or work (Olsson 1999, 90–95, 198–214; Nevala 2007, 70; Pohls & Latva-Äijö 2009, 125, 148–149).
41 According to literary scholar Kukku Melkas (2005), the position of a maid servant in the middle-class family was contentious because of the general conception of working-class girls' sexuality.
42 Relationships between two people of different classes were also a common theme in various forms of Finnish popular culture such as the films of the 1950s and 1960s (M. Peltonen 1992, 138–139).

43 Ethnologist Katriina Siivonen (2008) notes in her research on identity among the residents of the archipelago in Southwest Finland that the people who lived in close connection to nature and in harsh circumstances wanted to define themselves within the shores of the Island. They would not accept any guidance or rule from outsiders, only from the outside forces of nature.

44 Recently worked horseshoes and spikes formed from melted iron were still warm.

45 According to the documents of a local co-operative, Hermanni had studied in an adult education college, a dairy institute and an agricultural school. He was elected as accountant of the cooperative of Ähtäri village in 1923 (Ihamäki 2007, 68).

46 In this context, "sleek" refers to well-oiled and wash-proof leather. People who had a greasy skin were considered genuine and impermeable to outside influences. The idea is close to that expressed by the English idiom "dyed-in-the-wool".

5. Change and Continuity in a Life Narrative

1 Translated by E.K-K.

2 See Radley 1990; Basso 1996; Ljungström 1997; Skultans 1998; Cashman 2006; Tuomaala 2009b; Webber & Mullen 2011.

3 Industrial rationalization, time and motion studies of production line work arrived to Finland already in the beginning of 20th century, but spread wider after the Second World War (Kettunen 1994, 109). A time and motion study is a business efficiency technique used to reduce the number of motions in performing a task in order to increase productivity. It is a major part of *scientific management* (*Taylorism*), task-oriented optimization of work.

4 *The Safety First ideology* took root in the heavy industrial enterprises of the United States and arrived in Europe in the 1920s. The main idea of the movement was to contribute to an undisturbed production process in order to avoid accidents, thereby raising production efficiency. This was done by paying attention to individual workers, the human subjects working with machines, to their knowledge and their working conditions. According to this ideology, industrial safety, work efficiency, and industrial harmony were to be gained by the same means, by involving the working subjects in the process of production development and regulation.

5 On the importance of analyzing gestures in narration see for example Young 2000.

6 The female shipyard workers interviewed by Taina Ukkonen (2000) also described their working conditions and talked about the lack of industrial safety. These women who were also union activists had taken part in promoting new practices of industrial safety.

7 Also agrarian children whose childhood reminiscences Saara Tuomaala studied, carried their scars with pride; their bodily marks reminded them of their learning and thus helped to construct their identity as workers (Tuomaala 2004, 87).

8 The number of office workers grew significantly in Finland in the period after the Second World War. Consequently, the word *toimihenkilö*, meaning office worker, was adopted into Finnish political language at the end of the 1940s. (Kettunen 1997, 103–106; Kettunen 2001, 142–143; Alasuutari 1996, 122–123.)

9 At the same time, the narrative of change closes the past to history, giving today's people a power to claim that cultures and traditions are dead (Knuuttila 1994, 8–17; Mikkola 2009, 137–138). For more on the myth of progress see Taira 2006, 81; on pro-modern attitudes see Anttonen 2005, 40–42, 71.

10 Household work, too, was rationalized with the aim of easing and reducing women's workload at home (see for example Lönnqvist 1986; Sulkunen 1989; Ollila, 1993; Malinen 2007).

11 Electric washing machines became widespread throughout Finland in the 1950s. At Inha, the local branch of the Metal Workers' Union suggested that a new mod-

ern washing machine should be bought and placed to the factory's sauna building (Inhan metallityöväen ammattiosasto 100 vuotta 2009, 18).
12 One could nevertheless question whether nostalgia could ever be characterized as simple. It is a complex phenomenon that, according to sociologist Stuart Tannock (1995, 454), "responds to a diversity of personal needs and even political desires".
13 Empirical research on, and the analysis, of people's relations to particular spaces may reveal some of the positive elements of nostalgia. Studying the strategies of town-dwellers' reactions to the planning of a new school building, the ethnologist Pirjo Korkiakangas (2004) notes that nostalgia functioned as a resource which not only strengthened the identity of a place but also 'legitimated' moral grievances against those in power.
14 Studies of modernization often involve dichotomist views of change and continuity in which tradition becomes a metaphor for stability, and modernity becomes a metaphor of change and innovation. These views are also deeply rooted in the history of ethnology and folklore studies. Change and continuity are not, however, opposite concepts but should rather be seen as simultaneous and interactive processes. (Anttonen 2005, 34; Mikkola 2009, 39–40.)
15 The concept of *chronotope* is created by the literary theoretician Mikhail Bakhtin (1979, 1981). A chronotope, or in other words a *time-space*, stops time and captures events within a certain space, thus transforming the real life relations between time and space. In chronotopes, form and content, time and space become entangled with the whole storyline and the historical context (Bahtin 1979, 243–244). Examples of Bakhtin's chronotopes include "encounter"," road", "threshold", "salon" and "idyll". For an application of the concept of chronotope to the narrative analysis of oral histories see Skultans 1998; Savolainen 2009.
16 Time can not be directly described but requires metaphoric language (Ricoer 2000, 106; Sääskilahti 2012, 75)
17 On the collective nature of childhood experiences, see also Korkiakangas 1996, 241, 328.
18 One example of the help offered by the villagers was that they always brought food to a house in which somebody had died (1/12, 47, p. 30).
19 Children needed a written permit from their parents to join the girls' sections (Olsson 1999, 200; Nevala 2003, 348; Pohls & Latva-Äijö 2009, 123).
20 Oral history interviews attest to the fact that during the Second World War, some teachers pressured young working-class girls into taking part in the activities of the Lottas (see for example Lappalainen 2010, 253).
21 Bad shoes symbolize the family's low status., Good shoes, by contrast can function as a vehicle into the accepted normative habitus and status of the Lottas (for shoes as a metonym of family status, see also Tuomaala 2004, 288–292; Lindroth 2005; Virkkunen 2010, 91–94) For more on the status, clothing and social class of the Lottas, see for example Olsson 2005; Turunen 2011, 367; Heikkinen 2012, 178–190). Shoes are mentioned in other narratives told by Elsa, and they occupied a central place in the everyday life of the family since Elsa's father was a village cobbler, who repaired shoes in his spare time.
22 Bicycles were important vehicles for young persons in the Finnish countryside of the 1920s and 1930s. By enabling young people to work and join different activities in broader area, bicycles enhanced the mobility and independence of both young men and women. (Tuomaala 2009b, 60–62).
23 Vaasa is a partly Swedish-speaking city on the west coast of Finland.
24 On the integrating power of humour see also Bakhtin 1995, 13.

6. Conclusions

1 See e.g. Kemppainen 2006a; Holmila 2008; Hytönen 2012a, 2012b; 2014.

References

Interviews

Interviews of Elsa Koskinen 2001–2014 by the author (see Appendix 1). [The interviews will be archived in the Finnish Labour Archives in January 2015.]

Archival sources

The Finnish Labour Archives
Inha worker's association (Inhan Työväenyhdistys) / folder 2.
Sport Archives
Inhan Taimi / folder 1.

Unpublished

Fine, Gary Alan 2009: Accounting for Jokes: Jocular Performance in Critical Age. Keynote lecture at the 9th Conference of International Society for Folk Narrative Research "Narrative across Space and Time" June 21st–26th, Athens, Greece.
Koskinen, Eerika 2005: *Isoäitini elämänsä kertojana.* Pro gradu -tutkielma. Folkloristiikka. Jyväskylän yliopisto.
Verde, Filipe 2011: Brigding the Cultural Gap. Anthropogy and Hermeneutics. Paper presented at the II Jornadas Internacionales de Hermenéutica: La hermenéutica en diálogo con las ciencias humanes y sociales: convergencias, contraposiciones y tensiones. July 2011, Buenos Aires, Argentina URL: https://www.academia.edu/1172190/Bridging_the_Cultural_Gap_-_Anthropology_and_Hermeneutics (accessed 3.10.2014.)

Literature

Abbott, H. Porter 2002: *The Cambridge Introduction to Narrative.* Cambridge: Cambridge University Press.
Abrahams, Roger D. 1986: Ordinary and Extraordinary Experience. In Victor W. Turner & Edward M. Bruner (eds.). *The Anthropology of Experience,* 45–72. Urbana & Chicago: University of Illinois Press.
— 1993: Phantoms of Romantic Nationalism in Folkoristics. *Journal of American Folklore* 106, 3–37.
— 2005. *Everyday Life. A Poetics of Vernacular Practices.* Philadelphia: University of Pennsylvania Press.
Abu Lughod, Lila 1986: *Veiled Sentiments: Honor and Poetry in a Bedouin Society.* Berkeley and Los Angeles: University of California Press.
A Statement of Ethics for the American Folklore Society. *AFS News*, New Series 17(1) February. URL: http://www.afsnet.org/?page=Ethics (accessed 25.3.2013.)

Ahvenisto, Inkeri 2008: *Tehdas yhdistää ja erottaa. Verlassa 1880-luvulta 1960-luvulle.* Bibliotheca Historica 118. Helsinki: Suomalaisen Kirjallisuuden Seura.

Aikasalo, Päivi 2000: *Seuratkaamme järkevää ja terveellistä muotia. Naisten pukeutumisihanteet ja vaatevalinnat 1920-luvulta 1960-luvun lopulle.* Kansatieteellinen arkisto 47. Helsinki: Suomen muinaismuistoyhdistys.

Alapuro, Risto 1985: Yhteiskuntaluokat ja sosiaaliset kerrostumat 1870-luvulta toiseen maailmansotaan. In Tapani Valkonen & Risto Alapuro & Matti, Alestalo & Riitta, Jallinoja & Tom Sandlund (toim.). *Suomalaiset. Yhteiskunnan rakenne teollistumisen aikana*, 36–100. Helsinki: WSOY.

Alasuutari, Pertti 1996: *Toinen tasavalta: Suomi 1946–1994.* Tampere: Vastapaino.

Alestalo, Matti: Yhteiskuntaluokat ja sosiaaliset kerrostumat toisen maailmansodan jälkeen. In Tapani Valkonen & Risto Alapuro & Matti, Alestalo & Riitta, Jallinoja & Tom Sandlund (toim.). *Suomalaiset. Yhteiskunnan rakenne teollistumisen aikana*, 36–100. Helsinki: WSOY.

Alho, Linnea 2011: Miten naisten palkoista muodostuu palkkakuilu? Palkkojen muodostuminen ja sukupuoli Rosenlewin Porin konepajalla 1945–1961. In Kirsi-Maria Hytönen & Eerika Koskinen-Koivisto (toim.). *Työtä tekee mies, nainen.* Väki Voimakas 24, 81–101. Tampere: Työväen historian ja perinteen tutkimuksen seura.

Ambjörsson, Ronny 1988: *Den skötsamme arbetaren. Idéer och ideal i ett norrländskt såg- verkssamhälle 1880–1930.* Stockholm: Carlsons.

Andrews, Molly 2002: Counter-narratives and the Power to Oppose. *Narrative Inquiry* 12(1), 1–6.

Anttila, Anu-Hanna 2000: "Ja tahmeeta on kun Konosen kävely..."Työläismiehen rekonstruointi rituaalien avulla. In Joni Krekola & Kirsti Salmi-Niklander & Johanna Vallenius (toim.). *Naurava työläinen, naurettava työläinen. Näkökulmia työväen huumoriin.* Väki Voimakas 13, 131–157. Tampere: Työväen historian ja perinteen tutkimuksen seura.

Anttonen, Pertti J. 2005: *Tradition through Modernity. Postmodernism and the Nation State in Folklore Scholarship.* Studia Fennica Folkoristica 15. Helsinki: Finnish Literature Society.

Apo, Satu 1990: Kansansadut naisnäkökulmasta: suuren äidin palvontaa vai potkut Lumikille? In Aili Nenola & Senni Timonen (toim.). *Louhen sanat. Kirjoituksia kansanperinteen naisista.* Suomalaisen Kirjallisuuden Seuran Toimituksia 520, 24–35. Helsinki: Suomalaisen Kirjallisuuden Seura.

— 1995: *Naisen väki. Tutkimuksia suomalaisten kansanomaisesta kulttuurista ja ajattelusta.* Helsinki: Hanki ja jää.

— 2001: *Viinan voima. Näkökulmia suomalaisten kansanomaiseen alkoholiajatteluun ja -kulttuuriin.* Suomalaisen Kirjallisuuden Seuran Toimituksia 759. Helsinki: Suomalaisen Kirjallisuuden Seura.

Apo, Satu, Nenola, Aili & Stark-Arola, Laura 1998: *Gender and Folklore. Perspectives on Finnish and Karelian Culture.* Studia Fennica Folkloristica 4. Helsinki: Finnish Literature Society

Aro, Laura 1996: *Minä kylässä. Identiteettikertomus haastattelututkimuksen folklorena.* Suomalaisen Kirjallisuuden Seuran Toimituksia 650. Helsinki: Suomalaisen Kirjallisuuden Seura.

Arvastson, Gösta 1987: *Maskinmänniskan. Arbetets förvandlingar i 1900-talets storindustri.* Göteborg: Korpen.

Arvidsson, Alf 1998: *Livet som berättelse. Studier i levnadshistoriska intervjuer.* Lund: Studentlitteratur.

— 1999: *Folklorens former.* Lund: Studentlitteratur.

— 2001. *Etnologi: perspektiv och forskningsfält.* Lund: Studentlitteratur.

Assmuth, Laura 1997: *Women's Work, Women Worth. Changing Lifecourses in Highland Sardinia.* Transactions of the Finnish Anthropological Society No. 39. Helsinki: Finnish Anhtropological Society.

Atkinson, Robert 1998: *The Life Story Interview.* Qualitative Research Methods Series 44. Thousand Oaks, London, New Delhi: Sage Publications.
Bahtin, Mihail 1979: *Kirjallisuuden ja estetiikan ongelmia.* Suom. Kerttu Kyhälä-Juntunen & Veikko Airola. Moskova: Progress.
Bakhtin, Mihail 1981: *The Dialogic Imagination: Four Essays.* Transl. Caryl Emerson and Michael Holquist. Austin and London: University of Texas Press.
— 1984: *The Problems of Dostoevsky's Poetics.* Transl. by Caryl Emerson. Minneapolis: University of Minnesota Press.
Bal, Mieke 2009 [1985]: *Narratology. Introduction to the Theory of Narrative.* 3rd edition. Toronto: University of Toronto Press.
Bamberg, Michael & Georgakopoulou, Alexandra 2008: Small Stories as a New Perspective in Narrative and Identity Analysis. *Text & Talk*, 28(3), 377–396.
Bauman, Richard 1986: *Story, Performance, Event. Contextual Studies of Oral Narrative.* Cambridge: Cambridge University Press.
Behar, Ruth 1993: *Translated Woman: Crossing Border with Esperanza's Story.* Boston: Beacon Press.
Bergholm, Tapio & Teräs, Kari 1999: Female Dockers in Finland, c. 1900–1975: Gender and Change in the Finnish Waterfront. *International Journal of Maritime History*, XI: 2, 107–120.
Bertaux Daniel 1981 (ed.): *Biography and Society: the Life History Approach in Social Sciences.* Beverly Hills: Sage.
Borland, Katherine 1991: "That's Not What I said" Interpretive Conflict in Oral Narrative Research. In Sherna Berger Cluck & Daphne Patai (eds.). *Women's Words. The Feminist Practice of Oral History*, 63–75. London & New York: Routledge.
Bornat, Joanna 2006: Reminiscence and Oral History. Parallel Universes or Shared Endeavor? In Robert Perks & Alistair Thomson (eds.). *The Oral History Reader. Second edition*, 456–473. London & New York: Routledge.
Boydston, Jeanne 2008: Gender as a Question of Historical Analysis. *Gender & History* 20(3), 558–583.
Brah, Avtar & Phoenix, Ann 2004: Ain't I a Woman? Revisiting Intersectionality. *Journal of International Women Studies* 5(3), 75–86.
Brah, Avtar & Pattynama, 2006: Editorial. Intersectionality. *European Journal of Women's Studies* 13(3), 187–192.
Bringeus, Nils-Arvid 1990: *Människan som kulturvarelse. En introduktion till etnologin.* Stockholm: Carlssons.
Bruner, Edward M. 1986: Introduction. In Victor W. Turner & Edward M. Bruner (eds.). *The Anthropology of Experience*, 3–30. Urbana & Chicago: University of Illinois Press.
Butler, Judith 1990: *Gender Trouble: Feminism And the Subversion of Identity.* London: Routledge.
Butler, Robert N. 1964: The Life Review: An Interpretation of Reminiscence in the Aged. In Robert Kastenbaum (ed.). *New Thoughts on Old Age*, 3–18. New York: Springer.
Cashman, Ray 2006: Critical Nostalgia and Material Culture in Northern Ireland. *Journal of American Folklore* 119, 137–160.
Chase, Susan E. 2005: Narrative Inquiry. Multiple Lenses, Approaches, Voices. In Norman K. Denzin & Yvonna S. Lincoln (eds). *Sage Handbook of Qualitative Research*, 251–679. Thousand Oaks: Sage.
Clifford, James 1986: Introduction. Partial Truths. In James, Clifford & George E. Marcus (eds.): *Writing Culture: the Poetics and Politics of Ethnography, 1–26.* Berkeley: University of California Press.
Clifford, James & Marcus, George E. (eds.) 1986: *Writing Culture: the Poetics and Politics of Ethnography.* Berkeley: University of California Press.

Crapanzano, Vincent 1990: On Dialogue. In Tullio Maranhão (ed.). *The Interpretation of Dialogue*, 269–291. Chicago: The University of Chicago Press.
Davis, F. 1979: *Yearning for Yesterday: A Sosiology of Nostalgia*. London: the Free Press.
Dégh, Linda 1995: *Narratives in Society. A Performer-Centered Study of Narration*. Folklore Fellows Communications 255. Helsinki: Academica Scientiarium Fennica.
Denzin, Norman K. 1989: *Interpretive Biography*. Qualitative Research Methods Series 17. Newbury Park, London & New Delhi: Sage.
Ehn, Billy 1981: *Arbetets flytande gränser. En fabriksstudie*. Borås: Prisma.
— 1992: Livet som intervjukonstruktion. In C. Tigersted & Roos, J.P. & Vilkko Anni (reds.). *Självbiografi, kultur. liv*, 199–220. Stokholm: Symposion.
— 1996: Närhet och avstånd. In Billy Ehn & Orvar Löfgren (eds.). *Vardagslivets etnologi. Reflektioner kring en kulturvetenskap*, 89–182. Stockholm: Natur och Kultur.
Ehn, Billy & Löfgren, Orvar 1982: Kulturanalys: ett etnologiskt perspektiv. Lund: LiberFörlag.
— 2001: *Kulturanalyser*. Malmö: Gleerups.
Eldh, Christer 1996: A Body out of Step in Times in the Shadow of Greenlegs. In Susanne Lundin & Lynn Åkesson (eds.). *Bodytime. On the Interaction of Body, Identity and Society*. Lund Studies in European Ethnology 2, 127–140. Lund: Lund University Press.
Ellis, Bill 2001: *Aliens, Ghosts, and Cults: Legends We Live*. Jackson: University Press of Mississippi.
Erdmans, Mary Patrice 2004: *The Grasinski Girls: The Choices They Had and the Choices They Made*. Athens: Ohio University Press.
Eskola, Katarina 1997: Varhain kuolleiden äitien verhottu muisto: sosiaalista genealogiaa vai/ja yksityisen yleisyyttä? In Katarina Eskola & Eeva Peltonen (toim.). *Aina uusi muisto*. Nykykulttuurin tutkimusyksikön julkaisuja 54, 60–87. Jyväskylä: Jyväskylän yliopisto.
Felski, Rita 1995: *Gender of Modernity*. Cambridge & London: Harvard University Press.
Fine, Gary Alan & Michaela DeSoucey 2005: Joking Cultures: Humor Themes as Social Regulation in Group Life. *Humor* 18, 1–22.
Fingerroos, Outi 2003: Refleksiivinen paikantaminen kulttuurien tutkimuksessa. *Elore* 10(2). URL: http://www.elore.fi/arkisto/2_03/fin203c.html (accessed 11.8.2008.)
Fingerroos, Outi & Haanpää, Riina & Peltonen, Ulla-Maija (eds.) 2006: *Muistitietotutkimus. Metodologisia kysymyksiä*. Tietolipas 214. Helsinki: Suomalaisen Kirjallisuuden Seura.
Finnegan, Ruth 2006: Family Myths, Memories and Interviewing. In Robert Perks & Alistair Thomson (eds.). *The Oral History Reader*. Second edition, 177–183. London & New York: Routledge.
Foucault, Michel 2005 [1975]: *Tarkkailla ja rangaista*. Suom. Eevi Nivanka. Helsinki: Otava.
Frank, Arthur W. 1997 [1995]: *The Wounded Storyteller. Body, Illness and Ethics*. Chicago & London, University of Chicago Press.
Frisch, Michael 1990: *A Shared Authority. Essays on the Craft and Meaning of Oral and Public History*. Albany: State University of New York Press.
Frykman, Jonas 1998: *Ljusnande framtid! Skola, sociala mobilitet och kulturell identitet*. Lund: Historiska media.
Frykman, Jonas & Gilje, Nils 2003: Being There. An Introduction. In Jonas Frykman & Nils Gilje (eds.). *Being there. New Perspectives on Phenomenology and the Analysis of Culture*, 7–51. Lund: Nordic Academic Press.
Gadamer, Hans-Georg 2006 [1975]: *Truth and Method*. 2nd revised edition. Transl. by Joel Weinsheimer & Donald G. Marshall. London & New York: Continuum.

Gergen, Kenneth J. 1991: *The Saturated Self. Dilemmas of Identity in Contemporary Life.* New York: Basic Books.
— 1999: *An Invitation to Social Construction.* London: Sage.
Gergen, Kenneth J. & Gergen, Mary, M. 1991: Toward Reflexive Methodologies. In Frederick Steier (ed.). *Research and Reflexivity,* 76–96. London, Newbury Park & New Delhi: Sage.
Georgekopoulou, Alexandra 2007: *Small Stories, Interaction and Identities.* Amsterdam: John Benjamins Publishing Company.
Giddens, Anthony 1991: *Modernity and Self-Identity.* Standford: Standford University Press.
Giles, Judy 1992: 'Playing Hard to Get': working-class women, sexuality and respectability in Britain, 1918–40. *Women's History* 1(2), 239–255.
Glassie, Henry 1982: *Passing the Time in Ballymenone.* Philadelphia: University of Pennsylvania Press.
— 1998: *History's Dark Places. Distinguished Lecture of the Institute and Society for Advance Study given on October 4, 1996.* Distinguished Lecture Series 8. Bloomington: Indiana University Institute for Advanced Studies.
Gubrium, Jaber F. 1993: *Speaking of Life. Horizons of Meaning for Nursing Home Residents.* New York: Aldine von Gruyter.
Gubrium. Jaber F. & Holstein James A. 2003: Introduction. In James A. Holstein & Jaber F. Gubrium (eds.). *Inside Interviewing. New Lenses, New Concerns,* 4–20. Thousand Oaks & London & New Delhi: Sage.
— 2008: Narrative Ethnography. In Sharlene Nagy & Hesse-Biber &Patricia Leavy (eds.). *Handbook of Emergent Methods,* 241–264. New York: The Guilford Press.
— 2011: Introduction. Establishing a Balance. In James A. Holstein & Jaber F. Gubrium (eds.). *Varieties of Narrative Analysis,* 1–13. Thousand Oaks & London & New Delhi: Sage.
Gullestad, Marianne 1994: Sticking together or standing out? A Scandinavian life story. *Cultural Studies* 8(2), 253–268.
Haanpää, Riina 2005: Velisurmasta suvun muistoksi. Elore 12(1). URL: http://www.elore.fi/arkisto/1_05/haa1_05.pdf (accessed 11.9.2014.)
— 8: *Rikosten jäljet: etsivän työtä yhteisön, suvun ja perheen muistissa.* Turun yliopiston tutkimuksia C270. Turku: Turun yliopisto.
Haapala, Pertti 1986: *Tehtaan valossa. Teollistuminen ja työväestön muodostuminen Tampereella 1820–1920.* Historiallisia tutkimuksia 133. Helsinki: Suomen Historiallinen Seura.
— 1995: *Kun yhteiskunta hajosi. Suomi 1914–1920.* Helsinki: Edita.
Haavio-Mannila, Elina 1968: *Suomalainen nainen ja mies.* Helsinki: WSOY.
Hahne, Reino 1994: *Inhan ruukkiyhdyskunta 1833–1964.* Ähtäri: Reino Hahne.
Hall, Stuart 2002: *Identiteetti.* 2. painos. Suom. ja toim. Mikko Lehtonen ja Juha Herkman. Vastapaino: Tampere.
Halme, Anna 2006: Maaseudun piika suomalaisessa kaunokirjallisuudessa. In Marjatta Rahikainen & Kirsi Vainio-Korhonen (toim.). *Työteliäs ja uskollinen. Naiset piikoina ja palvelijoina keskiajalta nykyaikaan.* Suomalaisen Kirjallisuuden Seuran Toimituksia 1092, 176–223. Helsinki: Suomalaisen Kirjallisuuden Seura.
Heikkinen, Kaija 2007: Naiset, miehet ja Sukupuoli. In Pia Olsson & Terhi Willman (toim.) *Sukupuolen kohtaaminen etnologiassa.* Helsinki: Ethnos ry, 26–40.
— 2012: *Yksin vai yhdessä. Rintamanaisen monta sotaa.* Kultaneito X. Joensuu: Suomen Kansantietouden Tutkijain Seura.
Heikkinen, Sakari 1997: Palkollisesta proletaariin: työn ja luokan suomalaista käsitehistoriaa. In Raimo Parikka (toim.). *Työväestö ja kansakunta.* Väki Voimakas 10, 68–98. Tampere: Työväen historian ja perinteen tutkimuksen seura.
Heimo, Anne 2010: *Kapina Sammatissa. Vuoden 1918 paikalliset tulkinnat osana historian yhteiskunnallisen rakentamisen prosessia.* Suomalaisen Kirjallisuuden Seuran Toimituksia 1275. Helsinki: Suomalaisen Kirjallisuuden Seura.

Helén, Ilpo 1997: *Äidin elämän politiikka. Naissukupuolisuus, valta ja itsesuhde Suomessa 1880-luvulta 1960-luvulle.* Gaudeamus: Tampere.

Helén, Ilpo & Jauho, Mikko 2003: Terveyskansalaisuus ja elämänpolitiikka. In Ilpo Helén & Mikko Jauho (toim.). *Kansalaisuus ja kansanterveys,* 13–32. Helsinki: Gaudeamus.

Helsti, Hilkka 2000: *Kotisynnytysten aikaan. Etnologinen tutkimus äitiyden ja äitiysvalistuksen konflikteista.* Suomalaisen Kirjallisuuden Seuran Toimituksia 785. Helsinki: Suomalaisen Kirjallisuuden Seura.

Hirdman, Yvonne 1989: Genussystemet – teoretiska reflektioner kring kvinnors sociala underordning. Rapport / Maktutredningen 23. Uppsala: Maktutredningen.

— 1990: The gender system: theoretical reflections on the social subordination of women. *Report – Study of Power and Democracy in Sweden* 40. Uppsala: Maktutredningen.

Hjerppe, Reino et al. 1976: *Suomen teollisuus ja teollinen käsityö 1900–1965.* Kasvututkimuksia VII. Helsinki: Suomen pankki.

Holmila, Antero 2008: Jälleenrakennuksen narratiivit ja niiden muotoutuminen Suomen lehdistössä 1944–1945. *Elore* 15(2). URL: http://www.elore.fi/arkisto/2_08/hol2_08.pdf (accessed 12.12.2008.)

Honko, Lauri 1992: Dialogisesta kenttämetodista. *Sananjalka* 34.

Hoppu, Petri 2003: Tanssintutkimus tienhaarassa. In Helena Saarikoski (toim.). *Tanssi tanssi. Kulttuureja, tulkintoja.* Tietolipas 186, 19–51. Helsinki: Suomalaisen Kirjallisuuden Seura.

Hutcheon, Linda 1994: *Irony's Edge. The Theory and Politics of Irony.* Lnodn & New York: Routledge.

Hymes, Dell 1973: The Contribution of Folklore to Sociolinguistic Research. In Américo Paredes & Richard Bauman (eds.). *Toward New Perspective in Folklore,* 42–50. Austin: University of Texas.

— 1975: Breakthrough into performance. In Dan Ben-Amos & Kenneth Goldstein (eds). *Folklore: Performance and Communication.* Hague: Mouton, 11–74.

Hynninen, Anna 2004: Toisto ja variaatio omaelämäkerrallisessa kerronnassa. *Elore* 11(2) URL: http://www.elore.fi/arkisto/2_04/hyn204.html (accessed 3.5.2007.)

— 2011: Elämää kerroksittain. Arkistokirjoittamisen kontekstualisointi. In Sami Lakomäki & Pauliina Latvala & Kirsi Laurén (toim.). *Tekstien rajoilla. Monitieteisiä näkökulmia kirjoitettuihin aineistoihin.* Suomalaisen Kirjallisuuden Seuran Toimituksia 1314, 259–295. Helsinki: Suomalaisen Kirjallisuuden Seura.

Hyttinen, Elsi & Melkas, Kukku 2009: "Me olemme teidän luomianne olentoja" – prostituoidun hahmo kirjallisena kiistakuvana. In Kati Launis & Marko Tikka (toim.). *Työväki ja kokemus.* Väki voimakas 22, 122–137. Tampere: Työväen historian ja perinteen tutkimuksen seura.

Hytönen, Kirsi-Maria 2012a: Suomalaisen sotilaan vaimo: naisroolin rakentuminen avioparin jatkosodan aikaisessa kirjeenvaihdossa. In Jarkko Keskinen, Suvianna Seppälä, Kari Teräs (toim.).
Häkäpöntöistä nurkkatansseihin: arjen ilmiöitä sota-aikana, 26–57. Turku: Turun yliopisto.

— 2012b: Kannettu kaksoistaakka: äitiys työssäkäyvien naisten muistelukerronnassa 1940–1950 -luvuilta. In Pasi Saarimäki, Kirsi-Maria Hytönen & Heli Niskanen (toim.). *Lapsi matkalla maailmaan: historiallisia ja kulttuurisia näkökulmia syntymään.* Historiallinen arkisto 135, 321–352. Helsinki: Suomalaisen Kirjallisuuden Seura.

— 2013: Hardworking Women: Nostalgia and Women's Memories of Paid Work in Finland in the 1940s. *Oral History Journal* 87: Autumn, 87–99.

Hytönen, Kirsi-Maria & Koskinen-Koivisto, Eerika 2009: Hikeä, naurua ja nokea – naisten kokemuksia tehdastyöstä toisen maailmansodan aikana. In Kati Launis &

Marko Tikka (toim.). *Työväki ja kokemus.* Väki voimakas 22, 138–160. Tampere: Työväen historian ja perinteen tutkimuksen seura.

Hyvärinen, Matti 1994: *Viimeiset taistot.* Tampere: Vastapaino.

— 2008: "Life as Narrative" Revisited. *Partial Answers: Journal of the History of Ideas* 6(2), 261–277.

Hyvärinen, Matti & Peltonen, Eeva & Vilkko, Anni 1998: Johdanto. In Matti Hyvärinen, Eeva Peltonen & Anni Vilkko (eds.). *Liikkuvat erot – sukupuoli elämäkertatutkimuksessa,* 7–25. Tampere: Vastapaino.

Hyvärinen, Matti & Löyttyniemi, Varpu 2005: Kerronnallinen haastattelu. – Johanna Ruusuvuori & Liisa Tiittula (toim.). *Haastattelu: tutkimus, tilanteet ja vuorovaikutus,* 189–222. Tampere. Vastapaino.

Häggman, Kai 1994: *Perheen vuosisata. Perheen ihanne ja sivistyneistön elämäntapa Suomessa 1800-luvun Suomessa.* Historiallisia tutkimuksia 179. Helsinki: Suomen Historiallinen Seura.

— 2006: *Metsän tasavalta. Suomalainen metsäteollisuus politiikan ja markkinoiden ristiaallokossa 1920–1939.* Metsäteollisuudenmaa 2. Suomalaisen Kirjallisuuden Seuran Toimituksia 1055:2. Helsinki: Suomalaisen Kirjallisuuden Seura.

Häkkinen, Antti 1995: *Rahasta – vaan ei rakkaudesta: prostituutio Helsingissä 1867–1939.* Helsinki: Otava.

— 2002: Pula ja köyhyys Iisalmen maalaiskunnassa ja Alavudella 1930-luvulla. In Blomberg, Helena, Matti Hannikainen & Pauli Kettunen (toim.). *Lama: näkökulmia 1990-luvun talouskriisiin ja sen historiallisiin konteksteihin,* 129–168. Turku: Kirja-Aurora.

Hänninen, Vilma 1999: *Sisäinen tarina, elämä ja muutos.* Acta Universitatis Tamperensis 696. Tampere: Tampereen yliopisto.

Ihamäki, Kalevi 2007: *Aito ähtäriläinen. Ähtärin Osuuspankki 100 vuotta.* Ähtäri: Ähtärin Osuuspankki.

Inhan metallityöväen ammattiosasto 51 1,00 vuotta. 2009. Ähtäri: Inhan metallityöväenliitto.

Jaago, Tiiu 2002: Family narrators as reverbarator of history. In Tiiu Jaago (ed.). *Lives, histories and indentities* vol. 3, 405–426. Tarto: University of Tartu.

Johansson, Anna 2005: *Narrativ teori och metod: med livsberättelsen i focus.* Lund: Studenlitteratur.

Jordanova, Ludmilla 2002: Gender. In Peter Burke (ed.). *History and Historians in the Twentieth Century,* 120–140. Oxford: Oxford University Press.

Järvinen, Irma-Riitta 1993: Lapsuuden rajalla. In Ulla Piela (toim.). *Aikanaisia. Kirjoituksia naisten omaelämäkerroista,* 111–124.

Kaarninen, Mervi 1995: *Nykyajan tytöt. Koulutus, luokka ja sukupuoli 1920- ja 1930-luvun Suomessa.* Bibliotheca Historica 5. Helsinki: Suomen Historiallinen Seura.

Kaivola-Bregenhøj, Annikki 1988: *Kertomus ja kerronta.* Suomalaisen Kirjallisuuden Seuran Toimituksia 480. Helsinki: Suomalaisen Kirjallisuuden Seura.

— 1996: *Narrative and Narration. Variation in Juho Oksanen's Storytelling.* Folklore Fellows Communications 262. Helsinki: Academia Scientiarium Fennica.

— 1998: Pilako vai eroottinen viesti? Seksuaaliarvoitus on testi kuulijalle. In Jyrki Pöysä & Anna-Leena Siikala (toim.). *Amor, genus & familia. Kirjoituksia kansanperinteestä,* 193–215. Tietolipas 158. Helsinki: Suomalaisen Kirjallisuuden Seura.

Kaivola-Bregenhøj, Annikki & Klein, Barbro & Palmenfelt, Ulf (eds.) 2006: *Narrating, Doing, Experiencing. Nordic Folkloristic Perspectives.* Studia Fennica Folkloristica 16. Helsinki: Finnish Literature Society.

Karonen, Petri 2002: Johdanto: Moninainen patriarkaalisuus. Normien ja käytäntöjen solmukohdat. In Piia Einonen & Petri Karonen (toim.). *Arjen valta. Suomalaisen yhteiskunnan patriarkaalisesta järjestyksestä myöhäiskeskiajalta teollistumisen kynnykselle (v.1450–1860),* 10–23. Historiallinen arkisto 116. Helsinki: Suomalaisen Kirjallisuuden Seura.

References

— 2004: *Patruunat ja poliitikot. Yritysjohtajat taloudellisina ja poliittisina toimijoina Suomessa 1600–1920*. Historiallisia tutkimuksia 217. Helsinki: Suomalaisen Kirjallisuuden Seura.

Kauppila, Juha 1996: Koulutus elämänkulun rakentajana. In Ari Antikainen & Hannu Huotelin (toim.). *Oppiminen ja elämänhistoria*. Aikuiskasvatuksen vuosikirja 37, 45–108. Helsinki: Kansanvalistusseura & Aikuiskasvatuksen Tutkimusseura.

Kemppainen, Ilona 2006a: *Isänmaan uhrit. Sankarikuolema Suomessa toisen maailman sodan aikana*. Bibliotheca historica 102. Helsinki: Suomalaisen Kirjallisuuden Seura.

— 2006b: Isät, äidit ja isänmaan toivot – käsityksiä lapsista ja vanhemmista sotavuosien Suomessa. *Historiallinen Aikakauskirja* 104(2), 163–173.

— 2010: Arjen sankaruus. Naisten, miesten, suomalaisten näkökulmia. In Ilona Kemppainen & Ulla-Maija Peltonen (toim.). *Kirjoituksia sankaruudesta*. Suomalaisen Kirjallisuuden Seuran Toimituksia 1283,193–223. Helsinki: Suomalaisen Kirjallisuuden Seura.

Kettunen, Pauli 1994: *Suojelu, suoritus, subjekti. Työsuojelu teollistuvan Suomen yhteiskunnallisissa ajattelu- ja toimintatavoissa*. Historiallisia tutkimuksia 189. Helsinki: Suomen Historiallinen Seura.

— 1997. *Työjärjestys. Tutkielmia työn ja tiedon poliittisesta historiasta*. Helsinki: Tutkijaliitto.

— 2001. *Kansallinen työ: suomalaisen suorituskyvyn vaalimisesta*. Helsinki: Yliopistopaino.

Kilborne, Benjamin 1992: Fields of Shame: Anthropologists Abroad. *Ethos* 20(2), 230–253.

Kinnunen, Eeva-Liisa 1988: Kertovatko naiset tuhmia juttuja? Naisten seksuaalisen työpaikkahuumorin tarkastelua. In Irma-Riitta Järvinen, Jyrki Pöysä & Sinikka Vakimo (toim.). *Monikasvoinen folklore*. Helsingin yliopiston kansanrunoustieteen laitoksen toimite 8, 119–135. Helsinki: Helsingin yliopisto.

— 1993: Läskiä kantapäissä. Huumori naisten omaelämäkerroissa. In Ulla Piela (toim). *Aikanaisia. Kirjoituksia naisten omaelämäkerroista*. Helsinki: Suomalaisen Kirjallisuuden Seura, 188–212.

— 1996: Kvinnor i humorvetenskaplig samspill. In Ulf Palmenfelt (red.). *Humor och kultur*, 103–115. Åbo: NIF Publications 34.

— 1998: Womens humour: conceptions and examples. In Satu Apo & Aili Nenola & Laura Stark-Arola (eds.). *Gender and Folklore. Perspectives on Finnish and Karelian Culture*. Studia Fennica Folkloristica 4. Helsinki: Finnish Literature Society, 403–427.

Kirshenblatt-Gimblett, Barbara 1989: Objects of Memory: Material Culture as Life Review. In Elliot Oring (ed.). *Folk Groups and Folklore Genres: A Reader*. Logan: Utah State University Press, 329–338.

Kirves, Jenni & Näre, Sari 2008: Nuorten talkoot: isänmaallinen työvelvollisuus. In *Uhrattu nuoruus. Sodassa koettua 2*. Porvoo: Weilin+Göös, 64–87.

Klein, Barbro 2006: Introduction. Telling, Doing, Experiencing. Nordic Folkloristic Perspectives. In Annikki Kaivola-Bregenhøj & Barbro Klein & Ulf Palmenfelt: *Narrating, Doing, Experiencing. Nordic Folkloristic Perspectives*, 6–28.

Knuuttila, Seppo 1984: Mitä sivakkalaiset itsestään kertovat. In Pertti Rannikko et al. *Yhteiskunta kylässä. Tutkimuksia Sivakasta ja Rasinmäestä*, 131–155, Joensuu: Joensuun yliopisto.

— 1989: Paluu nykyisyyteen. In Teppo Korhonen & Matti Räsänen (eds.). Kansa kuvastimessa. Etnisyys ja identiteetti, 92–102. Helsinki: Suomalaisen Kirjallisuuden Seura.

— 1992: *Kansanhuumorin mieli. Kaskut maailmankuvan aineksena*. Suomalaisen Kirjallisuuden Seuran Toimituksia 554. Helsinki: Suomalaisen Kirjallisuuden Seura.

— 1994: *Tyhmän kansan teoria. Näkökulmia menneestä tulevaan*. Tietolipas 129. Helsinki: Suomalaisen Kirjallisuuden Seura.

Koivisto, Johan 1963: *Suomen Metallityöväen Liitto 1899–1930*. Helsinki: Suomen Metallityöväen Liitto.
Koivunen, Anu & Liljeström, Marianne 1996: Paikantuminen. In Anu Koivunen & Marianne Liljeström (eds.) *Avainsanat. 10 askelta feministiseen tutkimukseen*, 271–292. Tampere: Vastapaino.
Koivuniemi, Jussi 2000: *Tehtaan pillin tahdissa. Nokian tehdasyhteiskunnan sosiaalinen järjestys 1870–1939*. Bibliotheca historica 64, Helsinki: Suomalaisen Kirjallisuuden Seura.
Komulainen, Katri 1998: *Kotihiiriä ja ihmisiä. Retorinen minä naisten koulutusta koskevissa elämänkertomuksissa*. Joensuu: Joensuun yliopiston yhteiskuntatieteellisiä julkaisuja N:o 35.
— 2001: Kansallisuus, perhe ja sukupuoli sotaa koskevissa kollektiivisissa kertomuksissa. *Naistutkimus* 14(2), 23–37.
Korkiakangas, Pirjo 1996: *Muistoista rakentuva lapsuus. Agraarinen perintö lapsuuden työnteon ja leikkien muistelussa*. Kansatieteellinen arkisto 42. Helsinki: Suomen muinaismuistoyhdistys.
— 2002: Muistelusta voimavaroja vanhuuteen. In Eino Heikkinen & Marjatta Marin (toim.). *Vanhuuden voimavarat*, 173–204. Helsinki: Tammi.
— 2004. Memories and the Identity of Place. Strategies of Town Residents in Jyväskylä. In Anna-Maria Åström & Pirjo Korkiakangas & Pia Olsson (eds.). *Memories of my Town. The Town Dwellers and Their Places in Three Finnish Towns*, 150–171. Helsinki: Finnish Literature Society.
Kortelainen, Kaisu 2006: Tehdasyhteisöstä kirjoitettu kartta. In Seppo Knuuttila & Pekka Laaksonen & Ulla Piela (toim.). *Paikka. Eletty, kuviteltu, kerrottu*. Kalevalaseuran vuosikirja 85, 291–307. Helsinki: Finnish Literature Society.
— 2008: *Penttilän sahayhteisö ja työläisyys. Muistitietotutkimus*. Suomalaisen Kirjallisuuden Seuran Toimituksia 1178. Helsinki: Suomalaisen Kirjallisuuden Seura.
Kortteinen, Matti 1992: *Kunnian kenttä. Suomalainen palkkatyö kulttuurisen muotona*. Helsinki: Hanki ja jää.
Koski, Kaarina & Ukkonen, Taina 2007: Folkloristiikka ja kertovat tekstit. Elore 14(1). URL: http://www.elore.fi/arkisto/1_07/kou1_07.pdf (accessed 1.6.2007.)
Koski, Leena 2011: Sivistystyön ihmiskäsitys: villi-ihmisestä aikuiseksi yksilöksi. In Pirkko Leino-Kaukiainen & Anja Heikkinen (toim.). *Valistus ja koulunpenkki. Kasvatus ja koulutus Suomessa 1860-luvulta 1960-luvulle*, 159–183. Helsinki: Suomalaisen Kirjallisuuden Seura.
Koskinen, Tarmo 1987: *Tehdasyhteisö: tutkimus tehtaan ja kylän kietoutumisesta tehdasyhteisöksi, kudelman säilymisestä ja purkautumisesta*. Vaasa: Vaasan korkeakoulun julkaisuja 123.
— 1993: *Elämää yhteisössä: muistijälkiä, ihmisääniä ja joukkosydämen lyöntejä tehdasyhteisön rakentumisen ja rapautumisen kausilta*. Vaasa: Vaasan yliopisto, 1993.
Koskinen-Koivisto, Eerika 2009: Healthy, Skilled, Disciplined – Modernizing Changes and the Sense of Self in the Embodied Experiences of a Female Factory Worker. *Ethnologia Fennica* 36, 72–83.
— 2011: Disappearing Landscapes. Embodied Experience and Metaphoric Space in the Life story of a Female Factory Worker. *Ethnologia Scandinavica* 41, 25–39.
Kreiswirth, Martin 1992: Trusting the Tale: The Narrativist Turn in the Human Sciences. *New Literary History* 23, 629–657.
Kurki, Tuulikki 2002: *Heikki Meriläinen ja keskusteluja kansanperinteestä*. Suomalaisen Kirjallisuuden Seuran Toimituksia 880. Helsinki: Suomalaisen Kirjallisuuden Seura.
Kurkowska-Budzan, Marta & Zamorski, Krzysztof (eds.) 2009: *Oral History. The Challenges of Dialogue*. Amsterdam & Philadelphia: John Benjamin's Publishing Company.

Laine, Juha 2005: Tanssiminen kansan huvina ja herrojen huolena – tanssilavakulttuurin synty Suomessa. In Henna Mikkola (toim.). *Tanssilavan luona. Huvielämää Jyväskylän Ainolassa*, 30–42. Jyväskylä: Minerva.

Laine, Leena & Markkola, Pirjo (toim.)1989: *Tuntematon työläisnainen*. Tampere: Vastapaino.

Laine, Timo 2007: Miten kokemusta voidaan tutkia? Fenomenologinen näkökulma. In Juha Aaltola & Raine Valli (toim.) *Ikkunoita tutkimusmetodeihin II. Näkökulmia aloittelevalle tutkijalle tutkimuksen teoreettisiin näkökohtiin ja analyysimenetelmiin*, 29–45. Jyväskylä: PS-kustannus.

Lappalainen, Niina 2008: Pilaa vai peliä? Miesten ja naisten välinen seksuaalihuumori työyhteisössä. In Tarja Tolonen (toim.). *Yhteiskuntaluokka ja sukupuoli, 58–79*. Nuorisotutkimusverkosto/ Nuorisotutkimusseura julkaisuja 83. Vastapaino: Tampere.

— 2010: Työn sankaruus. Sankaruus tehtaalaisyhteisön suullisessa perinteessä. In Ilona Kemppainen & Ulla-Maija Peltonen (toim.). *Kirjoituksia sankaruudesta*. Suomalaisen Kirjallisuuden Seuran Toimituksia 1283, 224–262. Helsinki: Suomalaisen Kirjallisuuden Seura.

Latvala, Pauliina 2005: *Katse menneisyyteen. Folkloristinen tutkimus suvun muistitiedosta*. Suomalaisen Kirjallisuuden Seuran Toimituksia 1024. Helsinki: Suomalaisen Kirjallisuuden Seura.

Lawless, Elaine 1992: "I was afraid someone like you... an outsider... would misunderstand" Negotiating interpretive differences between ethnographers and subjects. *Journal of American Folklore* 105, 302–314.

Lehtipuro, Outi 1980: On Sampling Folklore Competence. In Osmo Ikola (ed.). *Congressus Quintus Internationalis Fenno-Ugristarum*, Turku 21–27 VII, 1980. Turku: Suomen kielen seura.

Leino-Kaukiainen, Pirkko & Heikkinen, Anja 2011a: Johdanto. In Pirkko Leino-Kaukiainen & Anja Heikkinen (toim.). *Valistus ja koulunpenkki. Kasvatus ja koulutus Suomessa 1860-luvulta 1960-luvulle*, 11–15. Helsinki: Suomalaisen Kirjallisuuden Seura.

— 2011b: Yhteiskunta ja koulutus. In Pirkko Leino-Kaukiainen & Anja Heikkinen (toim.). *Valistus ja koulunpenkki. Kasvatus ja koulutus Suomessa 1860-luvulta 1960-luvulle*, 16–33. Helsinki: Suomalaisen Kirjallisuuden Seura.

Leminen, Pia 1996: Kohtaamisia ja väistöjä. Rajankäyntiä 1930-luvun tehdasyhteisössä. In Marjatta Rahikainen (ed.). *Matkoja moderniin. Lähikuvia suomalaisten elämästä*, 167–186.

Liljeström, Marianne 1996: Sukupuolijärjestelmä. In Anu Koivunen & Marianne Liljeström (toim.). *Avainsanat. 10 askelta feministiseen tutkimukseen*, 111–138. Tampere: Vastapaino.

Linde, Charlotte 1993: *Life Stories. The Creation of Coherence*. New York, Oxford: Oxford University Press.

Lloyd, Timothy C. & Mullen Patrick B. 1990: *Lake Erie Fishermen: Work, Identity, and Tradition*. Illinois: University of Illinois Press.

Lowenthal, David 1985: *The Past Is a Foreign Country*. Cambridge: Cambridge University Press.

Lyotard, Jean-François 1984: *The Postmodern Condition: A Report on Knowledge*. Trans. by Geoff Bennington and Brian Massumi. Minneapolis: University of Minnesota Press.

Lähteenmäki, Maria 1994: Ansioäidit arvossaan. Naimisissa olevat naiset ja palkkatyö 1940-luvun puolivälissä. Teoksessa Parikka, Raimo (toim.). *Työ ja työttömyys. Väki Voimakas 7*, 66–83. Tampere: Työväen historian ja perinteen tutkimuksen seura.

— 1995: *Mahdollisuuksien aika. Työläisnaiset ja yhteiskunnan muutos 1910–30-luvun Suomessa*. Bibliotheca Historica 2. Helsinki: Suomen Historiallinen Seura.

— 2000: *Vuosisadan naisliike. Naiset ja sosialidemokratia 1900-luvun Suomessa*. Helsinki: Sosialidemokraattiset Naiset.

Löfgren, Orvar 1987: Deconstructing Swedishness: culture and class in modern Sweden. In Anthony Jackson (ed.). *Anthropology at Home*, 74–93. London & New York: Tavistock.

Löyttyniemi, Varpu 2004: *Kerrottu identiteetti, neuvoteltu sukupuoli. Auscultatio medici*. SoPhi 90. Jyväskylä: Minerva.

Magnússon, Sigurður Gylfi 2011: The Life of a Working-Class Woman: selective modernization and microhistory in early 20th-century Iceland. *Scandinavian Journal of History* 36(2), 186–205.

Mahlamäki, Tiina 2005: *Naisia kansalaisuuden kynnyksellä. Eeva Joenpellon Lohjasarjan tulkinta*. Suomalaisen Kirjallisuuden Seuran Toimituksia 1030. Helsinki: Suomalaisen Kirjallisuuden Seura.

Marander-Eklund, Lena 2002: Narrative style. How to dramatize a story? *Arv* 2002, 113–123.

— 2011: Livet som hemmafru. In Lena Marander-Eklund & Ann-Catrin Östman (red.). *Biografiska betydelser. Norm och erfarenhet i levnadsberättelser*, 133–156. Möklinta: Gidlunds förlag.

Maranhão, Tullio 1986: *Therapeutic Discourse and Socratic Dialogue*. Madison: University of Wisconsin Press.

Marcus, George E. & Fischer, Michael M.J. 1986: *Anthropology as Cultural Critique: An Experimental Moment in the Human Sciences*. Chicago & London: The University of Chicago Press.

Markkola, Pirjo 1990: Women in Rural Society in the 19th and 20th century. In Merja Manninen & Päivi Setälä (eds.). *The Lady with the Bow: the Story of Finnish Women*, 17–29. Otava: Helsinki.

— 1994: *Työläiskodin synty. Tamperelaiset työläisperheet ja yhteiskunnallinen kysymys 1870-luvulta 1910-luvulle*. Historiallisia Tutkimuksia 187. Helsinki: Suomen Historiallinen Seura.

— 2002a: Vahva nainen ja kansallinen historia. In Tuula Gordon, Katri Komulainen & Kirsti Lempiäinen (toim.). *Suomineitonen hei! Kansallisuuden sukupuoli*, 75–90. Tampere: Vastapaino.

— 2002b: *Synti ja siveys. Naiset, uskonto ja sosiaalinen työ Suomessa 1860–1920*. Suomalaisen Kirjallisuuden Seuran Toimituksia 888. Helsinki: Suomalaisen Kirjallisuuden Seura.

Marttila, Juuso 2010: Beyond the Family and the Household: Occupational Family Networks. *Journal of Family History* 35(2), 128–146.

Massey, Doreen 2005: *For Space*. London: Sage.

McAdams, Dan P. 1993: *The Stories We Live by: Personal Myths and the Making of the Self*. New York: Morrow.

McCarl, 1997: Occupational Folklife/Folklore. In Thomas A. Green (ed.). *Folklore: an encyclopedia of beliefs, customs, tales, music, and art*. Vol. 2, I-Z. Santa Barbara: ABC-CLIO.

McIntyre, Alasdair 1985: *After Virtue*. Notre Dame: University of Notre Dame Press.

Melkas, Kukku 2005: Toisen palveluksessa. Palvelijat porvarillisen perheen ja työväenluokan välissä. In Olli Löytty (toim.). *Rajanylityksiä. Tutkimusreittejä toiseuden tuolle puolen*, 162–180. Helsinki: Gaudeamus.

Meriläinen-Hyvärinen, Anneli 2010: "Sanopa minulle, onko meijän hyvä olla täällä?" Paikkakokemukset kolmen talvivaaralaisen elämässä. *Elore* 17(1). URL: http://www.elore.fi/arkisto/1_10/art_merilainen_1_10.pdf (accessed 11.9.2010.)

Mikkola, Kati 2009: *Tulevaisuutta vastaan. Uutuuksien vastustus, kansantiedon keruu ja kansakunnan rakentaminen*. Suomalaisen Kirjallisuuden Seuran toimituksia 1251. Helsinki: Finnish Literature Society.

Modell, Judith & Hinshaw, John 1996: Male Work and Mill Work. Memory and Gender in Homestead, Pennsylvania. In Selma Leydesdorff & Luisa Passerini & Paul Thompson (eds.) *Gender and Memory*. International Yearbook of Oral History and Life Stories vol. IV, 133–149. Oxford: Oxford University Press.

Moore, Henrietta 1993: The Differences within and the Differences in-between. In Teresa del Valle (eds.) *Gendered Anthropology*, 193–204. London: Taylor & Francis.

Mullen, Patrick B. 1992: *Listening to Old Voices. Folklore, Life Stories and The Elderly*. Urbana & Chicago: University of Illinois Press.

— 2008: *The Man Who Adores the Negro. Race and American Folklore*. Urbana & Chicago: University of Illinois Press.

Myerhoff, Barbara 1978: *Number Our Days*. New York: Simon and Schuster.

Määttänen, Kirsi 1998: Sense of Self and Narrated mothers in Women's Autobiographies. In Satu Apo & Aili Nenola & Laura Stark-Arola (eds.). *Gender and Folklore. Perspectives on Finnish and Karelian Culture*. Studia Fennica Folkloristica 4. Helsinki: Finnish Literature Society, 217–331.

Nenola, Aili 1986: *Miessydäminen nainen: naisnäkökulmia kulttuuriin*. Tietolipas 102. Helsinki: Suomalaisen Kirjallisuuden Seura.

— 1990: Sukupuoli, kulttuuri ja perinne. In Aili Nenola & Senni Timonen (toim.). *Louhen sanat. Kirjoituksen kansanperinteen naisista*. Suomalaisen Kirjallisuuden Seuran Toimituksia 520, 11–23. Helsinki: Suomalaisen Kirjallisuuden Seura.

Nenola, Aili & Timonen, Senni (toim.) 1990: *Louhen sanat. Kirjoituksen kansanperinteen naisista*. Suomalaisen Kirjallisuuden Seuran Toimituksia 520. Helsinki: Suomalaisen Kirjallisuuden Seura.

Nevala, Seija-Leena 2003: Pikkulotat ja suojeluskuntapojat kansakuntaa rakentamassa. In *Nuoruuden vuosisata. Suomalaisen nuorison historiaa*. Suomalaisen Kirjallisuuden Seuran Toimituksia 909, 345–353. Helsinki: Suomalaisen Kirjallisuuden Seura.

— 2007: *Lottatytöt ja sotilaspojat*. Helsinki: Gummerus.

Nieminen, Juha 1995: *Nuorisossa tulevaisuus. Suomalaisen nuorisotyön historia*. Helsinki: Nuorisotutkimusseura & Lasten Keskus.

Norrena, Leevi 1993: *Talonpoika, pohjalainen – ja punainen: tutkimus Etelä-Pohjanmaan Järviseudun työväenliikkeestä vuoteen 1939*. Historiallisia tutkimuksia 178. Helsinki: Suomen historiallinen seura.

Nurmi, Virpi 1989: *Lasinvalmistajat ja lasinvalmistus Suomessa 1900-luvun alkupuolella*. Kansatieteellinen arkisto 36. Helsinki: Suomen Muinaismuistoyhdistys.

Nätkin, Ritva 1993: Äitiys ja sukupuolten väliset suhteet. In Ulla Piela (toim.). *Aikanaisia. Kirjoituksia naisten omaelämäkerroista*, 165–187.

— 1997. *Kamppailu suomalaisesta äitiydestä. Maternalismi, väestöpolitiikka ja naisten kertomukset*. Helsinki: Gaudeamus.

Ojanen, Karoliina 2008: Kenttäkokemuksesta tiedoksi. – *Elore* 15(1). URL: http://www.elore.fi/arkisto/1_08/oja1_08.pdf (11.9.2014.)

— 2011: *Tyttöjen toinen koti. Etnografinen tutkimus tyttökulttuurista ratsastustalleilla*. Suomalaisen Kirjallisuuden Seuran Toimituksia 1319. Helsinki: Suomalaisen Kirjallisuuden Seura.

Ollila, Anne 1993: *Suomen kotien päivä valkenee... Marttajärjestö suomalaisessa yhteiskunnassa vuoteen 1939*. Historiallisia tutkimuksia 173. Helsinki: Suomen Historiallinen Seura.

— 1998: *Jalo velvollisuus. Virkanaisena 1800-luvun lopun Suomessa*. Suomalaisen Kirjallisuuden Seuran Toimituksia 711. Helsinki: Suomalaisen Kirjallisuuden Seura.

Olney, James: 1980: *Autobiography. Essays Theoretical and Methodological*. Princeton. Princeton University Press.

Olsson, Pia 1999: *Eteen vapahan valkean Suomen Kansatieteellinen tutkimus lottatoiminnasta paikallisella tasolla vuoteen 1939*. Kansatieteellinen arkisto 45. Helsinki: Suomen muinaismuistoyhdistys.

— 2005: *Myytti ja kokemus. Lotta Svärd sodassa.* Helsinki: Otava.
— 2007: Vain lehtohuorat viheltävät. Siveys tyttöjen kasvatuksessa. In Pia Olsson & Terhi Willman (eds.). *Sukupuolen kohtaaminen etnologiassa*, 216–228. Helsinki. Ethnos ry.

Oring, Elliot 1987: Generating lives: The Construction of Autobiography. *Journal of Folklore Research* 24(3), 241–262.
— 2003: *Engaging Humor.* Urbana & Chicago: University of Illinois Press.

Paaskoski, Leena 2008: *Herrana metsässä. Kansatieteellinen tutkimus metsänhoitajuudesta.* Suomalaisen Kirjallisuuden Seuran Toimituksia 1170. Helsinki: Suomalaisen Kirjallisuuden Seura.

Palmenfelt, Ulf 2006a: The Dark Shadow of the Un-mentioned Event. Collapsing Taleworlds and Narrative Reparation. In Annikki Kaivola-Bregenhøj & Barbro Klein & Ulf Palmenfelt: *Narrating, Doing, Experiencing. Nordic Folkloristic Perspectives*, 101–116.
— 2006b: Från tre världar till många. Tankar om en berättandets etnografi. *Kulturella Perspektiv* 15(3), 4–13.
— 2007: Expanding Worlds: into the Ethnography of Narrating. *Folklore* 37, 7–18.

Passerini, Luisa 1988: *Fascism in Popular Memory. The Cultural Expekrience of the Turin Working Class.* Transl. Robert Lumley & Jude Bloomfield. Cambridge, New York: Cambridge University Press.
— 1989: Women's Personal narratives. Myths, Experiences, and Emotions. In Personal Narratives Group (ed.). *Interpreting Women's Lives. Feminist Theory and Personal Narratives*, 189–197. Bloomington & Indianapolis: Indiana University Press.

Patai, Daphne 1987: Ethical Problems of Personal Narratives, or Who Should Eat the Last Piece of Cake? *International Journal of Oral History* 8, 5–27.

Paunonen, Heikki 2005: *Tsennaaks stadia, bonjaats slangii. Stadin slangin suursanakirja.* Helsinki. Sanoma Pro.

Peacock, James L. & Holland, Dorothy C. 1993: The Narrated Self. Life Stories in Process. *Ethos* 21(4), 367–383.

Peltonen, Eeva 1993: Miten kotirintama kesti – miten siitä kerrotaan. In Riikka Raitis & Elina Haavio-Mannila (toim.). *Naisten aseet. Suomalaisena naisena talvi- ja jatkosodassa*, 26–70. Helsinki: WSOY.
— 1997: Muistojen sodat – muistien sodat. In Katariina Eskola & Eeva Peltonen (eds.). *Aina uusi muisto. Kirjoituksia menneen elämisestä meissä.* Nykykulttuurin tutkimusyksikön julkaisuja 54, 88–142. Jyväskylä: Jyväskylän yliopisto.

Peltonen, Matti 1992: *Matala katse. Kirjoituksia mentaliteettien historiasta.* Helsinki: Hanki ja jää.
— 2006. Mikrohistorian lajit. In Outi Fingerroos & Riina Haanpää & Ulla-Maija Peltonen (eds.). *Muistitetotutkimus. Metodologisia kysymyksiä.* Tietolipas 214, 145–171. Helsinki: Suomalaisen Kirjallisuuden Seura.

Peltonen, Ulla-Maija 1996: *Punakapinan muistot. Tutkimus työväen muistelukerronnan muotoutumisesta vuoden 1918 jälkeen.* Suomalaisen Kirjallisuuden Seuran Toimituksia 657. Helsinki: Suomalaisen Kirjallisuuden Seura.
— 2003: *Muistin paikat. Vuoden 1918 sisällissodan muistamisesta ja unohtamisesta.* Suomalaisen Kirjallisuuden Seuran Toimituksia 894. Helsinki: Suomalaisen Kirjallisuuden Seura.
— 2006: Muistitieto folkloristiikassa. In Outi Fingerroos & Riina Haanpää & Ulla-Maija Peltonen (eds.). *Muistitetotutkimus. Metodologisia kysymyksiä*, 93–119.

Pentikäinen, Juha 1971: *Marina Takalon uskonto. Uskontoantropologinen tutkimus.* Suomalaisen Kirjallisuuden Seuran Toimituksia 299. Helsinki: Suomalaisen Kirjallisuuden Seura.
— 1978: *Oral Repertoire and the World View. An Anthropological Study of Marina Takalo's Life History.* Folklore Fellows Communications 219. Helsinki: Academia Scientiarum Fennica.

Pesola, Sakari 1996: Tanssikiellosta lavatansseihin. In Matti Peltonen (toim.). *Rillumarei ja valistus*. Historiallinen arkisto 108, 105–126. Helsinki: Suomalaisen Kirjallisuuden Seura.

Phelan, James 2005: *Living to Tell about It. A Rhetoric and Ethics of Character Narration*. Ithaca: Cornell University Press.

Piela, Ulla (toim.) 1993: *Aikanaisia. Kirjoituksia naisten omaelämäkerroista*. Tietolipas 127. Helsinki: Suomalaisen Kirjallisuuden Seura.

— 1993: Arjen unelmat. In Ulla Piela (toim.). *Aikanaisia. Kirjoituksia naisten omaelämäkerroista*, 235–255.

Pohls, Marjatta & Latva-Äijö, Annika 2009: *Lotta Svärd. Käytännön isänmaallisuutta*. Helsinki: Otava.

Polkinghorne, Donald E. 2007: Validity Issues in Narrative Research. *Qualitative Inquiry* 13(4), 471–486.

Portelli, Alessandro 2006: What Makes Oral History Different. In Robert Perks & Alistair Thomson (eds.).*The Oral History Reader*. Second edition, 32–42. London & New York: Routledge.

Portes, Alejandro 1995: Economic Sociology and the Sociology of Immigration: A Conceptual Overview. Alejandro Portes (ed). In *The Economic Sociology of Immigration: Essays in Ethnic Entrepreneurship*. New York: Russell Sage Foundation.

Pöysä, Jyrki 1997: *Jätkän synty. Tutkimus sosiaalisen kategorian muotoutumisesta suomalaisessa kulttuurissa ja itäsuomalaisessa metsätyöperinteessä*. Suomalaisen Kirjallisuuden Seuran Toimituksia 669. Helsinki: Suomalaisen Kirjallisuuden Seura.

— 2012: *Työelämän alkeismuodot – Narratiivinen etnografia*. Kultaneito XI. Joensuu: Suomen Kansantietouden Tutkijain Seura.

Radley, Alan 1990: Artefacts, Memory, and the Sense of Belonging. In David Middleton & David Edwards (eds.). *Collective Remembering,* 47–58. London: Sage.

Rahikainen, Marjatta 1996 (toim.): *Matkoja moderniin. Lähikuvia suomalaisten elämästä*. Historiallinen Arkisto 107. Helsinki: Suomen Historiallinen Seura.

— 2003: Nuorena työhön. Lasten ja nuorten työnteko Suomessa 1900–1970. In Sinikka Aapola & Mervi Kaarninen (toim.). *Nuoruuden vuosisata. Suomalaisen nuorison historiaa*. Suomalaisen Kirjallisuuden Seuran Toimituksia 909, 161–185. Helsinki: Suomalaisen Kirjallisuuden Seura.

— 2006: Kotiapulaisena 1900-luvun kaupunkilaisperheessä. In Marjatta Rahikainen & Kirsi Vainio-Korhonen (toim.). Työteliäs ja uskollinen. Naiset piikoina ja palvelijoina keskiajalta nykyaikaan. Suomalaisen Kirjallisuuden Seuran Toimituksia 1092, 224–252. Helsinki: Suomalaisen Kirjallisuuden Seura.

Ranta, Matti 2006: *Aikamatka ruukin elämään*. Matti Ranta: Ähtäri.

Rantala, Pälvi: Erilaisia tapoja käyttää kylähullua. Kalkkimaan pappi aatteiden ja mentaliteettien tulkkina 1800-luvulta 2000-luvulle. Turku: k&h, Turun yliopisto.

Rautainen tarina 1991. Inhan tehtaat 150 vuotta.

Ricoeur, Paul 1984: *Time and Narrative. Vol. 1*. Transl.by Kathleen McLaughlin & David Pellauer. Chicago: University of Chicago Press.

— 1991: Narrative Identity. *Philosophy Today*, 35(1), 73–81.

— 1992: *History and Truth*. Transl. by Charles A. Kelbley. Evanston: Northwestern University Press.

Riessman, Catherine Kohler 1993: *Narrative Analysis*. Newbury Park: Sage.

Reinharz, Shulamit 1992: *Feminist Methods in Social Research*. Oxford: Oxford University Press.

— 2011: *Observing the Observer. Understanding Ourselves in Field Research*. Oxford and New York: Oxford University Press.

Rojola, Lea 1999: Työläiskodin onnea. Tyyne Salminen ja 1930-luvun työläisen arki. In Pentti Karkama & Hanne Koivisto (toim.). *Ajan paineessa. Kirjoituksia 1930-luvun*

suomalaisesta aatemaailmasta. Suomalaisen Kirjallisuuden Seuran Toimituksia 758, 342–365. Helsinki: Suomalaisen Kirjallisuuden Seura.
— 2011: Sivistymättömyyden häpeä. In Siru Kainulainen & Viola Parente-Čapková (toim.). *Häpeä vähän! Kriittisiä tutkimuksia häpeästä*, 202–224. Turku: Utukirjat (Turun yliopisto).
Ronkainen, Suvi 1999: *Ajan ja paikan merkitsemät: Subjektiviteetti, tieto ja toimijuus.* Helsinki: Gaudeamus.
Roos, J-P. 1987: *Suomalainen elämä. Tutkimus tavallisten suomalaisten elämäkerroista.* Suomalaisen Kirjallisuuden Seuran Toimituksia 454. Helsinki: Suomalaisen Kirjallisuuden Seura.
Roos, J-P. & Rotkirch, Anna (eds.) 1997: Vanhemmat ja lapset. Helsinki: Gaudeamus.
Rosen, Ilana 2008. *Sister in Sorrow. Life Histories of Female Holocaust Survivors from Hungary.* Transl. Dandy Bloom. Detroit: Wayne State University Press.
— 2011: *Soul of Saul. The Life, Narrative and Proverbs of a Transylvanian-Israeli Grandfather.* Supplement Series of *Proverbium.* The Yearbook of International Proverbs Scholarship. Burlington: The University of Vermont.
Rosenthal, Gabriela 1991: German War Memories: Narrability and Biographical and Social Functions of Remembering. *Oral History* 19(2), 24–48.
Rossi, Leena 1988: Initiation Rites among Finnish Factory Workers from the 1890s to the 1980s. *Ethnologia Scandinavica,* 61–66.
Ruoppila, Veikko 1954: *Kansa lasten kasvattajana.* Helsinki: WSOY.
Ruotsala, Helena 2002: *Muuttuvan palkiset: elo, työ ja ympäristö Kittilän Kyrön paliskunnassa ja Kuolan Luujärven poronhoitokollektiiveissa vuosina 1930–1995.* Kansatieteellinen arkisto 49. Helsinki: Suomen muinaismuistoyhdistys.
Räikkönen, Tuovi 1993: Läskisoosia ilman läskiä ja sitruunasoodalla ohukaisia. Kotirintaman monitaitureiden elämää. In Riikka Raitis & Elina Haavio-Mannila (toim.). *Naisten aseet. Suomalaisena naisena talvi- ja jatkosodassa*, 160–200. Helsinki: WSOY.
Saarenheimo, Marja 1997: *Jos etsit kadonnutta aikaa. Vanhuus ja oman elämän muisteleminen.* Tampere: Vastapaino.
Saarikangas, Kirsi 1993: *Model Houses for Model Families. The Type-Planned Houses of the 1940s in Finland.* Studia Historica 45. Helsinki: Societas Historica Finlandiae.
Saarikoski, Helena 1999: Tytön rakkaus ja häpeä huoran maineen säätelemänä. In Sari Näre (toim.). *Tunteiden sosiologiaa I. Elämyksiä & läheisyyttä.* Tietolipas 156, 108–130. Helsinki: Suomalaisen Kirjallisuuden Seura.
— 2011: Menneisyyden ruumiinkokemusten tutkiminen kirjoitetussa aineistossa. In Sami Lakomäki & Kirsi Laurén & Pauliina Latvala (toim.). *Tekstien rajoilla. Monitieteisiä näkökulmia kirjoitettuihin aineistoihin,* 117–136. Suomalaisen Kirjallisuuden Seuran Toimituksia 1314. Helsinki: Suomalaisen Kirjallisuuden Seura.
Saarinen, Tuija 2003: *Poikkeusyksilö ja kyläyhteisö: tutkimus Heikan Jussin (Juho Mäkäräisen) elämästä ja huumorista.* Suomalaisen Kirjallisuuden Seuran Toimituksia 917. Helsinki: Suomalaisen Kirjallisuuden Seura.
Saastamoinen, Mikko 2000: Elämänkaari, elämäkerta ja muisteleminen. In Pekka Kuusela ja Mikko Saastamoinen (toim.). *Ruumis, minä ja yhteisö. Sosiaalisen konstruktionismin näkökulma*, 135–197. Kuopio: Kuopion yliopisto.
Salmi-Niklander, Kirsti 2004: *Itsekasvatusta ja kapinaa. Tutkimus Karkkilan työläisnuorten kirjoittavasta keskusteluyhteisöstä 1910- ja 1920-luvuilla.* Suomalaisen Kirjallisuuden Seuran Toimituksia 967. Helsinki: Suomalaisen Kirjallisuuden Seura.
— 2007: Bitter Memories and Burst Soap Bubbles: Irony, Parody, and Satire in the Oral-Literary Tradition of Finnish Working-Class Youth at the Beginning of the Twentieth Century. *International Review of Social History* 52, supplement 15, 189–207.
Salokorpi, Asko 1999: *Suomen rautaruukit.* Helsinki: Otava.
Samuel, Raphael & Thompson, Paul 1990: Introduction. In Raphael Samuel & Paul Thompson (eds.). *The Myths We Live by,* 1–22. London & New York: Routledge.

Santino, Jack 1978: Characteristics of occupational narratives. *Western Folklore* 37, 199–212.

Sappinen, Eero 2000: *Arkielämän murros 1960- ja 1970-luvuilla. Tutkimus suomalaisen työväestön elämäntavoista ja niiden paikallisista raumalaisista piirteistä.* Kansatieteellinen arkisto 46. Helsinki: Suomen muinaismuistoyhdistys.

Saraste, Erja 1990: Talonpitoa rintaman varjossa – työvoima ja työmarkkinat vuosina 1941–44. Teoksessa *Kansakunta sodassa 2. Vyö kireällä,* 285–300. Valtion painatuskeskus, Helsinki.

Saresma, Tuija 2007: *Omaelämäkerran rajapinnoilla. Kuolema ja kirjoitus.* Nykykulttuurin tutkimuskeskuksen julkaisuja 92. Jyväskylä: Jyväskylän yliopisto.

— 2010: Kokemuksen houkutus. In Tuija Saresma, Leena-Maija Rossi & Tuula Juvonen (eds.). *Käsikirja sukupuoleen,* 59–74. Tampere: Vastapaino.

Satka, Mirja 1993: Sota-aika perhekäsitysten ja sukupuolten suhteiden murroksena. In Haapala, Pertti (toim.). *Hyvinvointivaltio ja historian oikut.* Väki voimakas 6, 57–73. Helsinki: Työväen historian ja perinteen tutkimuksen seura.

— 1994: Sota-ajan naiskansalaisen ihanteet naisjärjestöjen arjessa. In Anttonen, Anneli et al (eds.). *Naisten hyvinvointivaltio,* 73–96 Tampere: Vastapaino.

Savolainen, Ulla 2009: Kasvun tiellä ja muutosten kynnyksellä. Evakkopojan muistelukertomuksen kronotoopit. *Kasvatus & Aika* 3(3), 95–114. URL: http://www.kasvatus-ja-aika.fi/dokumentit/artikkeli_savolainen_2410091802.pdf (accessed 2.22.2010.)

Sawin, Patricia 2004: *Listening for a Life. A Dialogic Ethnography of Bessie Eldreth through Her Songs and Stories.* Logan: Utah State University Press.

Scott, James C. 1985: *Weapons of the Weak: Everyday Forms of Peasant Resistance.* New Haven: Yale University Press.

Scott, Joan W. 1986: Gender: A Useful Category in Historical Analysis. *American Historical Review* 91, 1056–1061.

— 1988: Some more Reflections on Gender and Politics. In Joan W. Scott (eds). *Gender and the Politics of History.* New York: University of Columbia Press, 199–206.

— 1991: The Evidence of Experience. *Critical Inquiry* 17, 773–798.

Seppänen, Anne 2000: *Populaarikulttuuri sosiaalistumisväylänä. Tampereen työväestön julkiset huvit 1860-luvulta vuoteen 1917.* Acta Universitatis Tamperensis 786. Tampere: Tampereen yliopisto.

Shilling, Chris 2005. *The Body in Culture, Technology and Society.* London & Thousand Oaks & Delhi: Sage.

Shostak, Marjorie 1989: 'What the wind won't take away' The genesis of Nisa – The Life and Words of a !Kung Woman. In Personal Narrative Group (ed.). *Interpreting Women's lives. Feminist theory and Personal Narratives,*228–240. Bloomington: Indiana University Press.

Shuman, Amy 2005: *Other People's Stories. Entitlement Claims and the Critique of Empathy.* Urbana & Chicago: University of Illinois Press.

Siikala, Anna-Leena 1984: *Tarina ja tulkinta: tutkimus kansankertojista.* Suomalaisen Kirjallisuuden Seuran Toimituksia 404. Helsinki: Suomalaisen Kirjallisuuden Seura.

Siivonen, Katriina 2008: *Saaristoidentiteetit merkkien virtoina.* Kansatieteellinen arkisto 51. Helsinki: Suomen muinaismuistoyhdistys.

Silvasti, Tiina 2001: *Talonpojan elämä. Tutkimus elämäntapaa jäsentävistä kulttuurisista malleista.* Suomalaisen Kirjallisuuden Seuran Toimituksia 821. Helsinki: Suomalaisen Kirjallisuuden Seura.

Skarin Frykman, Birgitta 1987: *Från yrkesfamilj till klassgemenskap. Om bagare i Göteborg 1800–1919.* Göteborg: Etnologiska föreningen i Västsverige.

— 1990: *Arbetarkultur, Göteborg 1890.* Göteborg: Etnologiska föreningen i Västsverige.

Skeggs, Beverley 1997: *Formations of Gender and Class. Becoming Respectable.* London: Sage.
— 2004: *Class, Self, Culture.* London & New York: Routledge.
Skultans, Vieda 1998: *The Testimony of Lives. Narrative and Memory in Post-Soviet Latvia.* London & New York: Routledge.
Smith, Sidonie 1998 [1995]: Performativity, Autobiographical Practice, Resistance. In Sidonie Smith & Julia Watson (eds). *Women, Autobiography, Theory: A Reader,* 108–115. Madison: University of Wisconsin Press.
Snellman, Hanna 1996: *Tukkilaisen tulo ja lähtö. Kansatieteellinen tutkimus Kemijoen metsä- ja uittotyöstä.* Oulu: Pohjoinen.
— 2003: *Sallan suurin kylä – Göteborg.* Suomalaisen Kirjallisuuden Seura Toimituksia 927. Helsinki: Suomalaisen Kirjallisuuden Seura.
— 2012: Pieni ihminen ja kansatiede. *Historiallinen aikakauskirja* 110: 4, 438–442.
Soikkanen, Hannu 1981: Vanha ja uusi yhteiskunta. – *När samhället förändras. Kun yhteiskunta muuttuu.* Historiallinen arkisto 76, 433–453. Helsinki: Suomen Historiallinen Seura.
Spoof, Sanna-Kaisa 1997: *Savikkojen valtias. Jokelan tiilitehtaan sosiaalinen ja fyysinen miljöö.* Kansatieteellinen arkisto 43. Helsinki: Suomen muinaismuistoyhdistys.
Stahl, Sandra 1977: The Personal Narrative as Folklore. *Journal of the Folklore Institute* 14(1–2), 9–30.
— 1989: *Literary Folkloristics and the Personal Narrative.* Bloomington & Indianapolis: Indiana University Press.
Stark, Eija 2005: Maalaisköyhälistö ja ryhmävastakohtaisuudet 1900-luvun Suomessa. In Matti Hannikainen (toim.). *Työväestön rajat.* Väki Voimakas 18, 25–53. Tampere: Työväen historian ja perinteen tutkimuksen seura.
— 2011: *Köyhyyden perintö. Tutkimus kulttuurisen tiedon sisällöistä ja jatkuvuuksista suomalaisissa elämäkerta- ja sananlaskuaineistossa.* Suomalaisen Kirjallisuuden Seuran Toimituksia 1320. Helsinki: Suomalaisen Kirjallisuuden Seura.
Stark-Arola, Laura 1998: *Magic, Body and Social Order. The Construction of Gender through Women's Private Rituals in Traditional Finland.* Studia Fennic Folkloristica 5. Helsinki: Finnish Literature Society.
— 2001: Vaginan tuntematon historia: naisen seksuaalisuuden kuvat suomalaisessa suullisessa kansanperinteessä. *Naistutkimus* 14(2), 4–22.
Stark, Laura: 2006a: Johdanto. Pitkospuita modernisaation suolle. In Hilkka Helsti Laura Stark & Saara Tuomaala (toim.). *Modernisaatio ja kansan kokemus suomessa 1860–1960.* Suomalaisen Kirjallisuuden Seuran Toimituksia 1101, 9–46. Helsinki: Suomalaisen Kirjallisuuden Seura.
— 2006b. Kansallinen herääminen ja sosiaalinen nousu maaseudulla. In Hilkka Helsti, Laura Stark & Saara Tuomaala (toim.). *Modernisaatio ja kansan kokemus suomessa 1860–1960,* 47–109. Suomalaisen Kirjallisuuden Seuran Toimituksia 1101. Helsinki: Suomalaisen Kirjallisuuden Seura.
— 2006c: *The Magical Self: Body, Society and the Supernatural in Early Modern Rural Finland.* Folklore Fellows Communications 290. Helsinki: Academia Scientiarum Fennica.
— 2009: Empowering practices. Perspectives on Modernization in Finland 1860–1960. *Ethnologia Fennica* 36, 4–16.
Steedman, Carolyn K. 1994 [1986]: *Landscape for a Good Woman. The Story of Two Lives.* New Brunswick & New Jersey Rutgers University Press.
Steel, Tytti 2011: Sataman Helmi. Sukupuolen risteävät erot satamatyöntekijän muistelukerronnassa. In Kirsi-Maria Hytönen & Eerika Koskinen-Koivisto (toim.). *Työtä tekee, mies, nainen.* Väki Voimakas 24, 102–137. Tampere: Työväen historian ja perinteen tutkimuksen seura.
Strandén, Sofie 2009: Trust in the Emphatic Interview. In Marta Kurkowska-Budzan & Krzysztof Zamorski (eds.) *Oral History. The Challenges of Dialogue,* 3–13.

— 2010: *I eld, I blod, I frost, I svält: möten med veteraners, lottors och sjuksköterskors berättande om krig.* Åbo: Åbo Akademi.
Sulkunen, Irma 1986: *Raittius kansalaisuskontona. Raittiusliike ja järjestäytyminen 1870-luvulta suurlakon jälkeisiin vuosiin.* Historiallisia Tutkimuksia 134. Helsinki: Suomen Historiallinen Seura.
— 1989a: *Naisen kutsumus. Miina Sillanpää ja sukupuolten maailmojen erkaantuminen.* Helsinki: Hanki ja jää.
— 1989b: Naisten järjestäytyminen ja kaksijakoinen kansalaisuus. In Risto Alapuro et al. (toim.). *Kansa liikkeessä,* 157–172. Helsinki: Kirjayhtymä.
Summerfield, Penny 1998: Reconstructing Women's Wartime Lives. Discourse and Subjectivity in Oral Histories of the Second World War. Manchester: Manchester University Press.
Suodenjoki, Sami 2010: *Kuriton suutari ja kiistämisen rajat. Työväenliikkeen läpimurto hämäläisessä maalaisyhteisössä 1899–1909.* Bibliotheca Historica. Helsinki: Suomalaisen Kirjallisuuden Seura.
Suojanen, Päivikki 1978: *Saarna, saarnaaja, tilanne: spontaanin saarnan tuottamisprosessi Länsi-Suomen rukoilevaisuudessa.* Suomalaisen Kirjallisuuden Seuran Toimituksia 343. Helsinki: Suomalaisen Kirjallisuuden Seura.
Suopajärvi, Tiina 2009: *Sukupuoli meni metsään.* Luonnon ja sukupuolen polkuja metsäammattilaisuudessa. Suomalaisen Kirjallisuuden Seuran Toimituksia 1255. Helsinki: Suomalaisen Kirjallisuuden Seura.
von Sydow, C. W. 1948: *Selected papers on folklore: published on the occasion of his 70th birthday.* Selected and edited by Laurits Bødker. Copenhagen: Rosenkilde and Bagger
Sykäri, Venla 2012: Dialogic Methodology and the Dialogic Space Created after an Interview. –*RMN newsletter* 4, 80–88. URL: http://www.helsinki.fi/folkloristiikka/English/RMN/RMNNewsletter_4_MAY_2012_Approaching_Methodology.pdf (9.9.2014.)
Sysiharju, Anna-Liisa et al. (toim.) 1997. *Työtytöt – naisten vapaaehtoinen työpalvelu 1941–1945.* Helsinki: Edita.
Sääskilahti, Nina 1999: Kansan kulttuurista arkipäivän merkityksiin. Bo Lönnqvist & Elina Kiuru & Eeva Uusitalo (toim.) *Kulttuurin muuttuvat kasvot.* Tietolipas 155, 145–154. Helsinki: Suomalaisen Kirjallisuuden Seura.
— 2012: Ajan partaalla: omaelämäkerrallinen aika, päiväkirja ja muistin kulttuuri. Nykykulttuurin tutkimuskeskuksen julkaisuja105. Jyväskylä: Jyväskylän yliopisto.
Taira, Teemu 2006: *Työkulttuurin arvomuutos työttömien kerronnassa.* Suomalaisen Kirjallisuuden Seuran Toimituksia 1097. Helsinki: Suomalaisen Kirjallisuuden Seura.
Talve, Ilmar 1997: *Finnish Folk Culture.* Studia Fennica Ethnologia 4. Transl. by Susan Sinisalo. Helsinki: Finnish Literature Society.
Tannock, Stuart 1995: Nostalgia Critique. *Cultural Studies* 9(3), 453–464.
Tervo, Katja 2008: *Metsän hiljaiset. Metsätyön rakennemuutosten kolme sukupolvea.* Suomalaisen Kirjallisuuden Seuran Toimituksia 1177. Helsinki: Suomalaisen Kirjallisuuden Seura.
Teräs, Kari 1999: Rankkaa käsityötä. Tarkkaa konetyötä. In Raimo Parikka (toim.). *Suomalaisen työn historiaa: Korvesta konttoriin,* 261–303. Helsinki: Suomalaisen Kirjallisuuden Seura.
— 2001: *Arjessa ja liikkeessä. Verkostonäkökulma modernisoituviin työelämän suhteisiin Suomessa 1880–1920.* Bibliotheca Historica 66. Helsinki: Suomalaisen Kirjallisuuden Seura.
Thomas, Jeannie B. 1997: *Featherless Chicken, Laughing Women, and Serious stories.* Charlottesville: The University of Virginia Press.
Thomson, Alistair 2010: Remembering in Later Life: Some Lessons from Oral History. In Joanna Bornat & Josie Tetley (eds.). *Oral History and Aging,* 26–42. London: Center for Policy of Aging.

Tiihonen, Kristiina 2000: Puhtaan nuoruuden ihanne. Sukupuolikasvatusta nuorison opaskirjoissa 1920- ja 1930-luvuilla. In Kari Immonen & Ritva Hapuli & Maarit Leskelä & Kaisa Vehkalahti (toim.). *Modernin lumo ja pelko. Kymmenen kirjoitusta 1800–1900-lukujen vaihteen sukupuolisuudesta*, 169–208. Helsinki. Suomalaisen Kirjallisuuden Seura.

Titon, Jeff Todd 1980: The Life Story. *Journal of American Folklore* 93: 276–292.

Torninoja-Latola, Jaana 2011: Omapäisesti valtaa vastaan. Elvi Sinervon arkipäivän politiikka vankilassa 1941–1944. In Ilana Aalto, Laura Boxberg, Ulla Iljäs & Heli Paalumäki (toim.). *Vallan teoriat historiantutkimuksessa*. Historia Miranbilis 7, 61–83. Turku: Turun historiallinen yhdistys ry.

Tuomaala, Saara 2004: *Työtätekevistä käsistä puhtaiksi ja kirjoittaviksi. Suomalaisen oppivelvollisuuskoulun ja maalaislasten kohtaaminen 1921–1939*. Bibliotheca Historica 89. Helsinki: Suomalaisen Kirjallisuuden Seura.

— 2006: Sukupuolen kokemuksista muistitietohistoriaan. In Outi Fingerroos & Riina Haanpää & Ulla-Maija Peltonen (eds.). *Muistitietotutkimus. Metodologisia kysymyksiä*, 271–291.

— 2009a: The Dialogues in-between. Phenomenological Perspective on Women's Oral History Interviews. In Marta Kurkowska-Budzan & Krzysztof Zamorski (eds.) *Oral history. The Challenges of Dialogue*, 77–86.

— 2009b: The Bicycle and Bodily Identities of Rural Finnish Youth from the 1920s to the 1940s. *Ethnologia Fennica* 36, 59–71.

Turner Victor W. & Bruner Edward M. (eds.) 1986. *The Anthropology of Experience*. Urbana & Chicago: University of Illinois Press.

Turunen, Arja 2005: Kun lauantai koitti..." Tansseihin valmistautuminen ja tanssilavapukeutuminen. In Henna Mikkola (toim.). *Tanssilavan luona. Huvielämää Jyväskylän Ainolassa*, 108–120. Jyväskylä: Minerva.

— 2009: Trousers and the Construction of a Modern Woman. *Ethnologia Fennica* 36, 48–58.

— 2011: *Hame, housut, hamehousut! Vai mikä on tulevaisuutemme. Naisten päällyshousujen käyttöä koskevat pukeutumisohjeet ja niissä rakentuvat naiseuden ihanteet suomalaisissa naistenlehdissä 1889–1945*. Kansatieteellinen arkisto 53. Helsinki: Suomen muinaismuistoyhdistys.

Ukkonen, Taina 2000: *Menneisyyden tulkinta kertomalla. Muistelupuhe oman historian ja kokemuskertomusten tuottamisprosessina*. Suomalaisen Kirjallisuuden Seuran Toimituksia 797. Helsinki: Suomalaisen Kirjallisuuden Seura.

Vakimo, Sinikka 2001: *Paljon kokeva, vähän näkyvä. Tutkimus vanhaa naista koskevista kulttuurisista käsityksistä ja vanhan naisen elämänkäytännöistä*. Suomalaisen Kirjallisuuden Seuran Toimituksia 818. Helsinki: Suomalaisen Kirjallisuuden Seura.

Valtonen, Heli 2004: *Minäkuvat, arvot ja mentaliteetit. Tutkimus 1900-luvun alussa syntyneiden toimihenkilönaisten elämäkerroista*. Jyväskylä Studies in Humanities 26. Jyväskylä: Jyväskylän yliopisto.

Vasara, Erkki 1997: *Valkoisen Suomen urheilevat soturit. Suojeluskuntajärjestön urheilu- ja kasvatustoiminta vuosina 1918–1939*. Bibliotheca Historica 23. Helsinki Suomen Historiallinen Seura.

Vasenkari, Maria 1996: Mitä se sanoo? Mistä se kertoo? Dialoginen näkökulma kenttätutkimusaineiston tuottamiseen. In Tuija Hovi & Lotte Tarkka (toim.). *Uskontotiede – Folkloristiikka. Kirjoituksia opinnäytteistä*. Etiäinen 3, 84–109. Turku: Turun yliopisto, kulttuurien tutkimuksen laitos.

Vasenkari, Maria & Pekkala, Armi 2000: Dialogic methodology. In Lauri Honko (eds.). *Thick Corpus, Organic Variation and Textuality in Oral Tradition*. Studia Fennica Folkloristica 7, 243–254. Helsinki: Finnish Literature Society.

Vattula, Kaarina 1989: Lähtöviivallako? Naisten ammatissa toimivuudesta, tilastoista ja kotitaloudesta. In Leena Laine & Pirjo Markkola (toim.). *Tuntematon työläisnainen*, 13–38. Tampere: Vastapaino.

Vehkalahti, Kaisa 2000: Jazz-tyttö ja naistenlehtien siveä katse. In Kari Immonen & Ritva Hapuli & Maarit Leskelä & Kaisa Vehkalahti (toim.). *Modernin lumo ja pelko. Kymmenen kirjoitusta 1800–1900-lukujen vaihteen sukupuolisuudesta*, 130–168. Helsinki. Suomalaisen Kirjallisuuden Seura.

Viertola, Juhani 1989: Ähtärin historia 1918–1980. *Vanhan Ruoveden historia* III: 6/1. Ähtäri: Ähtärin kaupunki.

— 1991: *Ähtärin historian lyhennelmä*. Ähtäri: Ähtärin kaupunki.

Vilkko, Anni 1993: Oman elämän kielikuvat. In Ulla Piela (toim.). *Aikanaisia. Kirjoituksia naisten omaelämäkerroista*, 54–72.

— 1997: *Omaelämäkerta kohtaamispaikkana. Naisen elämän kerronta ja luenta*. Helsinki: Suomalaisen Kirjallisuuden Seura.

Vilkuna, Kustaa H.J. 1996: *Arkielämää patriarkaalisessa työmiesyhteisössä. Rautaruukkilaiset suurvalta-ajan Suomessa*. Historiallisia tutkimuksia 196. Helsinki: Suomen Historiallinen Seura.

Virkkunen, Gia 2002: Köyhyyden omakuva ja toiseus. Suomalainen maalaisyhteisö 1930-luvun pula-aikana. In Helena Blomberg, Matti Hannikainen & Pauli Kettunen (toim.). *Lamakirja. Näkökulma 1990-luvun talouskriisiin ja sen historiallisiin konteksteihin*, 169–193. Turku. Kirja-Aurora.

— 2010: *"Köyhyydestä ei puhuttu, sitä vaan elettiin". Köyhyyden kokemus ja selviytyminen 1930-luvun pulan oloissa Suomen maaseudulla*. Bibliotheca Historica 127. Helsinki: Suomalaisen Kirjallisuuden Seura.

Virtanen, Leea 1982: Henkilökohtainen kerronta. In Irma-Riitta Järvinen ja Seppo Knuuttila (toim.). *Kertomusperinne. Kirjoituksia proosaperinteen lajeista ja tutkimuksesta*. Tietolipas 90, 171–205. Helsinki: Suomalaisen Kirjallisuuden Seura.

Vuorinen, Pihla 2002: Doing research among family and friends. Problems and advantages. In Tiiu Jaago, Mare Kõiva & K. Kärsna, (toim.). *Lives, Histories and Identities. Studies on Oral History, Life- and Family Stories*, 348–363. Tartu: University of Tartu; Estonian Literary Museum.

Wallace, J.B. 1992: Reconsidering the Life Review: The social construction of talk about the Past. *The Gerontologist* 32(1), 120–125.

Watson, Lawrence C. & Watson-Franke, Maria-Barbara 1985: *Interpreting Life Histories: An Anthropological Inquiry*. New Brunswick: Rutgers University Press.

Weber, Max 1980: *Protestanttinen etiikka ja kapitalismin henki*. Suom. Timo Kyntäjä. Helsinki: WSOY.

Webber, Sabra J. & Patrick B. Mullen 2011: Breakthrough into Comparison: "Moving" Stories, Local History and the Narrative Turn. *Journal of Folklore Studies* 48(3), 213–247.

Wegs, J. Robert 1982: Working Class Respectability. The Viennese Experience. *Journal of Social History* 15, 621–635.

Widdershoven, Guy A.M. 1993: The Story of Life. Hermeneutic Perspectives on the Relationship Between Narrative and Life Story. In Ruthellen Josselson & Amia Lieblich (eds.). *The Narrative Study of Lives*. Volume 1, 1–20. London: Sage.

Williams, Raymond 1976: *Keywords: A Vocabulary of Culture and Society*. New York: Oxford University Press.

Willis, Paul 1977: *Learning to Labour. How Working Class Kids Get Working Class Jobs*. Aldershot: Gower.

Wilson, William A. 1991: *Personal Narratives: the Family Novel*. Western Folklore 59(2), 127–149.

Vodopivec, Nina 2010: Textile Workers in Slovenia: From Nimble Fingers to Tired Bodies. *The Anthropology of East Europe Review* 28(1), 165–183.

Worthington, Kim L. 1996: *Self as Narrative: Subjectivity and Community in Contemporary Fiction*. Oxford: Clarendon Press.

Young, Iris 1990: *Throwing like a Girl and Other Essays in Feminist Philosophy and Social Theory*. Bloomington and Indianapolis: Indiana University Press.

Young, Katherine Galloway 1987: *Taleworlds and Storyrealms: The Phenomenology of Narrative.* Dordrecht & Boston & Lancaster: Martinus Nijhoff Publishers.
— 2000: Gestures and the Phenomenology of Emotion in Narrative. *Semiotica* 131(1/2), 79–112.
Yow, Valerie 2006: 'Do I like them too much?' Effects of the oral history interview on the interviewer and vice-versa. In Robert Perks & Alistair Thomson (eds.). *The Oral History Reader.* Second edition, 54–72. London & New York: Routledge.
Yuval- Davis, Nira 2006: Intersectionality and Feminist Politics. *European Journal of Women Studies* 13(3), 193–209.
Zerubavel, Yael 1995: *Recovered Roots. Collective Memory and the Making of Israeli National Tradition.* Chicago & London: University of Chicago Press.
Åström, Lissie 1985. Husmodern möter folkhemmet. – Frykman, Jonas et al. *Modärna tider. Vision och vardag i folkhemmet*, 196–255. Malmö: LiberFörlag.
Åström, Anna-Maria 1993: *Sockenboarne: herrgårdskultur i Savolax 1790–1850.* Helsingfors: Svenska litteratursällskapet i Finland, Folkkultursarkivet.
— 1995: Savon herrasväki kansan silmin. In Kimmo Katajala (toim.). *Manaajista maalaisaateliin. Tulkintoja toisesta historian, antropologian ja maantieteen välimaastossa,* Tietolipas 140, 208–235. Helsinki: Suomalaisen Kirjallisuuden Seura.

Appendix 1: Interviews

Interview and date		initial theme	other themes	duration (min), narratives, variants (%)		
1	25.1.2001	oral tradition	childhood, work, community	105	46	12 (26%)
2	March 2001	foodways	work, colleagues	30	16	7 (44%)
3	26.6.2001	shopping	wartime	45	9	3 (30%)
4	8.9.2001	work	work, wartime	60	18	5 (28%)
5	9.12.2001	life story	life stages, work, free time	90	35	15 (43%)
6	19.12.2001	youth	free time, supernatural	60	26	9 (35%)
7	1.1.2002	local dialect	childhood, social class	60	16	5 (31%)
8	6.1.2002	change	retirement, fishing, travelling	60	21	2 (10%)
9	16.2.2002	dreams	supernatural, family, humor	60	26	8 (31%)
10	24.5.2002	family	youth, free time, being old, bears	60	22	2 (9%)
11	28.9.2002	proverbs	family, wartime, clothes	60	22	5 (23%)
12	June 2004	work	gender relations, jokes, youth, work and free time activities	50	19	9 (47%)

Total amount of micro-narratives in all interviews 276, 82 (30%) variants

Appendix 2:
Key Events and Milestones of Elsa's Life

Year		Age
1927	Elsa Sanelma is born in Ähtäri during the lockout	
1934	Elsa goes to school	7
1939	Elsa passes the obligatory elementary school after the outbreak of the WWII and becomes a maid servant in the upper-class households	12
1942	Elsa begins work at Inha Ironworks	15
1948	Elsa marries Eino and their first child, daughter Raija is born	21
1952	Elsa's and Eino's second child, son Asko is born	25
1956	Elsa's and Eino's second child, daughter Marja-Terttu is born and dies	29
1959	Elsa's and Eino's third child, son Simo is born	32
1965*	Elsa goes back to factory work, Raija and Eino study	38
1984	Elsa and Eino retire and move to the municipal center of Ähtäri	57
1989	Eino dies	62
1998	Elsa gets a breast cancer diagnosis and treatments begin	71
2001	Eerika interviews Elsa for the first time	74
2004	Eerika interviews Elsa for the last time	77
2010	Elsa gets a diagnosis for Alzheimer's disease	83
2012	Elsa moves to nursing home	85

*) *Year estimated*

Appendix 3:
Commenting Letter from Elsa

Elsa's comment to the essay presented in the Master's Seminar of Folklore Studies (2002–2003), January 2003 (English/Finnish)

Comments to Eerika's work

Thank you Eerika!
I have read many times through this study of my life and found it engrossing. You have done a good job. I wanted you to realize that a person can be happy and satisfied in life with what God has given, without worldly wealth. Living only to meet the bare necessities. The old people said "children bring bread to the house". People believed that and did not grumble or complain, but resigned themselves, humbled themselves. Poverty and humility foster perseverance. The old people sometimes smelled like a mixture of camphor drops and arthritis salve. It was a remedy for pain. It also opened even the most congested noses. Reading through your study, I have relived the ironworks, *Hamarimäki*. It was beautiful in its own way. The scent and noise of the factory, the sound of work, nothing today can compare to it. There one could feel human closeness; I mean contact with one's fellow man, which is nowhere to be seen nowadays. People can be cruel to each other. Nowadays you can't trust anybody. It's better to be alone. I am alone, but not lonely. I have a rich life behind me. It was tough at the time, but memories do not vanish, memories are golden.

Can you see Eerika, my treasure chest of words has opened again. Old age makes me tired, my hand gets tired. I want you to know that my heart is sensitive to good and evil. It is like a clamshell, it only opens cautiously for good things. If some person's words deeply offend me, my clamshell closes up tight, I mean my heart, I can feel it. It will never open again for that person, although I feel no hatred. I hope that you will learn to distinguish good from evil. I don't want to pretend to be superior, but rather to advise another person on her life path in how to survive difficulties with perseverance, strength of will and a humble mind.

Your Grandmother Elsa Koskinen

Mielipide Eerikan työstä

Kiitos Eerika!
Olen lukenut moneen kertaan tämän elämästäni kertovan tutkimuksen, joka oli mukaansa tempaava. Olet tehnyt hyvän työn. Halusin sinun huomaavan, että ihminen voi olla onnellinen ja tyytyä siihen minkä on hänelle määrännyt, ilman maallista mammonaa, itse Luoja. Vain tarpeellisen elämän mahdollisuuksia eläen. Vanha kansa sanoi: "Lapsi tuo leivän tullessaan." Siihen uskottiin, ei purnattu, eikä valitettu vaan alistuttiin, nöyryttiin. Köyhyys ja nöyryys kasvattaa sisua. Vanhat ihmiset haisivat joskus kamfertille ja reumavoiteen sekoitukselle. Se oli lääkitys kipuihin. Siinä aukes tukkoisempikin nenä. Lukiessani sinun työsi olen elänyt Ruukilla Hamarimäillä. Se oli kaunis omalla tavallaan. Tehtaan tuoksu ja kolina, työn ääni, sitä ei voita mikään nykyaikana. Siellä sai tuntea ihmisen läheisyyden, siis lähimmäisen kosketuksen, jota tänä aikana ei ole näkyvissä. Ihminen on peto toiselle ihmiselle. Nykyään ei voi luottaa kehenkään. Yksinäisyys on valttia. Olen yksin, mutten yksinäinen. Minulla on rikas elämä takana. Se oli ajallaan kovaa, mutta muistot eivät häviä mihinkään, aika kultaa kaiken.

Huomaatko Eerika, mun sanainen arkkuni on taas auennut. Vanhuus väsyttää, käsi väsyy. Vielä mä sanon sulle, että mun sydän tuntee herkästi hyvän ja pahan. Se on kuin simpukka, hyville asioille avautuu varovasti. Jos joku henkilö puhuessaan loukkaa pahasti, mun simpukkani supistuu ja menee suppuun, siis sydän, mä tunnen sen. Sille henkilölle se ei avaudu koskaan, en kuitenkaan vihaa. Mä toivon, että sä opit erottamaan hyvän pahasta. En halua korottaa itseäni, vaan neuvoa elämän tiellä kulkevaa henkilöä, vaikeistakin asioista selviytymään sisulla, tahdon voimalla, nöyrin mielin.

Mummusi Elsa Koskinen

Appendix 4:
Index of Micro-narratives

Interview (nr.): amount of micro narratives
(amount of narratives which have variants in other interviews)

1. Title in English/Title in Finnish

    Page of transcription (Chapter where quoted/referred to), theme and narrative tendency, actors

2. **Narrative told more than once**

    Themes: W= Work C= Class G= Gender

3. Narrative 1: Title = part of a series of narratives about the same topic

    Tendencies: P = Personal experience H= Humor B= Belief Cited/mentioned *

Interview 1: 46 **(12)**

1. I Was Born during the Lockout / Oma syntymä sulun aikaan	p. 1 (4) C, S Father, Capitalist *
2. Jesus, It's a Whore / Jessus, so'n huora	p. 2–3 (3) G Old man *
3. People from Ähtäri Don't Have Bikes / Ähtäriläisille ei ole pyöriä	p. 3 Villagers
4. Automobile 1: A Car with Stripes / Auto 1: Viiva-auto	p. 3–4 Villager
5. **" 2: A Car Which Looked Like It was made of Gutta-Percha / " 2: Kuttaperkkainen auto**	p. 4 Villagers
6. **Children Too Close to the Manor House 1: Playing Upper-class/ Lapset herrojen mailla 1: Hieno leikki**	p. 5 C, P Children *
7. " 2: Big Snake / " 2: Iso Käärme	p. 5 (5) C, P ", Housekeeper *
8. Ghost 1: Ghost of the Manor House / Aave 1: Pytingin kummitus	p. 6–7 (4) B Patron *
9. " 2: A Lamp Falls Down / " 2: Lamppu putoaa	p. 6–7 PB Elsa, friend
10. " 3: The Dog Is Afraid / " 3: Koira pelkää	p. 7 B
11. The Factory Owner's Dogs / Patruunan koirat	p. 8–9 (4) WC Patruuna, worker *
12. Bosses / Pomoista	p. 9 WC Workers
13. **Rude Names for Places / Rumia paikkojen nimiä**	p. 10 (3) W, H " *
14. Hiding at Work: The Big Big Boss / Piilosilla töissä 1: Iso herra	p. 11 WC, P (3) Fellow workers, boss*
15. **Different Levels of Authority: Cutting Firewood / Piilosilla töissä: Mottimehtä**	p. 11–12 WC, P ", " *
16. Having a Hard on / Värkki seisoo	p. 12 WG, H Women, male worker *
17. Old Men Teasing / Vanhat miehet kiusaavat	p. 12–13 WG, PH, Old men

18. Memories of the Market Days 1: Doll in the Lollipop / Muistoja toripäiviltä 1: Nukke tikkunekussa — p. 13–14 P Seller
19. " 2: Stye / " 2: Veripahka — p. 14 C, P Mother
20. " 3: Asking for Sweet Bread / " 3: Pullaa pyytämässä — p. 14 (4) C, P Friend, Gentlefolk *
21. " 4: Quarter Dollar / " 4: Hilikku — p. 15 P Villagers
22. " 5: Low Price / " 5: Halavalla — p. 15 H Seller
23. A Drunken Worker / Työläinen humalassa — p. 15 (4) H Worker, Boss *
24. Worker's Use of Language / Työläisen kielenkäyttöä — p. 15–16 (4) C, H ", " *
25. **Premonition 1: Father's Death / Enne 1: Isän kuolema ja enne** — p. 17 B Father
26. "2: Knocking Foretells Death / " 2: Koputus tietää kuolemaa — p. 17–18 B Mother
27. " 3: Chains / " 3: Kahleet — p. 18 B "
28. Hot Stone / Kuuma kivi — p. 19 P Parents
29. Anecdotes 1: Spring Came with Monkey-Martti / Anekdootti 1: Apina-Martti toi kevään — p. 20 W Workers, Visitor
30. " 2: I Want a Kiss / " 2: Pusun otan — p. 20 G, P "
31. " 3: The Vicar's Wife / " 3: Ruustinna — p. 20–21 GC, H "
32. " 4: Riikku-Heikki (a person's name) — p. 21 Children, Visitor
33. Christmas 1: Present from Aura / Joulu 1: Joululahja Auralta — p. 22–23 (4) C, P Siblings *
34. " 2: Santa and Grandpa's Shoes / " 2: Joulupukki ja papan kengät — p. 23 P family
35. " 3: Real Santas / " 3: Oikeat joulupukit — p. 23 C, P Gentlefolk, family
36. " 4: Treats / " 4: Kaikille joulupussit — p. 24 C, P ", villagers
37. Bikes Hoisted up the Flagpole / Pyörä tankoon — p. 25 (4) C, G Peers *
38. Smashed Skis / Sukset palasiksi — p. 26 (4) C, G " *
39. **A Invented Poem / Itse sepitetty runo** — p. 26 P Fellow workers
40. Bluebell and Daisy / Sinikellokukka ja päivänkakkara — p. 26–27
41. Father Sang / Isä lauloi — p. 27 Father
42. Father's Salve / Isän salva — p. 28 "
43. The Doctor's Advice / Lääkärin konsti — p. 28 Doctor
44. Midwife / Päästäjä — p. 28 Mother, Midwife
45. The Neighbor Died / Naapurin mies kuoli — p. 29 Neighbors
46. Food for the Mourning Family / Ruokaa kuolleen taloon — p. 30 ", villagers

Interview 2: 16 (7)

1. Eating Herring / Silakan syönti — p. 1–4 Father, family
2. The Ear Ache / Korvakivun parannuskonsti — p. 4–5 Neighbor
3. In the Sauna / Saunajuttuja — p. 7 Villagers
4. **Children Too Close to the Manor House / Lapset herrojen mailla** — p. 8 (5) C, P Children *
5. **Workers Visiting the Patrunessa / Työläiset Nessan puheilla** — p. 10 (4) C, H Patrunessa, Workers *
6. **Handprints on Your Backside / Sormenjäljet takapuolessa** — p. 10 (3) WG, P Fellow workers *
7. If it Started Raining / Jos rupeais satamaan — p. 10 WG, PH "
8. **Absurdities 1: Light Lunch / Absurdia 1: Kevyt lounas** — p. 11 (3) WCG, H " *
9. **" 2: Cleaning the Hallway / " 2: Tampuunin siivooja** — p. 11 (3) WCG, H " *

201

10. " 3: Flower Arrangements / " 3: Kukka-asetelma — p. 11 (3) WCG, H " *
11. **" 4: Pickled Gingerbread / " 4: Suolatut piparit** — p. 11 (3) WCG, H " *
12. **Mimicking / Näyttelijä** — p. 12 (3) WG, H "
13. **" 5: If I Became a Widow / " 5: Jos jäis leskeks** — p. 12 (3) WG, H " *
14. **Working on Saturday Night / Lauantai-iltana työssä** — p. 12 (3) WC, P Workers, foreman *
15. Fresh Air / Raitista ilmaa — p. 12 WC, P Workers, foreman
16. Behind the Furnace / Valsvärkin uunin takana — p. 13 W, P Fellow workers

Interview 3: 9 (3)

1. **Trading by the Classed Bias / Kastikauppaa** — pp. 4–5 (4) C, P Villagers *
2. Black Market 1: First time / Hamstruu 1: Ensimmäinen kokemus — p. 5 C, P Friend
3. **" 2: The Rocky Road / " 2: Kivinen tie** — p. 6 (5) C, P ", railroad workers *
4. **" 3: Big House and Small Cottage / " 3: Iso talo ja pieni mökki** — pp. 8–9 C, P Farmers *
5. Buying Dried Sweetbread / Korppuja hakemassa — p. 10 family
6. Shopkeeper Teltori / Kauppias Teltori — p. 12 Shopkeeper
7. Old Maid 1: The Saying / Vanhapiika kaupanmyyjä 1: Sanonta — pp. 12–13 ", man
8. " 2: Courting / " 2: Miehissä — p. 13 G, H Neighbor, shopkeeper
9. Frozen Ground / Rouvan rakkoon — pp. 18–19 H Father

Interview 4: 18 (5)

1. Frightened / Säikähdys — p. 1 W, P Visitor
2. Ironing Man's Shirt / Paidan silitys — p. 3 (3) WC, P Lady of the house
3. Ironing Goes Wrong / Silitys menee pieleen — p. 3 (3) WC, P "
4. The Perfect Household / Täydellinen huusholli — p. 3 (3) WG, P " *
5. Cooking Game Dishes / Metsälinnun laittaminen — pp. 3–4 WGC, P Master "
6. A Born Gentleman / Synnynnäinen herra — p. 4 (4) WGC, P " *
7. A Maid Servant Worth a Hundred / Satasen piiat — p. 5 WGC, P Friend
8. A Maid Servant with the Latva Family 1; Professor / Maist. Latvalla piikana 1: Prohvessori — p. 5 WC, P Gentlefolk *
9. " 2: Gift to the Member of Women's Auxiliary / " 2: Lahja pikku-Lotalle — p. 6 (5) WC, P Lady of the house *
10. Elsa's Service with the Amberg Family / Elsa jää Ambergille — p. 6 (4) WC, P " *
11. A Maid servant and a Young Man / Piika ja nuori herra — pp. 6–7 WGC, P ", Young man
12. Working with Sister Aili and the Old Men / Aili-siskon ja vanhojen miesten kanssa töissä — p. 7 WG P Old men, sibling
13. **Tired Worker / Väsynyt työntekijä** — p. 9 WG, PH Old men
14. **How's the Hammer Doing? / Mitä vasaralle kuuluu?** — p. 9 (3) WGC, P Workers, visitors *
15. **Rude Names for Places / Rumia paikkojen nimiä** — p. 10 (4) W " *
16. **Hiding at Work: Cutting Firewood / Piilosilla töissä: Mottimehtä** — p. 10 WC, P Workers, boss *
17. **Asking for a Raise / Palkankorotusta pyytämässä** — pp. 10–11 (3) WGC, P (H?) ", " *
18. **Memories of Wartime / Sotamuistoja kaatuneista** — pp. 14–15 (4) Villagers

Appendix 4

*Interview 5: 35 **(15)***

1.	Memories of Schooldays / Koulumuistoja	pp. 1–2 (5) C, P Family
2.	War Broke Out and Work Began / Sota ja työt alkoivat	p. 2 W, P *
3.	**From a Dogsbody's Dogsbody to Operating a Machine / Sällin sällistä koneelle**	pp. 2–3 (4) W, P Foreman *
4.	Legacies of the Factory /Tehtaan mahaleita	p. 3 (4) W, P Friends *
5.	**Waiting for the Wages / Palkan odottaminen**	p. 3 (4) WGC, P *
6.	Black Paths / Mustat polut	p. 4 W Workers
7.	**Memories of the Market Days 1: Low Prices / Muistoja toripäiviltä 1: Halavalla**	p. 4 H Seller
8.	**" 2: Quarter Dollar / " 2: Hilikku**	p. 4 P Villagers
9.	**" 3: Stye / " 3: Veripahka**	pp. 4–5 (4) C, P Seller
10.	Food Rationing / Ruoan jako	p. 5 C Villagers, mother
11.	**Shoes Too Fine to Wear / Liian hienot kengät**	p. 5 (5) C, P Father *
12.	**At Haapamäki Station / Haapamäellä**	p. 6 Peers, German soldiers
13.	**An Old Maid Nurse / Vanhapiika terveyssisar**	p. 6 (3) CG, P Nurse *
14.	At the Hospital / Sairastamassa	pp. 6–7 P Doctors, nurses
15.	**Fathers' Death / Isän kuolema ja enne**	p. 7 B Father
16.	My Wedding / Omat häät	p. 8 G, P Peers
17.	Christmas Party / Joulujuhlat	p. 8 P Villagers, Children
18.	**Black Market 1: Rocky Road/ Hamstruu 1: Kivinen tie**	p. 9 (5) GC, P Friend, railroad workers*
19.	**" 2: Big House and Small Cottage / " 2: Iso talo ja pieni mökki**	p. 10 (4) C Friend, farmers *
20.	" 3: Not Dangerous / " 3 Ei vaarallinen	p. 10 P ", "
21.	**Clothes under the Counter / Vaatetta tiskin alta**	p. 10 (4) G, P Old people, sellers *
22.	The Girl from Next Door Got Nylons / Naapurin tyttö sai nailonit	pp. 10–11 (4) GC Neighbor *
23.	Silk Stockings and Hemp Leggings / (Silkkisukkia ja hamppua)	p. 11 (4) GC, P Railroad workers *
24.	**Fare Dodging 1: A Stye in My Eye / Pummilla junassa 1: Silmä**	p. 11 (5) P, Conductor, Peers *
25.	**" 2: Swedish Magazines / " 2: Ruotsalainen lehti**	p. 11 (5) C ", " *
26.	Potluck / Nyyttikestit	p. 12 Peers, old man
27.	How Hurutlinna Got Its Name / Miten Hurutlinna sai nimensä	p. 14 Patruuna
28.	Dryer / Linko	p. 15 (5) P, H Friend *
29.	Wild Grandson / Villi lapsenlapsi	p. 16 P Family
30.	Sister's Letters / Siskon kirjeitä viemässä	p. 17 Siblings
31.	**War Memories / Sotamuistoja kaatuneista**	pp. 17 P, Siblings
32.	Frightened on the Train 1: Shady-looking Men / Pelkoa junassa 1: hämärät miehet	pp. 17–18 (5) G, P Unknown men *
33.	Frightened in Helsinki / Pelkoa Helsingissä	p. 18 (5) P Siblings *
34.	Frightened on the Train 2 / Pelkoa junassa 2	p.18 P Family
35.	A Worried Mother / Äidillistä huolenpitoa	p.18 (5) P "

Appendix 4

Interview 6: 26 (9)

1. Soldier at the Window / Sotilas ikkunassa	p. 1 (3) P Soldier *
2. The River Rushes / Koskikin kuohuu aina	p. 2 G, P Soldier
3. **Absurdities 1: Pickled Gingerbread / Absurdia 1: Suolatut piparit**	pp. 3–4 (3) WCG, H Fellow worker *
4. **" 2: Cleaning the Hallway / " 2: Tampuunin siivooja**	pp. 3–4 (3)WCG, H " *
5. **" 3: If I Became a Widow / " 3: Jos jäis leskeks**	p. 4 (3) WG, H " *
6. **An Invented Poem / Itse sepitetty runo**	p. 4 P Fellow workers
7. Dancing 1: Lights off / Tanssimuistoja 1: Valot pois	p. 5 G, P Peers
8. " 2: Is It You? / " 2: Oletko se sinä	p. 5 G, P "
9. I Watched Raija / Kyttäsin Raijaa	pp. 5–6, P Family
10. Courting: Raija & Kalevi / Riiustelua: Raija & Kalevi	p. 6 G "
11. Ghost 1: The Clatter of Dishes / Aave 1: Kolistelija	p. 7 PB
12. **" 2: Wake Up / " 2: Herättäjä**	p. 7 PB
13. " 3: Frightened Neighbor / " 3: Naapurin säikyttäjä	p. 8 PB Neighbor
14. " 4: Frightened Niece / " 4: Siskontytön säikäyttäjä	p. 8 PB Family
15. " 5: Don't Be Afraid / " 5: Älä ole huolissasi	p. 9 PB
16. **" 6: Sound of Footsteps at the Manor House / " 6 Pytingin askeleet**	p. 9 (4) PB Friend
17. **" 7: A Lamp Falls Down / " 7: Lamppu putoaa**	p. 10 PB Friend
18. **" 8: The Dog Was Afraid / " 8: Koira pelkää**	p. 11 B
19. " 9: The Dog Saw Dead People / " 9: Koira näki kuolleita	p. 11B Neighbor
20. Dead Man Wakes up / Kuollut herää eloon	p. 12 B Unknown man
21. Man Sleeps in a Coffin / Mies nukkuu arkussa	p. 12 B "
22. **Old Maid Nurse / Vanhapiika sairaanhoitaja**	p. 15 (3) CG. P Nurse
23. Inconsiderate Advice / Terveyssisaren ajattelematon neuvo	p. 15 (3) CG, P " *
24. Visiting the Doctor / Lääkärissä	p. 15 WCG Fellow worker, doctor *
25. Help from Worker's Sick Fund / Kipukassa apuna	p. 16 W, P Eino
26. Mimicking / Näyttelijä	p. 26 W, H Fellow worker

Interview 7: 16 (5)

1. Viivi and Her Children on the Train / Viivi ja lapset junassa	p. 1 Villagers, siblings
2. Letters / Kirjeistä	p. 5 P Siblings
3. The Vicar and Morality / Kirkkoherra ja moraali	p. 7 G Uncle, Vicar
4. **Courtesy Forms of Address / Teitittelyä**	p. 7 (3) Family, siblings *
5. The Heroic Mother / Sisukas äiti	pp. 8–9 (3) GC Mother *
6. Sointu and the Gingerbread / Sointu ja renikat	p. 10 Siblings
7. **Mum's Discipline / Äiti piti kuria**	p. 11 (3) G, P Mother *
8. Children Swimming / Lapset uimassa	pp. 12–13 C, P Chridren, villagers
9. The Sewing Machine / Naalimakone	p. 13 C ", "
10. The Days of Log-Floating / Uittopäivät	pp. 13–14 G ", Lumberjacks
11. **A Car Which Looked Like It Was Made of Gutta-percha / Kuttaperkkainen auto**	p. 15 Villagers

204

12. A Maid servant at Parties / Piikana juhlien alla	p. 15–16 C, P Man, Lady of the house
13. Time and Motion Analysts / Kellokallet	p. 17 (5) W, P Workers *
14. **Workers and the *Patronessa*** / Työläiset Nessan puheilla	pp. 19–20 (4) C, H Workers, the Patronessa *
15. Wealthy Girl Wonders about Patched Clothes / Rikas tyttö ihmettelee housun paikkoja	p. 20 (4) C Children, siblings *
16. **Trading by the Classed Bias / Kastikauppaa**	pp. 21–22 (4) C Shop-owner, villager *

Interview 8: 21 (2)

1. Back to Work / Takaisin töihin	pp. 1–3 (3) WCG, P Elsa, Eino *
2. **Waiting for the Wages / Palkan odottaminen**	p. 3 (4) WC, P Workers *
3. Retiring / Eläkkeelle jäänti	p. 4 (4) WC, P Workers
4. Visiting the Social Insurance Institution / Kelalla käynti	p. 4 (4) WC, P Office worker *
5. Sliding on the Floor / Lattialla luistelua	p. 5 P Eerika *
6. Old Mill Bridge / Myllysilta	pp. 5–6 P Villagers
7. Salmon Season 1: Action in and in front of the Tent / Lohiaikana 1: Teltan edessä ja sisällä tapahtuu	p. 6 P Visitors
8. " 2: Eager Fisherman / " 2: Innokas kalamies	p. 6 P Villager
9. Uncle and Traders of Craw Fish and /Ravun ostajat ja Setä	p. 7 "
10. Getting Bites / Syöttejä hankkimassa	pp. 7–8 P
11. Salmon Season 3: Wood from the Dam Was Burned / Lohiaikana 3: Lussit poltettiin	p. 8 Visitors
12. Nursing Home of Kaija / Kaija oli kauhistus	p. 8 Villagers
13. The Demolished Smokestack / Tehtaan piippu kaatuu	p. 9 (5) W, P (Old) workers *
14. Touring / Kierroksella	pp. 9–10 C Children
15. An Old Man's Suicide / Vanhuksen itsemurha	pp. 10–11 Children, old man
16. Road Trip Narrative 1: The Ghost of Turku Castle / Autoreissulla 1: Turun linnan kummitus	p. 11 P Siblings
17. " 2: At the Vaasa Market Square / " 2: Vaasan torilla	pp. 11–12 (5) PH ", Family *
18. " 3: Who Is the Last to Swim / " 3: Kuka kastelee viimeisenä	p. 12 PH ", "
19. " 4: High-heeled Shoe Gets Stuck / " 4: Kengänkorko jää kiinni	p. 12 PH ", "
20. " 5: Making Faces in the Back of the Car / " 5: Ilveilyä takaikkunassa	p. 12 (5) PH ", " *
21. **Fare Dodging / Pummilla junassa**	p. 13 (5) P Peers *

Interview 9: 26 (8)

1. Dream 1: Contact Us Twice a Day / Uni 1: Ota yhteys aamuin illoin	p. 1 PB
2. Dream 2: Illnesses / Uni 2: Sairaudet	p. 1–2 PB
3. Dream 3: Small Mattress / Uni 3: Pieni patja	pp. 2–3 PB
4. Dream 4: Concussion / Uni 4: Aivotärähdys	pp. 3–4 PB
5. **Ghost 1: Wake up / Aave 1: Herättäjä**	p. 4 PB
6. " 2: Dead Person Having a Meal / " 2: Vainaja ruokailee	p. 4 PB Siblings, Mother

Appendix 4

7. Cattle Go Missing / Karja katoaa — p. 5 B Villagers
8. **Ghost 3: A Lamp Falls Down / Aave 3: Lamppu putoaa** — p. 5 PB Friend
9. " 4: Man Walks towards the Manor House / " 4: Mies kävelee Pytingille — p. 5 PB Children
10. **" 5: Sound of Footsteps at the Manor House / " 5: Pytingin askeleet** — p. 6 PB (3) Friend
11. Home Sickness 1: Visiting Uncle Hermanni / Koti-ikävä 1: Hauta-aholla kylässä — p. 6 P, Uncle
12. " 2: Siblings Leave Home / " 2: Sisaret lähtevät — p. 6 (5) P, Family *
13. The Curtseying Girl / Niiaava tyttö — p. 7 Children (of today)
14. **Courtesy Forms of Address / Teitittelyä** — p. 7 (3) Family, siblings *
15. At the Hospital 1: Some Excitement in Life / Sairaalassa 1: Vipinää elämään — p. 8 (5) PH Nurses *
16. " 2: Downtown / " 2: Kirkonkylälle — p. 8 (5) PH Friend
17. **Brother Esko Returns Home on Sunday Morning / Esko-veli riiuureissulla** — p. 9 G, H Siblings, old women
18. Buying Cough Mixture / Tippojen haussa — p. 9 WC, H Old man
19. Call of Nature / Hankaniemen mettässä pikkutakkipaskalla — p. 9 C, H Worker
20. Fighting Neighbors / Naapurit tappelee — p. 10 G, H Neighbor
21. Advising a Younger Worker / Nuorempaa työntekijää neuvomassa — p. 11 W, P Fellow worker
22. Slapping Colleague / Työkaveri hakkaa — pp. 11–12 W, P "
23. **Working on Saturday Night / Lauantai-iltana työssä** — p. 12 WC, P Fellow worker, foreman*
24. **Absurdities 1: Light lunch / Absurdia 1: Kevyt illallinen** — p. 12 WCG, H Fellow worker *
25. **" 2: Cleaning the Hallway / " 2: Tampuunin siivooja** — p. 12 WG, H " *
26. Uncle Hermanni and Runeberg / Hermanni-eno ja Runeberg — p. 13 Uncle

Interview 10: 22 (2)

1. Mum Prepared Tasty Coffee / Äiti keitti hyvät kahvit — p. 1 Mother
2. The Flywheel / Varppi — p. 2 W, Fellow workers
3. Beauty Contest / Kauneuskilpailut — p. 3 G, P Old woman
4. The Hair Net over the Chignon / Verkko kampauksen päälle — p. 4 P
5. Electric Curls / Sähkökiharat — p. 5 G, P Friend, family
6. Photo / Valokuvassa — p. 6 P
7. Taxi to the Church / Taksilla rippikirkolle — p. 6–7 P
8. Your Life's Path / Sinun polkusi — p. 7 P Friend, Friend's mother
9. Let the Others Study / Muut lukevat — p. 8–9 (5) C, P Family *
10. Illness as a Highlight / Sairaudesta kohokohta — p. 9 (5) PH *
11. Illness as a Ghost / Sairaus kuin aave — p. 10 P, Other old women
12. A Bear Whistled / Karhu vihelsi siellä — p. 10 P
13. A Bear Tried to Escape Its Cage / Karhu yritti karata häkistä — p. 11
14. Invitation Dances / Kutsutanssit — p. 12 G, P Peers
15. The Floppy Hat / Räysähattu — p. 13 (3) GH ", Visitor

16. Worried Brother / Huolestunut veli	p. 13 (3) G Siblings
17. **Performing Sardas and Old Maidens / Mustalaisleiri ja Raatikko**	p. 14 Peers
18. Song of the Street Boys / Laulu katupoikien	p. 15 C ", gentlefolk *
19. **Performing at Alavus / Alavuden nuorisoseura**	pp. 15 Peers, farmers
20. **Girls of Taimi on the Train / Taimen tytöt junassa**	p. 16 Peers, passangers
21. Why Don't You Come to Dance? / Mikset sää tuu tanssiin?	p. 16 (6) PH *
22. I Know All about Chopping Wood / Mottimehtä on tuttu	p. 16 P Siblings, father *

Interview 11: 22 (5)

1. Too Tired to Speak / Mun kieleni väsyy	p. 1 Mother
2. **Mum's Discipline / Äiti piti kuria**	p. 1 (3) G, Mother *
3. Stuck in the Arm with an Awl / Naskali käsivartee	p. 1 (3) Father *
4. Girls to the Attic / Tytöt vinttii	p. 1 Father, siblings
5. Scary Little Sister / Pelottava pikkusisko	p. 2 Siblings
6. Worried about Pauli / Huoli Paulista	p. 2 (5) "
7. Father and the Bible / Isä luki Raamattua	p. 4 Father
8. **Brother Esko on Sunday morning / Esko-veli riiuureissulla**	p. 5 G Siblings
9. **Shoes Too Fine to Wear / Liian hienot kengät**	p. 6 (5) C Father *
10. New Skirt / Uusi kolttu	p. 6 C, P
11. Men on the Way to the Frontlines / Miehet matkalla rintamalle	p. 11 P Soldiers
12. The Evacuees / Evakot	p. 12 P Karelians
13. Whipped Cream / Kermavaahto	p. 13 P Karelians
14. **Clothes under the Counter / Vaatetta tiskin alta**	p. 15 (4), G, P Old people *
15. Boots with Curled Toes / Kippurakärkiset kengät	p. 15 C, P Siblings*
16. The Fur Collar / Karvakaulus	p. 16 P
17. The Georgette Coat / Sorsettitakki	p. 17 Friend
18. Paper Shoes and a Paper Hat / Puukengät ja hattu	p. 18 Peers
19. Cotton is Cheap / Retonki on halpa	p. 19 (3) GC, P Peers *
20. **Cockroaches / Russakat**	p. 20 C Old woman
21. Neighbor's Cockroaches / Naapurin russakat	p. 21 P Neighbors, Father
22. My Eyes Have Dried Out / Kuivaneet silmät	p. 22 P

Interview 12: 19 (9)

1. Meeri and Aarne / Meeri ja Aarne	p. 1 WG Fellow workers
2. You've Been Getting Some / Oot saanu	p. 2 (3) WG " *
3. Men Should Know Their Own Business / Kylläpä miehet tietää omasa	p. 2 (3) WG, P " *
4. **Tired Worker / Väsynyt työntekijä**	p. 3 WG, P Old men
5. University Students / Ylioppilaat	p. 3 (4) WCG, P Friend, Men *
6. Joking at the Station / Vitsin kerrontaa asemalla	p. 4 H Peers
7. Black Fox / Musta kettu	pp. 4–5 (3) W, G Men, Father *
8. **Fingerprints on Your Backside / Sormenjäljet takapuolessa**	p. 5 (3) WG, P fellow workers *
9. Prosthesis / Proteesi	p. 5 WG "

10. How to Have Children / Miten lapsia tehdään p. 5 WG, H "
11. **How's the Hammer Doing? / Mitä vasaralle kuuluu** p. 6 WCG, P Visitor *
12. **Big Big Boss / Iso herra** pp. 6–7 WC, P Workers, bosses *
13. **Asking for a Raise / Palkankorotusta pyytämässä** p. 7 (3) WCG, PH (?) *
14. **From a Dogsbody's Dogsbody to Operating a Machine / Sällin sällistä koneelle** p. 8 W, P Foreman *
15. You Have Eaten, Haven't you? / Kylläpä söitkin p. 8 WC, P " *
16. **Visiting the Alavus Youth Association's Hall / Alavuden nuorisoseuran talolla** p. 10 P Peers, farmers
17. **Performing Sardas / Mustalaisleiri** p. 10 P Peers
18. **Girls of Taimi on the Train / Taimen tytöt junassa** p. 10 P Peers
19. **At the Haapamäki Station / Haapamäellä** p. 11 P Peers, German soldiers

Appendix 5:
Actors of Elsa's Narratives

US	In the middle	THEM
Insiders	**In the middle**	**Gentlefolk**
Workers	Shop owners	Patruuna Keirkner
Fellow workers	Foremen (Masters)	Patronessa (Nessa)
(men/ women)	Office staff	Amberg, Old / Young
Old men (at work)	Housekeeper	(Manager /Technical
The old people	Teachers	Manager, Master of
(men/women)		the House)
Grandpa Vihtori	**Outsiders**	Illman (Manager, Master
Children, "we"	Sellers	of the House)
Friend/Peers (working-	Doctors	Mrs. Amberg
class youth, "we, the	Nurses	(Lady of the House)
girls of the ironworks"	Vicar	Mrs. Illman
Neighbors	Visitors	(Lady of the House)
Villagers	Farmers	Mr. Latva (Master of the
Railroad workers	Train Passengers	House, absent)
Conductors	Soldiers	Mrs. Latva
	German soldiers	(Lady of the House)
Family members	Unknown men/people	Mrs. Latva's Mother
Father / Mother		English Professor
Siblings		Big Bosses
Uncle Hermanni		University students
Eino		Students of the Forestry
Elsa's children		Institute
Granddaughter Eerika		

Abstract

Eerika Koskinen-Koivisto

Her Own Worth

Negotiations of Subjectivity in the Life
Narrative of a Female Labourer

In this study, I examine the life narrative of a female factory labourer, Elsa Koskinen (née Kiikkala, born in 1927). I analyze her account of her experiences related to work, class and gender because I seek to gain a better understanding of how changes in these aspects of life influenced the ways in which she saw her own worth at the time of the interviews and how she constructed her subjectivity. Elsa's life touches upon many of the core aspects of 20th-century social change: changes in women's roles, the entrance of middle-class women into working life, women's increasing participation in the public sphere, feminist movements, upward social mobility, the expansion of the middle class, the growth of welfare and the appearance of new technologies. What kind of trajectory did Elsa take in her life? What are the key narratives of her life? How does her narrative negotiate the shifting cultural ideals of the 20th century?

A life story, a retrospective evaluation of a life lived, is one means of constructing continuity and dealing with the changes that have affected one's life, identity and subjectivity. In narrating one's life, the narrator produces many different versions of her/him self in relation to other people and to the world. These dialogic selves and their relations to others may manifest internal contradictions. Contradictions may also occur in relation to other narratives and normative discourses. Both of these levels, subjective meaning making and the negotiation of social ideals and collective norms, are embedded in life narratives.

My interest in this study is in the ways in which gender and class intersect with paid labour in the life of an ordinary female factory worker. I approach gender, class and work from both an experiential and a relational perspective, considering the power of social relationships and subject formations that shape individual life at the micro-level. In her narratives Elsa discusses ambivalence related to gendered ideals, social class, and especially the phenomenon of social climbing as well as technological advance.

I approach Elsa's life and narratives *ethnographically*. The research material was acquired in a long-standing interview process and the analysis is based on *reflexivity* of the dialogic knowledge production and *contextualization* of Elsa's experiences. In other words I analyze Elsa's narratives in their situational but also socio-cultural and historical contexts. Specific episodes in one's life and other significant events constitute smaller narrative entities, which I call *micro-narratives*. The analysis of micro-narratives, key dialogues and cultural ideals embedded in the interview dialogues offers perspectives on experiences of social change and the narrator's sense of self.

Index

Actor 25, 48, 49, 52, 115, 153, 209
Adulthood 36, 60, 79, 142–147,
Age 27, 60, 78, 135, 147, 150, 151, 153–159
Agency 26, 29, 32, 34, 68–70, 77–78, 88, 119, 123
Alcohol, -ism 58–59, 91
Anecdote 15, 25, 72, 75
Antagonism 16, 84, 86, 90, 122
Authentic, -ity 38, 43, 92, 114, 125
Authority, -arian 42, 48, 54, 76–77, 86, 88, 89, 112, 137
Autobiography, -cal 24, 33, 25, 26, 28, 36, 48
Automation / mechanization 14, 22, 122

Black market 100–102, 137–139
Blue collar 78, 96–97
Bodily practices 28, 98
Bodily expressions 50, 114–115, 119
Bodily layering 113, 152
Boundaries 20, 73, 83, 95, 100, 103, 105, 127, 130, 145
Breadwinner 58, 65

Capitalist, -sm, 23, 84–86, 113, 118
Childhood 17, 27, 33, 34, 35, 36, 43, 133–135
Chronotope / time-space 132, 133, 139
Civil war 20–21, 23, 135, 136
Class 13, 16, 27, 28, 34, 36–37, 38–42, 51, 53, 60, 64, 65, 75, 82, 83–116, 125–129, 132–135, 136–137, 145, 150, 150–153, 156
Clothes 36, 82–83, 98–101, 11, 113, 136–137
Coherent, -nce 26, 35, 45, 52, 119, 125
Continuity 14, 117, 119, 129, 131, 135, 145, 150, 152–153, 156

Crystallized narrative 34, 48, 63, 101, 107
Cultural ideal / cultural (model) narrative 51–52, 57, 72, 153, 155–157

Deindustrial, -ed, -ization 23, 131
Dialogic 14, 15, 26, 31–32, 35, 49, 65, 156,
Dialogic anthropology 31
Dialogic methodology 13
Dialogic self 26
Dialogic ethnography 65
Dialogue, 26, 31–32, 34, 35, 41–43, 63, 77, 115, 155–156
Dignity 108–111
Dirt, -y 28, 61, 63, 67–68, 69–70, 78, 80–82, 110, 113
Distinction 39, 50, 84, 89, 94–95, 97, 98, 107, 136
Distancing 40, 50, 140, 145, 147
Doctor,-s 18, 32, 39, 72–73, 83, 111–112

Education 13, 38, 63, 95, 97, 99, 108–109,111, 113, 115, 121, 130, 131–132, 151, 157
Educator 37, 71
Eigensinn 75
Embodied 25, 80, 113, 118, 146, 153
Embodied memories, 50, 110, 132
Engineer, -s 121, 129
Epistemology 64, 31
Ethics 44–47
Ethnology 15–16, 36
Ethnography, -ic 31–32, 25, 38, 45
Ethnography of narrative 32
Ethnography of subjectivity 13
Ethos of work 112–113, 156
Experience
    Narrated Experience 24–25, 43
    Personal Experience 33, 52, 87, 119, 131–132, 150, 157

Factory work 17–18, 60–61, 80–82, 109–112, 118–121, 151–152
Factory village 18–22, 84
Factory owner 84, 85–88
Family 16–18, 22–24, 34, 35, 36–37, 42, 49, 52–53, 54–66, 67, 72, 83, 84, 85–86, 88, 95, 98–100, 105, 113, 114–115,124, 125, 133–135, 137, 142, 148, 150, 155
Father 16–17, 22–23, 54–59, 69, 84, 85, 98–99, 110, 134, 136–38
Feminine, -nity 80–82, 99, 150, 156
Folk, -ness 16, 38, 90
Folk culture /tradition 15, 69, 70
Folklore 41
Folklore Studies 15–16, 36, 45
Foreman 18, 76–77, 79, 80, 90, 97
Fragmentary, -iness 26, 125
Free / leisure time (activities) 21, 34, 35, 77, 82, 91, 92–95, 135–136

Generation 36–37, 39–40, 41–44, 46, 59, 62, 124, 129–130, 141, 148, 150, 154, 156–157
Gender 14, 16, 27–29, 36–37,53–82, 90–91, 93–95, 99, 105, 108, 114, 119–120, 135–137, 150–152, 156–157
Gender contract /system 29
Gentlefolk 83, 86, 100, 103, 105, 134–135
Grandmother 143, 40, 43, 12
Granddaughter 37, 43
Gymnastics 35, 136–137

Health, -y 26, 34, 46, 53, 57, 79, 135, 146–147
Health care 34, 72–73
Health care professionals 62, 72–73, 145
Hermeneutics 31, 35
Heroe, -ine, -ic,-ism 57–59, 120, 121, 133, 139
High(er) class 33, 39, 65, 94, 98, 100, 104, 107, 127, 132
Homemaker 22, 28, 53–59, 61–62, 145, 151, 153, 157
Housewife 63, 144–145, 151
Household work /chores 17, 27, 55, 58–60, 62, 63, 65, 67, 96, 150, 152
Humiliation 108
Humour 15, 34, 35, 47, 48, 50, 51–54, 66–77, 98, 145–146, 151–152, , 153, 155, 156

Identity 14, 18, 26–27, 38, 39, 41, 48, 49, 65, 81, 82, 84, 85, 98, 108–110, 112–116, 122, 125, 120, 133, 141, 146, 150–153
Identification 28, 39, 49, 50, 51, 54, 89, 98, 108–116, 151, 153–154
Illness 34, 47, 51, 120, 145–146, 155
Industrial safety 118–120
Industrial community 14, 19–22, 22–23, 68, 95, 84–85, 95, 129–133
Industrialization 18–20
In-depth interview 32–33
Intergenerational 41–43, 54
Intersectionality 28–29
Intersubjective, -vity 33
Intimate, -acy 33, 37, 47
Ironworks 84, 18–22
Irony, -ic 47, 48, 50, 72–73, 82, 123, 145, 147, 151, 155

Joke, -ing 54, 66–77, 81, 90, 93, 98, 106, 145–147, 155

Key narrative/dialogue 14, 47, 49, 63, 114, 153, 155, 157, 159

Landscape 50, 80, 117–118, 127–128, 129–133, 152
Life narrative / story 12, 13, 15, 24–25, 25–27, 32, 149, 152
Life history 24, 53
Life review 41
Life story interview 32–33, 49
Labour/ Workers' movement 20, 22, 84, 85
Labour/ trade union 75, 20–21, 22, 23, 84, 85
Language 46–47, 75, 78, 84, 86, 91, 96, 114
Lockout 16, 21, 85
Low(er)-class
Lotta Svärd Organization 104–105, 136–137

Machine, -s 77–78, 81, 109–110, 113, 117, 118–120, 122–123
Maid servant 33, 39, 104–105, 59–60, 62, 95–96, 106, 151
Marriage 46, 64, 94, 125
Managers, -rial, -ment 18, 19, 21, 75, 76, 83–85, 89, 92, 95, 97, 114, 126
Masculine, -nity 28, 54, 65, 68, 78–80, 81, 90–92, 114, 118, 152
Master narrative 51–52, 152
Materiality 82, 98–104, 113, 117, 124–126, 130–132, 137, 150–151

213

Index

Memory 28, 46–47, 52, 119, 124, 132, 152
Metal industry 14, 78, 122
Metaphor, -ic 41, 48, 50, 84, 109–110, 114, 132, 133, 152, 154
Micro-narrative 25, 34, 48–49, 153–155
Middle class 12, 28, 58, 59–60, 63, 72–73, 77, 83, 95, 97, 104–108, 135, 135, 151, 157
Modernisation 12, 13, 20, 51, 66, 84, 95, 156
Modern woman 53, 63, 115, 141, 157
Moral, -ity 24, 46, 50, 53, 66–67, 69–71, 73, 74, 82, 89, 91, 92–93, 94–95, 105–106, 112, 124, 132, 139, 140, 151, 154
Mother 17, 22, 28, 36, 45, 53, 54–59, 143, 150, 151
Motherhood 53–54, 59–63, 71–73, 141, 143, 156–157
Multi-vocal, -ility 13, 32, 153

Narration 24–27, 28, 32, 44, 48–49, 49–51, 51–52, 119, 153–154
Narrative 12, 24–25, 48
Narrative ethnography 32
Narrative identity 27, 156
Narrative key 48
Narrative orientation 50, 153
Narrative strategy 119, 151, 154
Narrative turn 36
Norms 12, 14, 28, 53, 54, 74, 75, 90, 97, 127, 145
Nostalgia, -ic 43–44, 46, 65, 117, 121–122, 123–124, 128, 130–131, 133, 135, 152, 153, 154
Nurse, -s 39, 62, 145

Pain, -full 51, 108, 120, 152, 156–157
Patriarchy, -cal 14, 28, 40, 65, 66, 75, 80, 85, 132, 152
Performance 48, 50, 77, 75, 114
Performativity 26, 77–78
Perroque 78
Personal (experience) narrative 15, 25, 31, 41, 47, 50, 51, 54, 132, 133, 154
Physical work 13, 17, 18, 27, 45, 51, 52, 60–61, 65, 78–80, 104–107, 108–112, 112–115, 119, 120–122, 123, 131, 140, 151, 152
Poverty 41, 98–103
Positioning 48–51, 133, 150, 153, 155, 156
Post-modern 26
Power 12, 27–29, 38, 63–66, 73–78, 79–80, 115, 140

Production line 61, 66, 78, 104, 107, 109, 118–119, 129

Rationing 82, 94, 100–101, 105, 110
Rationalization 118, 120
Reciprocal ethnography 46
Reflexive, -ity 26, 31, 32, 35, 36, 38–40
Reflexive turn 31
Reported speech 48, 65–66, 112
Respectability 58, 67, 106, 156
Rhetoric, -al 28, 51, 61, 124, 139
Rhetoric other 43
Ritual 74, 91
Romantic, -ize 38–39, 44

Scarcity 98–103, 137
School 17, 19, 21, 24, 59, 63, 77, 95, 99, 108, 110, 111, 113, 130, 135–136, 156, 157
Self 13, 14, 26–27, 49–50, 52, 66, 79–80, 98–116, 117, 119, 121, 131, 133, 136, 139, 141–142, 152–153
Self-control 79–80
Self-esteem 61, 109
Self-identification 38, 152
Self-image 105, 145, 149
Self-reflection 36, 49
Self-respect
Self-representation 13, 37, 47, 52, 62–63, 65, 88, 119, 136, 139, 146, 147, 148, 153–154, 156
Sense of self 13, 22, 52, 64, 84, 112–116, 132–133
Sense of community 52, 66, 83, 84, 98–105, 124, 128, 135, 150, 154
Sexual humour / joking / jokes 69, 70, 106, 151
Sexual norms / morals 54, 71, 82
Sexuality 27, 29, 67, 69, 10, 82, 140, 150
Shame 12, 65, 72, 74, 75, 82, 104, 107, 108, 152
Shoes 22, 43, 55, 80, 83, 99, 113, 136–137, 141
Significant others 49
Small narrative, -s 48, 114
Social hierarchy 12, 14, 38, 64, 73, 83–116, 132, 126–129, 135–136, 150
Social climbing / mobility 12, 14, 15, 37, 51, 65, 92, 95–98,
Solidarity 66, 75, 92–95, 124, 133–135, 140, 154
Space 26, 49, 67, 77, 78, 110, 117, 120, 125–128, 131, 132–133, 153,
Sport club 21–22, 92–93
Stability 129, 130–132

Stereotype 25, 49, 59, 84, 90–92
Stigmatized, -ation 98, 99, 108
Strike 16, 21, 83
Subject, -ivity 13, 14, 16, 25–27, 27–29, 36, 37, 48, 113, 115–116, 118, 119, 141, 148, 150–153, 155, 156
Subjective 28, 32, 36, 37, 41, 110, 118, 129, 150
Subordination 27, 79, 104, 106–107, 121, 106,

Technological advance 15, 22, 51, 118, 121, 122, 129, 156
The Second World War 14, 17, 21, 34, 45, 53, 61, 62, 82, 83, 95, 100–101, 108–109, 111, 125, 136, 153
Tradition 13, 14, 15, 16, 31, 33, 38, 41, 49, 69, 70, 75, 78, 87, 88, 90, 114, 117, 124, 129
Translation 30, 47
Transcription 30
Travelling 133–141, 144–146
Time 24, 25, 26, 33, 40, 41, 45, 46, 49–50, 78, 82, 110, 113, 117, 118, 120, 122, 125–133, 127, 131–132,

Time and motion analyst 120
Time-space 133

Wage 74–75, 106 –107
Wage labour / work 18, 27, 28, 63, 82, 100, 109
Wartime 62, 78, 79, 101–102, 109, 111, 137, 139, 141, 147, 153
Widow 18, 74, 125, 146
Worker identity 39, 64, 112–116, 118–120, 146, 151–153
Working class 39, 53, 58, 60, 77, 82, 83–116
Working-class youth 108–109, 112, 139–140, 151
Working-class women 36, 53, 60, 82, 91, 95, 104, 112, 141, 150

Young women 53, 61, 62, 73–77, 78–79, 80–82, 92–95, 101, 105–106, 139, 140, 141, 152
Youth 33, 34, 44, 50, 54, 60, 66–70, 73–77, 78–79, 82, 92–95, 108, 111–112, 124–125, 133–141, 144, 146, 151

Studia Fennica Ethnologica

Memories of My Town
The Identities of Town Dwellers and Their Places in Three Finnish Towns
Edited by Anna-Maria Åström, Pirjo Korkiakangas & Pia Olsson
Studia Fennica Ethnologica 8
2004

Passages Westward
Edited by Maria Lähteenmäki & Hanna Snellman
Studia Fennica Ethnologica 9
2006

Defining Self
Essays on emergent identities in Russia Seventeenth to Nineteenth Centuries
Edited by Michael Branch
Studia Fennica Ethnologica 10
2009

Touching Things
Ethnological Aspects of Modern Material Culture
Edited by Pirjo Korkiakangas, Tiina-Riitta Lappi & Heli Niskanen
Studia Fennica Ethnologica 11
2008

Gendered Rural Spaces
Edited by Pia Olsson & Helena Ruotsala
Studia Fennica Ethnologica 12
2009

Laura Stark
The Limits of Patriarchy
How Female Networks of Pilfering and Gossip Sparked the First Debates on Rural Gender Rights in the 19th-century Finnish-Language Press
Studia Fennica Ethnologica 13
2011

Where is the Field?
The Experience of Migration Viewed through the Prism of Ethnographic Fieldwork
Edited by Laura Hirvi & Hanna Snellman
Studia Fennica Ethnologica 14
2012

Laura Hirvi
Identities in Practice
A Trans-Atlantic Ethnography of Sikh Immigrants in Finland and in California
Studia Fennica Ethnologica 15
2013

Eerika Koskinen-Koivisto
Her Own Worth
Negotiations of Subjectivity in the Life Narrative of a Female Labourer
Studia Fennica Ethnologica 16
2014

Studia Fennica Folkloristica

Pertti J. Anttonen
Tradition through Modernity
Postmodernism and the Nation-State in Folklore Scholarship
Studia Fennica Folkloristica 15
2005

Narrating, Doing, Experiencing
Nordic Folkloristic Perspectives
Edited by Annikki Kaivola-Bregenhøj, Barbro Klein & Ulf Palmenfelt
Studia Fennica Folkloristica 16
2006

Mícheál Briody
The Irish Folklore Commission 1935–1970
History, ideology, methodology
Studia Fennica Folkloristica 17
2008

Venla Sykäri
Words as Events
Cretan Mantinádes in Performance and Composition
Studia Fennica Folkloristica 18
2011

Hidden Rituals and Public Performances
Traditions and Belonging among the Post-Soviet Khanty, Komi and Udmurts
Edited by Anna-Leena Siikala & Oleg Ulyashev
Studia Fennica Folkloristica 19
2011

Mythic Discourses
Studies in Uralic Traditions
Edited by Frog, Anna-Leena Siikala & Eila Stepanova
Studia Fennica Folkloristica 20
2012

Studia Fennica Historica

Medieval History Writing and Crusading Ideology
Edited by Tuomas M. S. Lehtonen & Kurt Villads Jensen with Janne Malkki and Katja Ritari
Studia Fennica Historica 9
2005

Moving in the USSR
Western anomalies and Northern wilderness
Edited by Pekka Hakamies
Studia Fennica Historica 10
2005

DEREK FEWSTER
Visions of Past Glory
Nationalism and the Construction of Early Finnish History
Studia Fennica Historica 11
2006

Modernisation in Russia since 1900
Edited by Markku Kangaspuro & Jeremy Smith
Studia Fennica Historica 12
2006

SEIJA-RIITTA LAAKSO
Across the Oceans
Development of Overseas Business Information Transmission 1815–1875
Studia Fennica Historica 13
2007

Industry and Modernism
Companies, Architecture and Identity in the Nordic and Baltic Countries during the High-Industrial Period
Edited by Anja Kervanto Nevanlinna
Studia Fennica Historica 14
2007

CHARLOTTA WOLFF
Noble conceptions of politics in eighteenth-century Sweden (ca 1740–1790)
Studia Fennica Historica 15
2008

Sport, Recreation and Green Space in the European City
Edited by Peter Clark, Marjaana Niemi & Jari Niemelä
Studia Fennica Historica 16
2009

Rhetorics of Nordic Democracy
Edited by Jussi Kurunmäki & Johan Strang
Studia Fennica Historica 17
2010

Fibula, Fabula, Fact
The Viking Age in Finland
Edited by Joonas Ahola and Frog with Clive Tolley
Studia Fennica Historica 18
2014

Studia Fennica Anthropologica

On Foreign Ground
Moving between Countries and Categories
Edited by Marie-Louise Karttunen & Minna Ruckenstein
Studia Fennica Anthropologica 1
2007

Beyond the Horizon
Essays on Myth, History, Travel and Society
Edited by Clifford Sather & Timo Kaartinen
Studia Fennica Anthropologica 2
2008

Studia Fennica Linguistica

Minimal reference
The use of pronouns in Finnish and Estonian discourse
Edited by Ritva Laury
Studia Fennica Linguistica 12
2005

ANTTI LEINO
On Toponymic Constructions as an Alternative to Naming Patterns in Describing Finnish Lake Names
Studia Fennica Linguistica 13
2007

Talk in interaction
Comparative dimensions
Edited by Markku Haakana, Minna Laakso & Jan Lindström
Studia Fennica Linguistica 14
2009

Planning a new standard language
Finnic minority languages meet the new millennium
Edited by Helena Sulkala & Harri Mantila
Studia Fennica Linguistica 15
2010

LOTTA WECKSTRÖM
Representations of Finnishness in Sweden
Studia Fennica Linguistica 16
2011

TERHI AINIALA, MINNA SAARELMA & PAULA SJÖBLOM
Names in Focus
An Introduction to Finnish Onomastics
Studia Fennica Linguistica 17
2012

Studia Fennica Litteraria

Changing Scenes
Encounters between European and Finnish Fin de Siècle
Edited by Pirjo Lyytikäinen
Studia Fennica Litteraria 1
2003

Women's Voices
Female Authors and Feminist Criticism in the Finnish Literary Tradition
Edited by Päivi Lappalainen & Lea Rojola
Studia Fennica Litteraria 2
2007

Metaliterary Layers in Finnish Literature
Edited by Samuli Hägg, Erkki Sevänen & Risto Turunen
Studia Fennica Litteraria 3
2008

AINO KALLAS
Negotiations with Modernity
Edited by Leena Kurvet-Käosaar & Lea Rojola
Studia Fennica Litteraria 4
2011

The Emergence of Finnish Book and Reading Culture in the 1700s
Edited by Cecilia af Forselles & Tuija Laine
Studia Fennica Litteraria 5
2011

Nodes of Contemporary Finnish Literature
Edited by Leena Kirstinä
Studia Fennica Litteraria 6
2012

White Field, Black Seeds
Nordic Literacy Practices in the Long Nineteenth Century
Edited by Anna Kuismin & M. J. Driscoll
Studia Fennica Litteraria 7
2013

LIEVEN AMEEL
Helsinki in Early Twentieth-Century Literature
Urban Experiences in Finnish Prose Fiction 1890–1940
Studia Fennica Litteraria 8
2014

www.ingramcontent.com/pod-product-compliance
Lightning Source LLC
Chambersburg PA
CBHW080805300426
44114CB00020B/2833